Lands End to John O Groats

ONLY MAD DOGS AND ENGLISHWOMEN

A cycling odyssey across the British Isles

Sarah Stinton

Visit us online at www.authorsonline.co.uk

An Authors OnLine Book

ISBN 978-07552-0498-4

Authors OnLine Ltd
19 The Cinques
Gamlingay, Sandy
Bedfordshire SG19 3NU
England

This book is also available in e-book format, details of which are available at www.authorsonline.co.uk

To: My Family

Authors Notes

I made my trip in 1997, since which I have had several aborted attempts to write this book. The first time I began typing, or should I say, bashing the words out on an ancient manual typewriter. No prizes for guessing what happened after hours of sore fingers and dozens of spelling mistakes! After several years and the purchase of an electric word processor from a charity shop, my enthusiasm was renewed. I was fired to finish the book. But alas, as many a budding author may already have discovered, the punishing world of publishing can mean just one rejection letter after another, and so the manuscript was once again abandoned to the dusty shelves of the spare room.

Hello 2008...and finally I catch up with the modern world by furnishing the dusted-down spare room with a P.C. I had great pleasure in putting the finishing touches to the manuscript and putting this book together, and this time I did it for me. Although it has been many years since the trip was made, rest assured I have not changed a thing. All that happened, all that I saw and witnessed, and my views on the world are just as I recorded them in my travel diaries, back at the youthful age of 21.

Introduction

There have been many theories through out history as to what dreams mean. My personal favourite is one which says; dreams are answers to questions we have not yet realised we need to ask ourselves.

> *I had never seen skies so blue in these parts before. And the only wind to be felt is a warm and gentle breeze. I close my eyes for a time, turning to face the full glare of the suns rays, feeling its power warming my soul and making me smile. Opening my eyes I see the rugged Scottish mountains that lure me to reach out and touch them with fingertips. My ears hear the distant bleating of sheep, and two black dots in the sky relinquish the squawking call of birds of prey. It fills me with a type of serenity only Mother Nature can offer. In this tranquil setting I am sat astride my bicycle, effortlessly free wheeling down the mountain road towards a tiny village I once stayed at with my parents, many years before. That trip had been my first to see the Scottish Highlands, and I had felt love and affinity with the place ever since.*

As I stirred from my dream, I thought of the Highlands and of the beauty of the area. And I felt a great unexpected pang.

'Now wouldn't that be a wonderful way to explore.' And a desire to see the world at the pace and level of a bicycle was unleashed in my mind.

And then there are dreams of the ambition kind. Sometimes they are what keep you going, they are what can give us a zest for life, and they bend and change with every experience and everyone we meet. As far back as I can remember my head has always been full of wild and ambitious dreams.

I remember when I was just twelve, I wanted to run away from Sussex, walk to Bangor, (which seemed at the time like a faraway mystical place in the Welsh mountains,) and live in the hills with my horses; eating berries and other wild foods. My route was already planned thoroughly in my parent's road atlas, (at the time, my favourite read). By fifteen this dream had changed. As soon as I was old enough I would pass my driving test, buy a transit van and join a convoy of New Age Travellers. The image that dominated my mind was swigging cider by the crackling fire, living in a like-minded community full of dreadlocked heads, and sleeping under the stars.

Life however, continued a little less adventurous. I went to college at sixteen. Did the usual bunking off lectures to swig cheap beer in the park, (although miraculously, I still passed my A levels). Half way through my course I met a man called Jason and the pendulum of my life once again began to swing. I had already become a keen environmentalist at the age of fifteen, swearing an allegiance to stick faithfully to public transport for the rest of my life. But then Jason introduced me to the concept of long distance cycling.

My rekindled passion with bicycles was not without its ups and downs. Jason gave me one of his old bikes, which I fondly named Bernard, (I still have this bike all these years later despite being stolen twice in Brighton and recovered). As I struggled, panting up hills on Bernard's solid, heavy old steel frame, and with only Jason's looks of dismay at how unfit I was for encouragement, I may have jacked it in there and then. But persistence prevailed and slowly my fitness and eagerness increased, so much so that at the age of 18 I found myself stood on Sevenoaks train station unwrapping my very own plush new touring bike. I named this one Lucy. From there on in I was unstoppable.

Bizarrely up to now, the travel bug had never bitten me, but a trip to Thailand to visit my sister soon changed that. Ironically it was whilst searching through the airport lounge for some good plane and beach reading material that I fell upon the travel writing section. Here I found several books written by different women of different ages, whom had been cycle touring alone in different parts of the globe. I was spellbound for most the trip, I just couldn't get enough of reading about their adventures. That coupled with the fact my hols turned into a three-week trip of a lifetime and I came back a changed women. Jason and I parted company soon after, and I took up with another kindred spirit, Alex. I should have realised that life after all this couldn't continue as it had. Something had to give. Things all came to a head six months later in the spring of 1997. I sat at work staring into space, trying and failing not to think of Alex who had recently left us for another. I found myself reaching for pen and paper and through tears, drafted my letter of resignation. This being the first stable job I'd had that I actually liked, I carried that letter around in my bag for some weeks. For weeks I contemplated, for weeks I naval gazed, and for weeks I drove everyone I knew mad by asking him or her what on earth I should do. Finally Jason came to the rescue with a suggestion.

'Toss a coin' he said. There is more logic to this loony sounding suggestion than meets the eye. When faced with what seems like an impossible decision, toss a coin. Only the once mind, with a resolve that whichever side it comes down on is the decision you will stick with. The idea being that once the coin goes up in the air, in that split second you will know for sure which side you want the coin to come down on. Decision made! Within another month I had said goodbye to all my work colleagues at my leaving do, (a bit of a wrench,) and had packed up the contents of my crummy bed-sit, (definitely not a wrench,) and taken everything I owned back to my parents place. I still remember to this day what it felt like to leave work, as I closed the door firmly behind me (and a metaphorical one too), picked up Lucy and cycled the fifteen miles back to my mothers. As I cycled through the sunshine baked fields of Kent and then back into Sussex, I sensed a feeling of relief and freedom, as never I have before. No more alarm clocks, routine, or living by other people's rules, schedules and expectations. Just me, left to my own devices, and for the first time in my life, a chance to explore my own self. No concrete plans; just listen to my desires and follow my own initiatives.

The first half of the summer of 97 was spent bumming around Europe, hot off the track of the over worn backpacker's trail. I spent two months living with a charming German teacher named Stephan, learning German and regularly making his aging mother fish and chips. I saw Ziggy Marley (Bob's son) perform live in Amsterdam at a concert full of the Dutch black community, complete with spliff in hand. I taught Basic English to Russian soldiers I met in Poland. I visited the original Bran Castle in Transylvania, sat in steaming natural spas in Hungary and got rat-arsed with polish soldiers on my way back to France. I made a whole heap of friends and surprised myself with my newfound confidence, having shaken off my old enemies, timidness and fear of the unknown. It was with a lump in my throat that I returned to Blighty, my rail tickets having expired. On the up side, I whooped with joy when I checked my bank account, so much time spent in Eastern Europe had saved me from bankruptcy. I still had plenty of funds to last me the summer. Subconsciously I think I was searching for a way to challenge myself again, but this time in a different way and a little closer to home.

I wanted to use this precious period of freedom to explore my own country, and to visit all those places I had not yet seen. The seed had been sown one barmy night in Budapest. Sat outside the youth hostel, I was in full flow, taking the piss out of an American traveller. I couldn't believe he had never been to see the Grand Canyon, to me, one of the natural wonders of the world. He was hastily defending himself. Describing the huge distances in the states, (always in hours drive and never in miles) when he suddenly stopped and said, 'Hang on woman, you haven't even been to the Lake District before...and your country is tiny!!'

He had a point. The idea for Part B of the summer of 97 was born.

The growing desire to explore this green and pleasant land, before it disappeared under a bulldozer became a very urgent one. And what was more, I would go by bicycle, so at the same time, I would be making a bold and 'green' statement.

My idea swelled in my head. I saw a romantic image, myself as a cycling nomad, drifting where I liked, sleeping in fields, and visiting beautiful and historic places. Spreading the word of the bicycle and environmental awareness, and spiritually looking for a place to lay down routes for the rest of my life. In fact, the more I looked at my maps, the more I couldn't believe how many fantastic places I hadn't seen as yet. By time I had finished planning a rough idea of my route, I had a wibbly-wobbly line from south-west to north-east that was anything but the shortest distance, usually favoured by most 'End to Enders.'

I was excited too by the prospect of the chance meetings I would have along the way. What did I know of my fellow countrymen and women, their changing counties, accents and lifestyles? Perhaps I was too cynical for the age of just twenty-one years old, but my favourite view of my home soil had become, 'This is a wonderful country, it's just a shame about the people who live in it'. From where I had lived all my life in the South-East, I had formed the opinion that I lived on an island full of rude, pompous bigoted and arrogant people. Would that view change on my travels?

It wasn't long before I realised it was only natural to set out on such escapades with the added aim of raising funds for charity. I could have spent a long time agonising over all the deserving charities and needy causes, but it would have been too tough a decision. So I cut out all thought and went straight with my heart, choosing Landmines Clearance International. I had recently read that there were enough unexploded land mines to kill every man women and child from the countries they are still prolific in, (Cambodia, Rwanda, Angola to name just a few). This was, at the time, a problem largely unknown and little reported on by the international press, so I decided to give this newly emerging cause a helping hand. It was ironic that a few days later I put on the television and saw that Princess Diana had also decided to lend her hand to bringing the world's attention to the landmines problem. I'd be a liar if I said I hadn't thought of doing a U turn on my choice of charity, I guess I didn't like the idea of people thinking I was just following a celebrity cause. But I told myself not to be daft and the cause was what mattered here. Land Mines Clearance International said they would be delighted to receive any funds I raised.

And finally, there were the personal reasons involved in such a journey. Was I physically capable of cycling thirty or forty miles? Not just once, but day in, day out? What would it feel like to actually do it? And what on earth would friends and family say? As it turned out people said very little, or certainly little in the way of encouragement. My ex boss said 'You won't do it'

Charming! But even worse was a friend who said 'Oh everybody does that.'

Really? And how many did she know of? None as it turned out, but that was my first encounter with (what I call) 'Traveller's snobbery.' (When people think of more and more extreme expeditions to test themselves, which is fine, but then insist on scoffing at what they deem as other peoples less exotic adventures).

My final inquisition was as to whether I would become philosophical? Time and again on my travels I would be dogged with the same old questions from the people I met…

'On your own? Don't you get bored?'

So what on earth does one think about, alone with ones head, cycling across the country with no one to talk to most of the time? I remember listening to a radio interview with a young monk who had gone off to the hills to live alone and meditate for a month. He lived off rice water and never saw nor spoke to another soul in all that time. On his return he found he had become a bit of a local celebrity and was interviewed by a local radio station. He was asked the predictable question,

'So what did you do all that time alone?'

To which the monk replied quite honestly,

'Well one day, I spent the entire day thinking about roast chicken.'

And later in the interview he was asked the equally predictable question,

'So what will you do next?'

Again he replied honestly and said,

'Probably go and eat some roast chicken.'

My journey, I decided, would be interesting.

Early days on 'Bernard'

The arrival of Lucy

Part1.
England.
My Green and
Pleasant Land.

Route Map 1 : The West Country

Main Features =

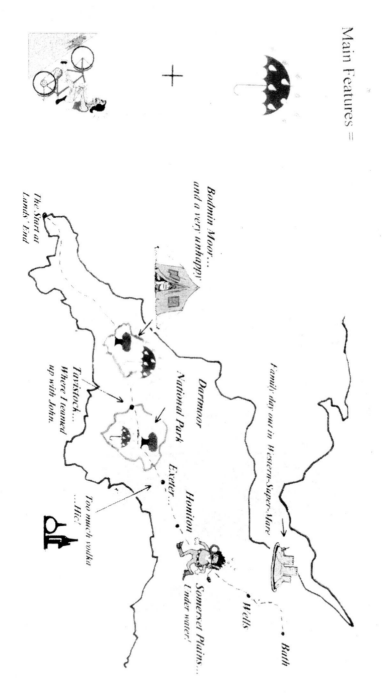

Family day out in Western-Super-Mare

Bodmin Moor....
and a very unhappy

Dartmoor
National Park

Tavistock....
Where I teamed
up with John.

The Start at
Lands' End

Exeter....

Too much vodka
...Hic!

Honiton

Somerset Plains....
Under water!

Wells

Bath

10

DAY 1   (38.7 miles)

I would hazard a guess that we are not the only nation of crazy folk in Europe. But due to our notoriety of stepping out across the globe at one time in history, I think we are one of the most infamous for being 'Mad Dogs.' Maybe that's why every year on this tiny Isle, hundreds and hundreds of people travel hundreds and hundreds of miles to a point in the U.K, just because it is considered the most westerly point on the mainland.

And not only this, but only a Mad Dog, having travelled so far to get to this grey, often rainy and always windy headland, would then about turn and spend the next few; weeks, months, hell…even years getting as far away as is possible from this point without actually crossing the sea, be it by driving, cycling, running, walking, even crawling. And what is the big amazing reward? You would find just another desolate headland as windy, rainy and grey as the one you left behind all those weeks ago. It's got to be madness?

And so it began, at 10am on July 30th of the year 1997. I was 21 years old. The weather was surprise, surprise, windy and grey. I wheedled my way through the handful of exotic sounding attractions; 'Smugglers Cove,' 'Shipwreck Supreme' and 'Fond Fumblings at the Bottom of the Sea' and other nauseating tourist traps, before I found what I was looking for, The official 'Lands End' signpost. I guess at this stage it wasn't the 874 miles it read to John O'Groats that made me draw breathe, (such a vast distance was incomprehensible to me at this point.) No it was probably more like the ten pounds the official photographer wanted to charge me for a personalised photograph.

The idea for this long slog had been dreamt up around the pretext of fun and adventure. Child-like emotions had stirred within me on the run up to this trip, and on the long train journey from London down to Penzance. Feelings of adventure and of running away, these days it was no longer from home, Enid Blyton style. (Of which I used to cram my head with as a child,) but more from ties and responsibilities aka the sixteen years old who longed to live with the New Age Travellers. And so this boldness was what brought me to a little, but extortionate campsite half a mile from Lands End. As darkness set in around my tent, pinpoints of doubt began to cloud the dream, as I prepared for my first night ever camping alone. I listened while a tiny smattering of rain fell on the tent and I watched intently at Lucy's silhouette on the canvas, just in case someone tried to hotfoot it with my only means of transportation. I wondered what sort of project I'd created for myself, what did I hope to gain from spending the next month cycling alone? I just didn't know. Next morning I felt little better as I sat on my rolled up sleeping bag, sipping black coffee. I had not slept a wink. Bleary eyes counted seagulls overhead and watched distances above only measurable in grey clouds…if they too were off to John O'Groats, they would be there long before me. My tired mind tried to avoid a distinct prickle that told me my training for this trip was seriously lacking. Were my childhood fantasies about to turn into grim, endurance-like hell?

As my first solo cycle tour of the U.K lacked interest from, well anybody really, I counted myself down. 5. Avoid all manner of commercial rubbish at the 'Land's End Experience,' which certainly did not compliment an otherwise naturally beautiful, albeit grey headland. No prizes there go to multi-millionaire Peter de Savary for his wholly unsympathetic rejuvenation project. 4. Whirl a screw driver around in one hand and set of instructions around in other, none of which seemed to be in English, and try to fit milometer to bike. 3. Don with pride my 'Blue Peter' style bib I'd made myself for this trip, which explained in simple terms what I was doing (despite it's uneven lettering and a grammatical error.) 2. Politely decline the Land's End photographer's kind offer to rip me off. Instead, thrust my camera into the hands of the nearest passing tourist and get them to take a photo for me. 1. Take a final look about at this peculiar place, as I am sure so many End to Enders have done before me, pray I'd not bitten off more than I could chew, and begin my quest…

Actually I didn't get very far at all, because half a mile up the road I realised I hadn't fitted my milometer correctly so I stopped to try and sort it out. Fortunate or not, I'm not sure, but another cycle tourist, a very lean man on a racer, had stopped to look over my shoulder to watch the operation.

'Here let me' he said promptly taking over. Still young and proud I wished he wouldn't, I guess I didn't like to think of anyone seeing me as an incapable girl...And I guess he just couldn't bear to see my bike getting a butchering. Whatever his reasons it was soon fitted properly. I thanked him profusely and got on my way.

As I sailed forth the first of many cars slowed to overtake, and as it did the driver called out 'good luck' through the open window. No one was as shocked as I was when I felt myself welling up. I hadn't expected this! And as one car driver after the next repeated this show of moral support, I had to wipe away several tears from my eyes. This would be one hell of a journey.

The road back to Penzance was a lot easier on the legs in this direction. Far more downhill's and with the wind behind me, and in no time at all I was back in the town. I decided to skirt the centre to avoid traffic and not break my rhythm, (see I knew the cycling lingo already!) It was on a road just east of Penzance that I saw a man walking along the road towards me. He held a John O'Groats to Land's End banner above his head, and his pace hinted at his seriousness. As I got closer, I read the anti-abortion message that was screamed out across his placard and I involuntarily shuddered. 'Here we go' thought I. In a complex world, nothing is black and white. There are exceptions to every rule, and I do not believe this notion portrayed by certain right wing or strict religious groups that abortion is taken lightly by women, or used as a convenient form of contraception. It is not up to a man like this to judge or to spout irrational and emotionally tapered arguments that suggest bringing unwanted children into this world is always the better option.

As we passed our eyes met briefly and I saw his tiredness. He looked glad his long journey was over. I wondered what lessons the road had taught him. Maybe he could now see a wider perspective. I wondered what lessons it would teach me. I certainly hadn't missed the irony of my first meeting out on the road.

Lunchtime came and passed. I swooped down through a beautiful spot named Marazion. A long sandy beach, holiday blue seas and St Michael's Mount, a small national trust island bobbing on the sea complete with castle, lured many a tourist to the expensive beach front car parks. Not me. The local pub also tried to tantalise me to stop, with a sign declaring pub grub and real ales, here too I fought temptation and won. After crossing the main road again I wound my way inland and up across the county. I was sad to leave the coast so soon. All of the Cornish waters I saw seemed to possess an extra deep shade of blue that spellbound me. Who needs the Mediterranean? I found out later that my father's side of the family all descended from around Penzance, so I guess in a way I was popping home.

I settled for lunch bought from a small local shop a little later on. I leaned Lucy up outside in the sun and stood munching a sarnie. A peek at my milometer had me beaming with pride…27 miles and I wasn't even tired yet. I had visions I might yet catch those clouds up. However, I was new to all this and about to learn a severe lesson. I couldn't believe what a difference just a few miles made! Within the space of half an hour, I had gone from zippy racehorse full of energy, to bedraggled donkey, totally done in!! Consulting the map I looked for a good place to call it the end of day. I was spot on because my map showed the area I stood in as being almost littered with campsites. Strange then that I should have such trouble actually finding one. I followed small wooden arrows, each inscribed with a tent symbol, and the corresponding number of miles to go. But at the end of each road, no campsite would materialise, just another small wooden arrow with tent and the number would change…2 then 2.5, which was followed by 1.45, and then back up to 3. Whether it was the same campsite badly signposted, or a different one it was leading me to each time, I have no idea. Up hill and down dale I cycled, growing more and more exhausted and agitated by the second. (At this stage no one had explained to me The Cornish Mile). Only the sight of a place named Crossroads Motel managed to lift my spirits. Finally, I stumbled across one of the buggers, though more by luck than design I might add.

It was a decent campsite with friendly management but I suddenly hit a snag. I had thought it was just last night's campsite that had seemed rather expensive. This I'd put down to it being in a famous tourist place, but alas this one was about the same price too. When planning this trip, because I was financing myself, I hadn't planned on spending more than around five pounds per day…two to three on food and the same again for pitching up of an evening. Alarmingly I realised most campsites being five or six pounds in themselves, meant I would seriously have to reconsider my budget.

I had been looking forward to a pint all day and the receptionist drew me a map to a pub that was a pleasant mile and a half walk across the hills. Who was I kidding? By time I'd pitched my tent, had supper and a shower, I didn't even have the strength to go and use the campsite telephone to call my mother. I crawled into my sleeping bag before it was even dark, but once more found I could not sleep on my alien and uncomfortable camping mat.

DAY 2   (40 miles)

I was approaching the top of the first hill of the day, and my first fifty miles. Such an occasion couldn't go unmarked so I stopped in a lay-by to celebrate with an apple. As I pulled over to regain breath, it appeared a family in a car had been awaiting my arrival. 'Are you just starting or finishing your tour?' they asked leaping from their car, producing a shiny coin. Pleased as punch to have just raised my first pound for charity I stayed to chat as I crunched on my apple.

The husband worked for London Underground, and as an ex British Rail worker myself, we compared notes. His wife was a Scottish Lass, and after a quick bit of mental arithmetic they worked out I'd be arriving in the Highlands just in time for 'Mozzie season.' Chuckling away like mad, they proceeded to relay full gruesome details of the severity of airborne attacks I'd be plagued by. 'Enough' they said, 'to drive even the sanest person stark raving bonkers...' I've always thought how nice it is to receive some encouraging, friendly local knowledge!

Whilst we chatted and giggled, another car pulled over and a smart businessman got out to stretch his legs. Before he had time to blink my new friends were upon him.

'Look at this lass here...cycling all this way...just started out...all for charity...'etc, etc. He had little choice but to donate to the charity box swinging from my handlebars. I should have employed these folks as my personal fundraisers, as they were far more bold and cheeky than I at asking for money. But all they wanted was to take my photograph against a backdrop of wind turbines (in case I was ever famous they guffawed,) before they bid me farewell. Happy now that I had two things in my charity tin that rattled, I sped on my way.

The busy A30 wound its way through a valley, where on either side loomed the tall rather stark formations of dozens of wind turbines. Cornwall, I read later off the back of a postcard, hosts the first wind powered farm to be built in the U.K. Now here is a contentious issue if ever I heard one. The thought of hundreds of wind farms popping up around the U.K have produced cries of; "blot on the landscape, noise pollutants, a danger to human health"...and other ramblings of the half witted, 'not in my back yard, can't see further than the end of my nose, don't look at the bigger picture' brigade that gives me my rather sceptic view of the British population as a whole. And as a consequence of people worrying about house prices and their daily dose of radio 4 being interfered with, wind powered farms, rather than being embraced as a viable option to a clean and safe future for generations to come, have instead had their planning permission refused in places such the windy Peak District and the mountains of North Wales. Meanwhile planning permission is granted regularly nationwide to build countless roads through areas of outstanding beauty and sites of special scientific interest, whilst nuclear waste, being dumped in some of Scotland's National Parks, goes on unchallenged. To me, this is pure hypocrisy.

Personally, the sight of the forces of nature being utilised in such a simple, yet clever and non-destructive way, and bringing about an unseen change for the better, brings a lump to my throat every time. Inside it bought about a mixture of sadness that it signalled the change needed was coming too slow, and of quiet hope, that there are those who understand and might yet save things. Far from the opinion they are a pollutant in itself, I could quite easily sit under the things for many an hour, gazing up awe struck at these majestic whirring giants, and listening to the wind murmuring away, just as I did when I lived near wind turbines for many months in Germany. On my travels around Europe, particularly: Germany, Switzerland and the Netherlands, wind turbines were a far more common sight. If these modern efficient nations could recognise the benefits and get their finger out and actually use this viable alternative to fossil fuels, why can't Britain?

After cycling a whole and unexpected 38 miles yesterday, another day pushing myself certainly wasn't on my agenda. To put it simply, my legs ached. And not just a dull ache, but a…wince every time I had to move…ache. It didn't take a genius to work out this was largely due to the Cornish geography. The roads all across Cornwall followed a very specific pattern. One minute you are coming down a near vertical drop, wearing away serious amounts of brake pad, for fear that to let go of the breaks on these steep narrow roads may mean a meet with a car coming the other way, and could all end with bicycle and body, a twisted and bloody wreck. And once you've made it safely to the bottom, you have joy of joys, the next up hill to contend with. Just as narrow and just as steep, (think the upper slopes of Snowdon,) only this time I was now worrying about car collisions from the rear, as I sweated and struggled up the hill. It was at times like these, I thought very fondly of my deep heat rub in my panniers. I had discovered the use of 'Tiger Balm' in Thailand, and had bought back dozens of jars from Asia. You name

16

the ailment and I slapped it on; mosquito bites, backache, period pains, headaches (probably not recommended as the close proximity to the eyes makes them sore,) strained muscles, and sore feet. I had visions of me finishing the jar before the end of the West Country. The back roads I desperately tried to stick to, to avoid suicide on the A30, were like a maze. But it was not just the steepness of the roads that caused me such grief that morning. I found I was becoming more and more frustrated with the road signs, and now I had a milometer, just a little angry at the alleged distances they showed. To anyone who has been to Cornwall, you are probably now smirking and thinking…'Ah the Cornish Mile.' For those of you who have not had the pleasure, let me explain. I would arrive at a T-junction and examine the signpost. To reach destination A, it would clearly say turn left, and for destination B turn right. Heading for destination B, and most definitely away from destination A, right I would turn. Only to find that half a mile up the road, it now said destination A, the opposite way in that I should be heading, was suddenly and mysteriously the place I was headed to! And as for the mileage…give me strength, how can somewhere you have been pushing towards for the last half an hour, suddenly be signed as being 2 miles further away than it was 30 minutes ago? Even I wasn't travelling that slowly!

Luckily there was some comic relief to be found, even on a day like today when weather, muscles, miles and maps all seemed hideously against me. Through a tiny hamlet I stopped to look at somebody's amazing collection of old Landrovers and Military tanks. A formidable sight and a far cry from the usual collection of garden gnomes. Unfortunately the owner wasn't about to ask more. I also noticed that in this area it seemed to be occupied by folk who were fiercely patriotic to their corner of the world. The Cornish flag of St Piran (black with a white cross) was flown on many a house and farm cottage. I wondered if these were proud families, long standing occupiers of their county, even though the flag is not more than a few hundred years old, or whether it seemed as it did to me, like some sort of defiant stance against the increasing tirade of encroachment on to their traditions and way of life by townies, and their insatiable desire for holiday homes in Cornwall (Kernow). Somewhere up one of these forever winding back roads, a man raking his lawn stopped to watch me cycle past, and I saw his eyes read my charity bib with, I noted, great amusement. Leaning on his rake he called out, 'You won't find John O'Groats up here.' I smiled my best tolerating smile back at him, unsure whether this had been a sarcastic comment, or just meant as friendly banter, and pushed harder down on the pedals in defiance of any doubts he had on my abilities.

After a morning spent getting lost and adding an unnecessary 10 miles to my already weary legs, I gave in and headed on to the A30, consoling myself with the thought that at least now it would be a straight road into Bodmin town. My father had given me grave warnings about this road, and said it was the main speed link down to the West Country. In typical 'child listening to parent' situation, my mouth had said, 'O.k. dad,' whilst the brain continued route planning, oblivious to his words. But they were about to return to haunt me.

I pulled up where minor road hit 'A' road, and did a double take. Three lanes of traffic roared past me in either direction, approaching speeds that looked to me suspiciously like 90mph. Gulp. I pulled out my map to check this wasn't a motorway I was about to wander on to and risk arrest. But no, this was it, either this or more of the leg aching, muscle wrecking, lung exploding, soul destroying Cornish mile. The former just about won. To begin with, I tried to stay as close to the edge as possible, virtually picking my way along in the gutter, but it didn't take long to realise that this course of action made things worse. The more I moved over, the closer the motorists seemed to overtake. I was suddenly aware of just how fragile the human body is, particularly my head which, no matter how hard I tried, kept feeling like a freshly laid

egg ready to be smashed and smeared all over the tarmac. For the first time ever, I wished I had a cycle helmet. The constant roar of engines drowned out the sounds of the world around me, and before long I could feel my head banging. My eyes span in their sockets as I tried to watch the traffic coming at me from all angles.

But it wasn't just the imminent threat of death that bothered me. I started to notice that the speed of the vehicles passing me by just made me feel like I was cycling slower and slower and rapidly getting nowhere fast. This began to be a hindrance in itself. My luck certainly wasn't in that day, especially when I began to see sign posts for road works up ahead, warning traffic would be down to just one lane…great.

By the time I hit the outskirts of Bodmin town, the milometer read thirty-eight miles. So much for taking things easy today. I honestly felt at that time, I had never been so exhausted in all my life. A pub appeared around the corner and I wobbled into the beer garden, collapsing on to a picnic bench. I indulged in a pint of beer and scoffed the largest baked potato I have ever eaten. The carbohydrate hit was exactly what my body craved and I fed it well. Besides, I mused, food will always taste better if you've had to cover a marathon to get to it. As I slurped and scoffed, it clouded over and I found myself pulling on my coat once again. All day the weather had been, well so typically bloody British. Hot sun followed by downpours, had left me struggling on and off with jumpers and coats all day, trying to maintain the perfect temperature for a cyclist. I wandered if other riders found it as much of a pain as I did? Perhaps I thought amused, the serious ones have some sort of all-weather automatic cycling suit that they use?

As I slowly supped the last of my pint, feeling the liquid anaesthetic gently begin to work it's magic, I watched a large group of loud, but friendly 'Northerners' also arriving on two wheels. Even the little ones with them looked remarkably fresh faced after a thirty-mile day ride around the area. It wasn't long at all before they knew my quest. They laughed, they joked. They patted my back, and so kindly remarked that I looked fit for my bed rather than a marathon cycle. Feeling a little embarrassed because I knew they were right, I nodded, or as best as I could nod without actually raising my chin out my hands. 'So' asked one, 'Which charity are you raising money for?'

'Landmine's Clearance International' I beamed back, sensing another donation heading my way. But only blank faces stared back…

'Princess Di's thing' I added hopefully. Ah, nods of understanding. Bloody Celeb cause, thought I!

I had been hoping, as per my map, to see my campsite for the night right next door to the pub, but a chat with the barmaid revealed it no longer existed. She was able to direct me to one she thought was further on towards town. Lucky for me, she turned out to be correct. Unlucky for me, it was at the top of another Cornish style hill. Drat. No longer capable of anymore pedal-power that day, I made do with pushing Lucy, oh so slowly, to the top.

The over enthusiastic campsite manager came rushing out of his office when he saw me arrive. He greeted me, said he'd lead me to a favourable spot by the ladies wash block, and tried to recruit me into 'The Caravan and Camping Club.' (I politely resisted.) I must admit having to hide a smirk when I watched the look of surprise, and then sheer panic on his face, as he tried to pick Lucy up off the floor where I had left her, lost balance, fell and landed with a crunch on top of bike and panniers. People really are unprepared for the sheer weight of a fully loaded touring bicycle! My pitch was, as promised, very favourable, and in that state of weariness, it took me a good hour of fiddling and stumbling around to set up camp for the night...

...So I cannot begin to repeat the language I wanted to scream, when that same over enthusiastic manager reappeared some time later and gleefully told me I had pitched up closer than the recommended six paces away from my neighbours tent, ordering me to re-pitch further back. Far too 'job's worth' to listen to: reason, pleas or promises not to set anything alight, and far, far too oblivious to my 'Can't you tell I don't give a shit about your fire recommendations' face, I eventually admitted defeat and complied.

Later that evening, finally nestled into my warm sleeping bag, the couple from a neighbouring caravan brought me out a cup of tea. I thought this very sweet, but couldn't help but wonder if they'd seen me alone and just felt sorry for me. This set off a chain of thought that lasted some time. It is a well known fact then when you travel in a group or as a couple, folk think you are quite o.k. and leave you alone. So to travel on one's own, means you appear more approachable and, hopefully, get to interact with others you meet far more, surely the whole idea, (well certainly mine,) of travelling and exploring. I certainly don't think people should be feeling sorry for me just because I am by myself. There is a world of difference between being lonely and being alone. I suppose it helps that I am a natural loner. As a teenager, I worried that I wasn't capable of socialising as well as some of my peers appeared able to, but I now realise, I do enjoy company, if it's of good quality. And if not, I am more than happy to go it solo for a time. I noticed when travelling around Europe, that being alone, my senses sharpened, I certainly observed far more than the gangs of travellers that clung together in pairs or groups. And ironically, I ended up meeting and interacting with people far more than a lot of others I met.

However, on this very subject, the evening did hold a bit of a sting in the tail. I made my way to the pay phone to ring my mother for the first time since setting out, only to be informed that my elder sister, due to fly out to Copenhagen to start a new English teaching job with her boyfriend, would now have to start the job several weeks early. The upshot of which was she probably wouldn't be able to come out to visit me next week, meaning I wouldn't get to see her for months. I lay back in my sleeping bag, suddenly overcome with the blues. I also found myself thinking of Stephan, the guy I had fallen for in Germany. All I knew of his whereabouts was that he was somewhere in Russia, another person close to my heart that seemed so far away. I find at times like these, the only way to get rid of these blues is to let it out. I lay in my tent for a while, sobbing like a homesick child.

I distracted myself by thinking about the dream I had had the previous night. I usually find that when I go away, I start to dream about people I thought I'd left behind. Last night it was the turn of an ex boyfriend, who in all honesty I had treated rather badly. He had been totally besotted with me, heaven knows why, and I suppose I had seen him more as a rebound guy when Alex trashed my heart, because when I went off to Europe in the spring, I just never bothered to contact him again, not even to say it was over. I think by dreaming about him, it was my conscience telling me there were ghosts here that needed laying to rest. I got out my scribble pad, and set about writing him a letter of explanation from the heart, until there was not enough light left with which to write.

DAY 3 (15 miles)

I decided this morning to add to my collection of equipment that varied from the 'ingeniously handy' into the, 'as good as useless' camp. In my mind I had already played out terrifying scenarios of what might become of me, should I have a tyre puncture across the wilds of Bodmin Moor. I saw myself being stuck miles from anywhere, in the wind and rain, with night fast approaching, hungry, thirsty and exhausted. As a last resort I'd be forced to bang on the door of a lonely old farmhouse, where some ancient old bugger would direct me towards a hotel by taking a short cut across the fields. So off I'd dubiously set, pushing my bicycle and wading in knee deep mud, through field after field, cutting my hand on barbed wire, stumbling blindly through the night, whilst unseen wild animals would be heard snarling as I passed, and I'd be trying to cling on to the old man's last directions...'and you'll come to a tree...'

I took a reality check. O.k. so this was dear old safe England, after all. And no matter how many times I looked at the map, Bodmin Moor was never going to look like Death Valley, or the Nullabor Plain come to think of it. But, just in case, I thought it wise to purchase a few spare inner tubes first.

I managed to track down the only cycle shop in town. However, once inside I found myself staring helplessly at a wall of different inner tube boxes. The kind shopkeeper pointed out the correct size I would need for my mount...and her 26" wheels. It was at this point that I suddenly had that dawning sense of realisation that I had done something very, very dim. Casting my mind back to two days ago, I distinctly remembered setting my milometer for bicycle wheels of the 16" variety...how could I have been so stupid. By now any self-respecting cyclist will be throwing this book down in disgust at my ignorance at the most basic of bicycle knowledge. But unfortunately, ignorant I was, in those early days of touring anyway. I paid for my goods and went outside to examine the Speedo, but felt even more puzzled. The mileage I had recorded so far all seemed reasonably accurate. I flicked through the instructions manual once again, following exactly what I had done, when I realised a second fortuitous mistake. I had misread the table, and had set the clock for a bicycle with 26" wheels after all...who says two wrongs don't make a right!

Moving on to my second shopping expedition of the morning, I bought a portable radio to give myself a treat when I made camp of an evening. The two old men in the local electrical shop patiently pointing to the things I requested in a non-committal, very non interested fashion, barely looking up from their tasks to smile their gratitude at my custom, or even to acknowledge my presence in their shop at all. Perhaps they were just having a bad day, or worried they were going out of business. But I did find this nonchalant attitude fairly consistent with the locals around Bodmin. The locals certainly weren't hiding their aversion to the tourists in this tiny town. All morning I had suffered a series of irritating setbacks, and I guess I should have taken it as warning to the type of day I was about to have. First off, my new found neat trick I had devised to save time and gas, (by cooking my boiled eggs and then pouring the water straight into my tea mug) had gone wrong as both eggs had burst open, leaving a whitish mess floating unappetisingly in the water, and I had to start again. Still, the nice lady who had bought me a cup of tea last night called out as I left to say she'd put a couple of pounds in my collection tin… the one I had carelessly left on Lucy's handle bars all night. But that was about it as far as happy events went that day. It was time to reluctantly roll out on to the road for another gruelling day.

Back on the A30, Bodmin Moor was invisible below a damp thick fog, one that seemed to lay heavy over the land, and felt curiously claustrophobic against my chest, which heaved in and out in protest against the hills. It was far too mild to wear my cagoule, and cycling without, it was not long before my clothes were as wet as the moors. A stray mat of damp hair dangled in my vision and I was faced with the irritating task of sweeping it out of my eyes every thirty seconds. The night alas had brought no relief to my aching leg muscles, and every push on the pedals was a grim reminder of the one hundred miles so far covered, and worse still, the nine hundred left to go. A familiar red-hot flair of temper began to well up inside, bought on by frustration and annoyance at my own stupidity. Why hadn't I given myself a day of rest? Why did I think I was capable of covering another thirty miles in this state?

This time I was sure it wasn't just an illusion created by the high-speed cars overtaking. I really was moving at a snails pace. Trying to ignore the fact that one's legs are turning to jelly was, I discovered, quite hard to do. (I never realised until three years later, just how steep the hills, disguised by the fog, actually were.) I was even more worried for my safety. Suffice to say, the poor visibility had no effect on car speeds whatsoever. I wore my fluorescent bib and kept my back light on flash mode to boost my morale.

Exhaustion…shit weather…busy roads. These unappetising statistics swam around my brain until I could think of little else. Self-pity had set in and was here to stay. Stopping for breath in a lay-by, I pulled out my soggy map and traced my finger along the A30, expecting to see, I don't know what, maybe some sign from the gods for inspiration. And then

I found it. There, nestled in the soggy folds of the map was a smudged sign for a tent and a caravan. This is where I'd be heading. Measured in thumbnails, it was only another eight miles up the road. I put the map away. Miraculously, now that I had an achievable goal in mind, the cycling was easier and I set out a little less troubled. My new plan might just work. 'That's it' I encouraged myself, 'Cycle at least as far as the next campsite…and then give up.'

The rest of the journey passed in a blur. My mind was lost to the sweet pleasure of daydreaming. In another world I was a gallant eco warrior, leaping from my bicycle to tear across the road and halt all traffic, coaxing the villainous drivers from their cars. But before long my imagination had adapted itself to thinking about a place where I could peel off my sodden clothes and slip into the largest, hottest bubble bath one had ever seen, where a tray of nibbles and a glass of Chardonnay had kindly been left for me. Mmmm bliss! This losing myself to daydreams must have worked, because when I looked up again, the brown tourist sign marking the campsite was just ahead of me. I had zero energy left for whoops of joy, only a sad sigh of relief.

When the girl on reception at the 'Colford Woods Campsite' (described by the leaflet as an 'Oasis' on Bodmin Moor) heard I was cycling for charity, she happily announced my tent pitch for the night would be free. I later placed the cost of that pitch into the charity tin myself, something I made a habit of doing throughout my trip. But to be honest, I must have looked to her like the most exhausted cyclist; she would put money on not completing their trip, near corpse she had ever seen. But she could see I looked distressed and was kind enough not to make any ill timed, morale zapping quips at my expense.

Back out in the rain again, and I spent another precious few minutes getting wetter still, in order to find the perfect place to pitch my tent. Three quarters of an hour later and my home was complete. My tent had been perfectly pitched in the most sheltered spot I could find, Lucy was propped up under the shelter of the ornamental pine trees, and I had even taken the liberty of tying one of my luggage straps between the branches where I had draped every sodden article of clothing I had over my new washing line to dry. I don't suppose they would dry much, but there again I didn't really care. I was curled up like a cat inside my tent, snug in my sleeping bag, so glad today's ordeal was over. As I dozed

I dreamt peculiar dreams of legs flailing round and round on a bicycle that was going nowhere.

'Hello?' A voice from just outside the canvas door startled me awake. Unzipping the door and poking my nose outside, I was surprised to see the receptionist standing in the rain clutching a brolley and looking rather peeved, whilst behind her stood a monstrously huge motor home. 'Look I'm sorry,' she said, 'but you weren't supposed to pitch here. This spot is reserved for caravans who pay for electrical hook ups. I'm afraid you'll have to move to the other side of the trees.'

'F#**#** B***#*#*!' How can the same shit happen to the same girl twice?

Under the eyes of the sneering caravan occupants whose spot I'd occupied, I made it policy to move my tent and all of my gear as slowly as possible, so I could be of maximum annoyance to them. I was forced to pitch my tent again on the windy, rain lashed side of the trees, where unfortunately things were not going to look up for me today. As physical exhaustion didn't seem to make sleeping on the unfamiliar and not very comfortable sleeping mat any easier, I came up with a new tactic in a bid to get at least one nights decent kip. Ten minutes later I was making myself comfortable in the on-site bar. I settled down, pint in one hand, and pen to write my daily diary in the other. It was time to get tough on myself. O.k. thought I, if my no good soft body refused to accept sleeping on less than luxurious surfaces for the next month, I was going to give it a hand. Tonight I would get totally sozzled and then nothing would keep me awake. At least that was the plan.

Settled into the corner I began writing up my diary, but every time I looked up to take a slurp, it was to find a different pair of eyes gawping at me in a manner that made me feel as though I'd just popped in from the moon for a pint. I can only guess that to these family and friends, it was incomprehensible why or how on earth a young girl came to be sat in a bar, drinking alone in the middle of Bodmin Moor, (perhaps I should have been wondering this myself?) But the real reason my plan was doomed to fail was just this. It only took the duration of one pint to realise I could no longer stand the suffocation of artificial heat. For the last four days I had been living and breathing the outdoor life. I felt claustrophobic and cramped inside, and I itched to get back out into the fresh air, rain or no rain. I returned to my tent completely sober, and settled down for bed. It was comforting to know I had already begun to adjust to the hardiness needed for the rough and ready life of an outdoor

expedition across the U.K. But alas I still tossed and turned for most of the night.

Looking back now, I realised that those fifteen miles across Bodmin Moor on the A30, was when I had reached my lowest ebb of the trip, both mentally and physically. From now on, things, as they say, could only look up.

DAY 4   (30 miles)

Awake roughly an hour after dawn, and it took a while to figure out what the thing that was missing actually was. Certain it wasn't my mind or sanity, (having lost those years ago.) I turned my attention to my body, and realised what it was. That dreadful ache in my legs, back and posterior that had accompanied me these last few days had gone. Happily I stretched a pain free stretch and beamed with personal triumph. In yesterday's hours of despair, my decision to push myself on for just a few more miles up the road, rather than say to myself I couldn't go anywhere that day, had given me the moral boosting sense of achievement I had needed, and a short fifteen miles meant in essence my legs had had the rest they needed after all.

I crawled out of the tent, stretching and yawning in the fresh air. The rain was gone and it was nice to be able to distinguish colour in the sky again, it made me realise just what an effect the climate can have on the psyche of a whole nation, particularly somewhere like the British Isles where we obsess constantly about the weather. Now in a far lighter mood, I could mull over the prospect of a day of rest, without suffering the after pangs of doubt about my abilities and commitment to this journey. But it wasn't just the sudden break in the weather that made me want to push on. The simple truth was I did not want to stay here. Maybe it was just me being slightly paranoid after my experience in the bar last night, but I felt as though my every move was being watched. As I passed back and forth between tent and shower block, I was sure all eyes were upon me, but as in the horror movies, when I turned around to look, there was no one there. However I had a strong feeling what was being said behind twitching caravan awnings. Something along the lines of…'Oh, look at that girl over there, I think she's on her own.'

'On here own? Why is she on her own?'

'I don't know, but we were only saying last night that it was a bit peculiar.'

'Yes, never right that, well maybe she's a bit of a, you know…odd ball.'

'Or maybe her whole family is?'

'Perhaps she's, well you know…'

'Know what?'

(Whispering) 'Hoping to find a fella?'

(Gasps of horror follow.) Not surprisingly I felt a strong urge to leave this campsite with its unfortunately disagreeable clientele. But even more so, no one was as surprised as me when I realised that I itched to be back on the road once more.

As I cycled out of the 'oasis' and on to Bodmin Moor, I mulled over a pattern I had begun to notice in my cycling days. When I started out of a morning, the first few miles were a terrible struggle, for both body and soul. My legs felt like rusted lead weights and Lucy as though an elephant had been smuggled into my bike panniers over night. Whilst my brained groaned, 'I can't do this.' However, once I had pushed on through those first few difficult miles, the wheels seem to turn with extra fluency, my anxieties relaxed and with it my body, and I was able to find my own comfortable rhythm. Once I fell into this, I could stop seeing this as a gruelling test, and begin to enjoy the pedalling, even the hills I encountered.

The misty morning cleared, and Bodmin Moor was transformed from the dank depressing place of yesterday into a green and picturesque landscape. I wished hard for the sun to emerge to complete my tranquillity. Some way on down the road, I stopped to have a 'chat' with the native ponies of Bodmin Moor. Like all of Britain's native ponies, these herds are feral; domestic animals turned loose. Like a lot of horses, they seemed most perplexed by my bicycle. I often wander if they think it to be some kind of headless horse, and I watched them watching me with amusement. As if to prove my theory, a handsome stallion, bobbed and weaved his head as he studied me anxiously, before turning tail and jealously herding his mares away. Unfortunately the picturesque scene of Britain's native ponies is marred by a tinge of sadness. The herds are left to over breed, are often riddled with worms and quite undernourished under those cute woolly coats, and sadly for a lot of them, they will end their days being rounded up for the meat van.

Today, I was back on a maze of Cornish back roads, and it was beginning to tell. Twice I took a wrong turning and ended up on the main road I was trying to avoid. I altogether missed the miner's memorial I wanted to visit, (another wrong turn) and unfortunately, the caves I planned to stop at for lunch with the intention of exploring after, where, to my surprise, closed on a Saturday. But any frustrations I felt that day where overridden by an inner glow of satisfaction. Some of the quite monstrous hills I was clearing left me astounded, as I would reach the top with heart, legs and lungs in reasonably functioning order. I quite got into a rhythm of self-hypnosis that day. As I ploughed on up the hills, I would lose myself in a trance of deep thought that went along these lines: remember old whatsis face that used to sit at the back of the classroom and fart… I can't believe what a shit my ex boyfriend was, (guaranteed to get you to the top, that one ladies!)…What was the name of that U2 song I loved as a kid…or you could even ponder over, why do people think cycling is such hard work? The idea being that rather than dwell on the hard work of your task ahead it was better to detach mind, and leave the body to do the work, so when you finally snap back to the here and now, you will be delighted to discover you have just pedalled up 'Ben Cornwall.'

Along the A390 towards Tavistock, the sun, at last, broke forth, and I revelled in the warming rays of gold that hit me face on. I mindlessly hummed a ditty or two as I sailed effortlessly along this stretch of the road, which having risen sharply for the last twenty minutes, now rewarded me with a long flat stretch across the top of the ridge. It gave me a golden opportunity to gaze out across the West Country landscape, a land I can only best describe as 'Real England.' Where I am from in the southeast, traditional hedgerows, (as well as much wildlife with it) had long since disappeared to make arable farming easier and more profitable. Fields of 200 acres plus were not an uncommon sight, fields more likely to be associated with Kansas State than Sussex or Kent. Where as here, as far as my eye could see, I saw small gentle rolling fields, fields which made me want to reminisce about a bygone era usually seen in history books, where men not machines worked the earth. And a flattering yellow sun completed the scene making it picture perfect.

It was at the bottom of this stretch, I spied a fully loaded up touring bicycle, albeit a riderless one, propped up against a bench. I felt a pang of excitement as I stopped to make myself comfortable and wait for 'John' to emerge from his leak in the bushes. We introduced ourselves and I listened intently as he told me in his thick Leeds accent that he too was cycling the 'End to End.' Not only this but he was also cycling alone and unsupported, carrying all his gear and camping equipment, just like myself. Delighted to find a fellow maniac, I listened whilst he told me of his charity fund raising attempts. He was raising money for his local school for deaf children, whilst his wife, who was a presenter for their local radio station, would be interviewing him daily in order to boost sponsorship. He had tried the usual writing off to many companies for sponsorship, but found as I had that they were only interested in funding large or famous events. We chatted away about the tiresome Cornish roads, and I felt greatly comforted to know I wasn't the only one struggling. John soon had to rush off in order to top the next hill ready for his next live interview with "The Mrs." It was then I realised with shock that not only was he cycling with all his gear and camping equipment, but he was lugging around a heavy transmitter in his panniers too. Fair play to the guy! But his efforts were certainly paying off. So far they had raised around £1300, (I tried not to think of my measly few pounds rattling around the bottom of my near empty handlebar collection tin.)

I watched John cycle off and stayed on the bench a few minutes longer to finish my apple. I eyed the speeding cars with an almost pitying air. How unaware, thought I, those occupants were of what had just occurred. How ignorant they were to the determination of two cyclists, battling on against the difficulties, not to mention the wonderful, beautiful chance meeting on that bench. What were the odds, I wondered? In four days I'd encountered just one cyclist, and goodness knows how many hundreds, if not thousands of cars.

A cyclist's vision is of the whole world…the long road snaking into the distance which would always lead to John O'Groats, the valleys that fell away on either side, hills that enveloped my vision in greenery, a sky devoid of clouds and my overwhelming desire to be here.

It wasn't long before I spied a speck in the distance, which as I got nearer manifested itself into a cyclist, which in turn manifested itself into John. Together we 'struggled' into Tavistock. I have to admit to being secretly chuffed when I found I could cycle to the top of some hills that John could only struggle to push his load up, (he put this down to my bike having a lower gear ratio than his.) It gave me a boost also because he then informed me, through gasping breathes, that he was planning on finishing the End to End in just sixteen days. If that were possible for him, then surely I could easily complete the journey in my allotted time frame of four weeks?

Freewheeling into Tavistock, it felt as though we were part of a team, and we hunted around for the local tourist information. Almost at once, I could literally 'feel' the difference in people's attitudes towards me, now I was no longer on my own. Although folk who sat about in the afternoon sun still watched John and myself with our bicycles, it was no more than looks of mild friendly interest. A stark comparison to the usual goggle-eyed, almost threatening stares I had experienced up to now. We finally tracked down the tourist office, only to be told that the YHA marked clearly on both our maps, had never actually existed. Instead, together we made tracks to the east side of Tavistock, where a campsite, was, we were told, most definitely situated on the edge of Dartmoor National Park. We arrived sometime later, both complaining bitterly at the hilly West Country, no easier despite having passed from Cornwall into Devon. But as true cyclists, we both glowed with triumph and self-satisfaction at another day of hills conquered. I personally felt as high as a kite, as if each turn on the pedals had got easier and easier, the opposite of what I'd been feeling at the end of previous days.

I pitched my tent in a sunny corner of the large camping field between John and a friendly couple from London, who told us they frequented this particular campsite on a regular basis. It was a welcome change, no make that a blessed relief, to be sat outside my tent at the end of the day, writing my diary and munching through an entire malt loaf, (much to John's amusement,) rather than being squashed inside trying to stay warm and dry. Not that I got an awful lot of writing done, as the hilarious banter between the three camps flew back and forth all evening, making this one of the most joyous campsites of the whole trip. And a particular pleasure after last night's campsite experience. Later I jumped at the chance to join everybody in the campsite bar to toast the completion of our first county.

The on site bar was small and dingy, but most comfortable, with a smart restaurant next door. I settled myself perched on a bar stool and took a swig of my pint, and listened whilst around me, many other holiday regulars took up the reins of the loud but comical banter going on. Quite naturally, to me, this meant one or two pints became a sociable four or five. Probably not the best move by someone who has to tackle Dartmoor by bike in the morning.

I very much enjoyed talking 'bike' with John too. And we gassed like old time CTCer's (that is, members of the long established Cyclists Touring Club.) He seemed rather envious when I revealed I had dreams of cycle tours in Scandinavia and Eastern Europe, and he predictably asked me if I had read books by Josie Dew, the very book I had taken to Thailand two years ago. We both agreed she was an admirable and inspiring cycling wonder. I tried to hide how chuffed I felt when John said he had seen many a good cyclist get off to push up hills he'd seen me pedal up today, but the beer as well as the compliment made me beam. I teased him that the reason was because whilst he was sat there filling up the ashtray, I on the other hand had not smoked a single cigarette since setting out. As the evening drew on I watched him puff through nearly a whole packet of Superking Lights, whilst he waved them temptingly under my nose. I think it was somewhere between pint number three and four, that I succumbed to my addiction.

Above: Fresh faced at the start

Below: A place of firsts…my first fifty miles, first donation received and Cornwall's first wind turbine farm

Above: Leaving Cornwall for Devon…alas the hills
stay with me!

Below: That's good advice!

Above: The hills of Dartmoor national park...

Below: ...not to mention the rain

Above: Flooded roads in Somerset block the way

Right: Glastonbury Tor

DAY 5   (8 miles)

If any persons present in the bar last night, had sat me down and laid
out in no uncertain terms, exactly how crap I would be feeling the next
morning, and thus prevented me from suffering 'Satan's Hangover,' I
would now be shaking them firmly by the hand, no, I think I would
probably now be writing them into my will. As I lay staring at the
sagging roof of my tent, I made a quick mental run down of the world
around me. Mouth…as dry as a bone and tasting as though I'd licked out
an ashtray. Head…danced over by a herd of pregnant hippos. Legs…
having braved 30 very hilly miles yesterday, the painful dispiriting
aches and pains of previous days had, alas, returned. Wallet…no doubt
empty. And finally the weather. I pushed an experimental finger into
the sagging canvas above and realised copious amounts of rainwater
were sat just over my head. The sides of the tent would every now and
again flap violently, as if it were a ship's topsail out at sea, and as my
fuzzy, alcohol blocked senses slowly began to clear, I could hear the
lashing of the rain outside.

Half of me didn't want to move, but the other half of me was very
aware of the liquor from last night still sloshing around my, otherwise
empty stomach. Action was needed now. Somehow I got myself
together to get dressed and venture outside. With my only protection
my cheap cagoule, I crouched in the rain and managed to rustle up a
couple of boiled eggs with my last remaining piece of bread. It was a
far cry from the full English veggie breakfast I craved and that thought
made me all the more miserable. As I bent over the stove watching the
water simmering, I tried not to look at the watery world around me for
fear of depressing myself still further. I cursed the rain, and I cursed
my own stupidity.

After a bit of sustenance, I packed up my soggy tent and the last of
my belongings as fast as I could, but it didn't slip my attention that a
wet tent was even more of an upheaval, the saturated canvas felt twice
as heavy as normal and I groaned at the added hindrance of yet more
weight to pedal with. John gave me a quick wave goodbye as he swung
his leg over the crossbar, muttering that he would make it to Bristol
today if it killed him, anything to leave the hills behind. And then he
was gone. I made ready to leave shortly after. The happy couple from
London came to wave me off. They brushed off the weather as a typical

day in Dartmoor, but I wondered if they might not give up and head for a hotel once I was gone. She kindly put money into my collection tin, whilst he handed me a ready-made survival meal of rice pudding. Just heat up the bag in boiling water and serve. I guessed they weren't confident of my survival in the storm either.

The problem with this particular campsite was its location. Out of the main entrance, turn right, and immediately you are looking at one of those hills so steep, it is often marked on maps with small black arrows, that might as well denote…"only four wheel drives need bother!" I stood at the bottom in a puddle, and alarmingly found I had to crane my neck right back to see the top. Slipping Lucy into the lowest gear, I gritted my teeth and, ever so slowly, began toiling heavenwards. What had also occurred to me was I didn't even know where I was heading for. Not direction wise, for this was the only road heading this way, but a place to aim for. There were two youth hostels perfectly located across the moor, but disappointingly, an answer phone message last night informed me they were both fully booked out for the next month.

In gasping breathes I struggled on up and up, but just as I topped the rise and was feeling thankful to have made it, I was lashed across the face by a gust of driven rain that made me draw in a sharp breath. Sorrowfully, I realised that far from having got the 'difficult bit' out of the way, actually the hell had only just begun. The wilderness of Dartmoor Park lay at my feet, it was my first ever glimpse, and my heart sank. It was far higher and more exposed than I had imagined. But worse than that was, (of course) the hills. I stood at the top of the rise looking at the road snaking away into the murky distance. They looked far longer and steeper than anything I had encountered up to now. The wind, gusty in strength when I left the campsite, was now, on top of the moor, reaching near gale force. I need not explain to any regular cyclists what cruel trick of fate would await me now, but for those still novices to the notion of cycling in windy conditions, it can be explained in just two words…HEAD WIND!!

With head down, legs on autopilot, mind, well I tried to keep it blank, I began the battle. Water fell in torrents on my head, ran down my face, dripped off the end of my nose and into my mouth. It leaked through my coat saturating every article of clothing I wore. It filled my boots too. It ran in rivers down the road, and as I passed drainage ditches it roared in an ever-constant waterfall off the moors. Breathing was becoming increasingly difficult. I not only panted hard up the hills, but the weather was making my nose run, and as nose blowing was out of the question, (any tissues I had just became saturated and disintegrated in my hand) I began to feel as though I was drowning in a sea of rain water and snot. I can in all honesty say there was not one part of me that was dry that morning. For a while I tried singing to raise my spirits, but instead the line from my favourite poem, 'The Rhyme of The Ancient Mariner' kept repeating itself in my head...'water water everywhere'... I found myself reminiscing about a not dissimilar pickle I got myself into a few years back, cycle touring around the Isle of Skye. One that left me stranded and on the brink of hypothermia. At least I could reassure myself that it was fortunately now August, and not frozen February like last time. The wind blew so hard into my front that I had to get off Lucy at regular intervals, just to try to regain my breath. I wasn't even making any progress on the downhill stretches either, the head wind would slow me down so much that I had zero momentum left to even try getting up the next side. At one stage I found myself screaming into the wind. 'Oh for crying out loud, just ease up will you' as a flying piece of twig smacked me in the face. Then 'Please...' I begged, almost in a whisper. '...Just for a few minutes.'

After nearly two hours of this, I glanced down at my milometer and saw I'd only managed a soul destroying eight miles. I could have walked the same distance in that time. A welcome sign on the road ahead for 'Princetown' and, joy of joys, a campsite shone through the murkiness. I had no desire to go on any further that day. My progress in the wind was so incredibly slow, it hardly seemed worth it, and it certainly wasn't worth the discomfort. I took a right turn at the junction and rolled on down the track towards the town. Dartmoor prison appeared eerily out of the swirling mists. Dartmoor prison was first built in 1809 to hold French and American prisoners of war before it became a criminal prison in 1850. It was reckoned to be the most hardest and

severe prison in Victorian England, and until recently, it housed some of the most dangerous and notorious inmates in Britain's history. I wondered if it was always this grey and depressing here? Stepping inside the campsite bar was like stepping inside another world. It was warm and dry in here, and was full of normal people doing normal Sunday things, like having a few pints, chatting with friends or watching the afternoon football match on the box. Perhaps I should have felt a little foolish, standing there pink faced in my own little puddle as water dripped off every angle of me, where as the people in the bar seemed to know better than to be out cycling in this weather. But I certainly didn't feel foolish at all; more inwardly satisfied at having got there at all, despite all the elements nature had thrown my way. O.k. so I had only managed eight miles, but it was still better than nothing, and as the other day through Bodmin had shown me, it was better to try for a while and then quit for the day whilst I was ahead, and make up the distance tomorrow.

I thought the landlady might have been a bit cross at the mess I was making on her carpet, but she didn't seem to notice. In fact she very kindly told me to go and sort myself out and come back and pay later. I was delighted to learn that the pub offered another cheap option, a bed in the bunkhouse out the back for only two pounds more than a camping pitch. I jumped at the chance. For just seven pounds I was delighted to get a bunk bed in a room I had all to myself, and not only that, there was enough room to hang every last sodden item of clothes and equipment I had up to dry, tent and all. I spent half hour in a deliciously warm shower examining with some amusement my wrinkled and pruned skin. Then I dried my hair and went down to the bar to treat myself to a bit of T.L.C.

I dined on veggie burger and chips, and supped a few pints, whilst my boots dried out beside the roaring log fire. There was no shortage of interesting characters to chat to. A Danish couple sat morosely with their pints, clutching a soggy copy of the 'Lonely Plant Guide to Walking in Britain.' They had been hoping to sit out the rain in the pub, but couldn't hide their disappointment at the British weather. Later we were joined by another couple from Scotland who too were walking, but were obviously more acquainted with this type of climate, and seemed to be taking the prospect of an afternoon in the pub with considerable more cheer then their cousins from across the North Sea. That afternoon, my collection tin, which I had got into the habit of taking everywhere with me, swelled by several more pounds. Land Mines Clearance International would be some of the people glad of the rain that day.

That night I was to share my bunkhouse with a large group of youngsters, who in the morning were attempting part of their Duke of Edinburgh gold award. This particular part of the challenge involved walking fifty miles across Dartmoor over three days, living under self built shelters and putting their map and compass skills into practise. It all sounded like terrific fun. I chatted to the team leaders, who seemed most impressed, not that I was cycling the End to End, but that I was doing it alone and without any back up support. They were all banging around till late that night, preparing all their equipment for the next day, and were all up again at the crack of dawn. They felt guilty in case they'd disturbed me, and so as a (literal) peace offering, they gave me some of their supplies for breakfast. I was more than happy to take them up on their offer and dined on tea, toast, cereal and eggs. But really there was no need for them to feel bad. An earthquake wouldn't have kept me awake that night. After five nights of disturbed and uncomfortable sleep in my tent, and five days of physically pushing myself further than I ever have in my life, I was exhausted. I was climbing into bed as early as seven o'clock, and as I lay in the softest warmest and cosiest bed in days, I fell asleep listening to a couple outside the pub opposite having a jealous row over another man. I slept like a baby for twelve hours.

DAY 6 (34 miles)

Dartmoor…A wild and windswept landscape, with miles of breathtaking rugged views. Well at least that was what I imagined. I had to make do with seeing only fifteen yards in front of my face; any further was blocked out by swirling mists. I had a feeling the poor visibility was probably a godsend, for the sheer steepness of those switchback hills were hidden from view, and psychologically I think this made the pedalling easier. It would have been hell if I were constantly struggling to the top of one hill, only to sight the next one and the next. Setting out from Princetown I quickly discovered with some relief that things would be easier than the previous days struggle. The road ran ever so slightly northeast, meaning the gale still blowing from the east was now hitting me side on, which although unbalancing, was still preferable to a head wind. As I settled into a rhythm I began to find that cycling alone and cocooned in a thick blanket of mist, strangely pleasurable. I saw no person, not even a car that morning and I began to have a strange notion that, for all I knew, the rest of the world wasn't even there anymore. The only sound was the constant buffeting wind. I pulled out my scarf and tied it tight over my head and ears. Every now and again I would see small signs of life, mainly crows and sparrows. I watched intently as they flapped their wings, fighting their own battle with the elements, as they fought to get somewhere before the mighty wind deposited them back from whence they'd came. I could certainly sympathise with them as I struggled on like this for another fifteen miles.

Just as I had expected, the mist quickly cleared once I came off the higher more exposed grounds of Dartmoor, leaving the world suddenly lighter. Thankfully, the wind also dropped and the rain ceased. Sadly though the hills did not abate with the bad weather, so I took all this as a cue for a break. In Moretonhampstead I bought and devoured six large bananas and an entire malt loaf in one go, malt loaf was fast becoming my favourite cycling food.

As I sat on a bench in the village centre, once again assessing just how much water had seeped through my inadequate rain mack, I found the village was made up mainly of two distinct groups. The first were tourists, easy to differentiate from the rest as they wandered about, by the usual look they gave me that said 'Ah, you must be an alien?' Locals on the other hand just ignored me and generally refused any eye contact whatsoever, be it when buying stuff from their shops, or sitting only feet away from them in the village centre. I guessed they must be quite used to tourists, and probably even a little sick of them, and had long ago taken to ignoring anyone who was a stranger to their community. I tried to imagine this paradox going on throughout modern day Devon and Cornwall. Employment rates and particularly wages are quite low compared to more affluent areas in the south of England, and yet Devon and Cornwall still remain an ever-popular holiday destination. So whilst a lot of areas are to some extent reliant on the tourist pound, it also meant constant disruption to daily life in the community. I can only imagine how begrudged I'd feel if the only means of local employment was to have to serve other folk on holiday all the time, but at the same time having to come to terms with the fact that the same hoards keeping you in brass, also meant there would never be a chance for a quick, stress free 'pop to the shops' on a Saturday morning for knowing you would be tripping over tourists in every shop doorway. Nor could you go for a quiet restful picnic at the local gardens with the family on a Sunday, for the same reasons. Many years ago, holidays were taken with the family, and spent relaxing around the home. How things have changed in our modern world. What I wandered would be the advantages and disadvantages to return to a life of those before the First World War, aka, Flora Thompson's 'Lark Rise to Candleford.'

On leaving Moretonhampstead, I unwittingly took the first of many a wrong turn, so was relieved to bump into 'Dave,' a grey bearded cycle tourist going in the opposite direction. He, with the help of his more detailed Ordinance Survey map, was able to put me straight on my whereabouts and following his sensible sounding advice, I decided to head for the Exeter Youth Hostel, which he reliably informed me allowed campers in the back garden, and provided breakfast. Now that sounded like a plan! Unlike others I met along the way, Dave was delighted I was cycling my route independent of back up and in self-sufficiency style. I was patted on the back and had several more coins placed into my charity tin. This made me grin like a Cheshire cat. As Dave was heading the way I had just come from and vice-versa, we quite naturally enquired about any geographical difficulties we may encounter, i.e. how many hills? Dave's answer made me want to burst into fits of giggles. 'Oh I've definitely come up more hills than I've come down today, so you should have an easy time of it to Exeter.' It was funny because I would have said exactly the same about my morning. Whether we said this just to encourage each other I don't know. More than likely it just felt that way, for it really were true, that would have meant we were standing on the highest point on Devon!

Despite the dismal weather it was to be a memorable day for meeting fellow psycho (cycle) tourists. When I finally wheeled into Exeter tourist information for directions to the hostel, (incidentally definitely more down then up...sorry Dave!) I met a chap from South Africa called Andrew. He had been living in London for the past five years, and was now on his way towards Plymouth, to catch a boat to Spain for a two wheeled adventure in the sun. One of the first things he did was ask if I had read Josie Dew's books. I congratulate the lass for inspiring all sorts of people to get up and use their maybe otherwise forgotten two wheeled friends. I followed hot on Andrew's tail all the way to the youth hostel, a modern building with a whole host of characters. Most memorable was a father and his ten year old daughter, who were cycling around England on a custom made tandem, little and large, to the rear and helm respectively. I found this so intriguing that a girl so young could think nothing of cycling right around the country with her dad. I hoped she wouldn't grow out of this beautiful affliction and at eighteen exchange her bicycle for a motorcar instead. So many of the holidaymakers I had met along the way all complained about the same thing…the traffic. But all failed to see that they were just adding to the problem. I had met many a physically able person who drove hundreds of miles to look around some traffic infested village or beauty spot, get out for ten minutes to stroll around, just to drive back again. But if I dare to mention them having a go at an alternative, like cycling, it was almost always met with a barrage of excuses or reasons why this was impossible for them. This ten-year-old girl would have put them all to shame.

I struck lucky with Andrew that night, that is to say he turned out to be a chef by trade, my favourite kind of person. And I certainly didn't say no when he started cooking up a huge saucepan of pasta, for which there was plenty for me to replenish my fuel tanks. After dinner I stood in the youth hostel's power shower, blasting my chilled body in deliciously hot water. The distance I had come today with, surprising ease over the hills was a wonderful sign that I was getting fitter by the day, and I noted, I still had energy to spare. I couldn't work out if it was this extra energy or just the elation of achievement that was giving rise to some quite comical thoughts. For example, as I stood warming myself up in that shower, I found myself thinking, 'if only the rain would fall from the sky this warm, cycling in extreme weather would never be a problem again.' Seconds later I realised what a daft thought this was. I could imagine the sheer terror if it really did rain hot rain. Thoughts of nuclear fallout came to mind, and I melted into peels of giggles at my daftness. I'm sure the girl in the next shower cubicle must have thought I was high on drugs.

Clean and fed and with my little house pitched up in the hostels garden I joined Andrew for a few pints in the public house down the road. I was keen to find out what life in South Africa was like. It was one of those almost infamous places that seemed so different, even daunting and a million miles away. But strangely Andrew did not seem so keen to divulge. About the only thing he said about it before he clammed up, was that he actually found Britain more racist than South Africa.

After a stroll back to the hostel in the dark I bid Andrew good night, and was about to walk back to my tent when I spotted some figures in the courtyard. With all of this extra energy charging around my body, and spending so much time alone in the saddle during the daytime, I felt I was ready for a bit more socialising before bedtime. I sidled up to the party, causally asking for a cigarette and introduced myself. I met Anna, Stephan and Ivan who were backpackers from Germany, and Roy, their English friend they had teamed up with. The four of them were very friendly and clutching three bottles of cheap Russian vodka, insisted I join them for a tipple. My sensible head thought, 'just the one won't hurt.'

Two hours later, I vaguely recall my rusty German improving with each glass I knocked back. Though things began to get a bit out of hand when a member of staff came out to yell at us for making too much noise, from where, we retired to the kitchen and sat laughing whilst Anna and Stephan began boiling up great saucepans of tea and vodka mixes. I can honestly say I have never tasted anything quite so disgusting in my life. Somewhere around one in the morning, a young French man showed up looking very forlorn. The lad, having just arrived in the country only a few hours ago, had managed to lose his friends already. Not only this but he hardly spoke any of the lingo and now faced a youth hostel that was closed. The others said they'd let him in with their key and he should just go in and help himself to a bed, but I thought this might not be wise and gallantly (and drunkenly) offered him a space in my tent. I thought it was about time I got a chance to repay some of the kindness that I'd been shown along the way. Though thinking back now, it probably would have been more practical if he'd just helped himself to a bed. We drunkenly debated this for a time, and in the end I took the young lad off and pointed out my tent, before heading back to the party.

Heaven knows what time later, when I couldn't physically get any more liquid down my throat, I stumbled back to my tent giggling loudly at nothing in particular, only to find that the Frenchman had not only helped himself to my tent but placed his enormous rucksack across the entrance as well. I think it took me a good ten minutes and several attempts before I could coordinate my giggling, drunken wreck of a body over the obstacle and into my sleeping bag. I'm guessing the Frenchman must have been wide-awake with all the noise I was making but if he was, he made no sign. In fact I got the distinct impression he was hiding in the depths of his sleeping bag, scared of what this mad drunken women might do next. But he need not have feared. The only thing I was interested in was sleep, and to prove my point, in seconds I was happily passed out, and aware of absolutely nothing.

DAY 7 (28 soggy miles)

I awoke to find the young French lad had gone, and I was alone in my tent once more. I lay still for a while and listened to a deluge falling outside. As my watch read five minutes to eight, thoughts turned to the veggie fry-up I had ordered. Feeling very dizzy and faint, I some how got myself up and inside the hostel dining room. But the excess of vodka killed off any taste sensations I may have had, and sadly the food tasted of nothing more than cardboard. I thought it may at least have made me feel better but I just felt exhausted. I went back to my tent hoping another few hours of sleep would do the trick, but dehydration prevented even this respite, so up I got again and made my way back into the hostel kitchen. Inside I found my fellow party friends also nursing hangovers, and suitable banter and piss taking about the night's events were bandied around.

I was sorely tempted to stay another night. All the signs were pointing in the right direction; the awful weather (again,) my hangover (er... again,) the splendid breakfast the hostel would no doubt lay on again tomorrow morning, and now an invite from my new found friends, who invited me to join them as they went out to explore for the day. But when I learnt they intended to drive in their car across Dartmoor, back the exact way I had cycled, I knew it wasn't for me.

Somehow, as if on autopilot, I began packing up my belongings and folding up the tent in a torrential downpour that clearly wasn't going to go away. I'm not sure who seemed more surprised at my eagerness to get going, myself or the three lads who stood astonished, watching me pack every last item on to my bike. I said goodbye and half-heartedly swung my leg over the crossbar. By now I suppose I was beginning to realise just how much I loved this trip. Of course I had always enjoyed pedalling, or else I would never have made it as far as Lands End. But now the rhythm of the road had got me well and truly hooked. I was no longer cycling just to cover the miles, but cycling also for the love of it. It was as though I had found a new purpose in my life. Every hill I topped with my heavily laden bike, I topped with a smile on my face and song on my lips as I breezed down the other side, looking forward to seeing what awaited me around the next corner.

It was to be a peculiar day, and one of many interesting encounters, where a whole manner of people stopped to question my sanity for making this a trip alone. A French biker clad in all his shiny leathers was the first. As I pedalled away from Exeter youth hostel, he pulled over on his motorbike. 'Don't you get bored, lonely, frightened?' he asked. He then went on to tell me that whilst travelling in South East Asia last year, he noticed then that any women he encountered who travelled alone all turned out to be British.

I found his observations interesting, but not really surprising. Maybe it is in our nature, or is it the way modern culture in this country now teaches girls to behave, to take a fiercely independent approach to life? Maybe it is just a select few of us that were born this way and once long ago maybe we would have been part of a team of early pioneers, trotting out across the globe. I certainly noticed whilst in Europe for the summer that even in other western cultures, France, Germany etc, that the women there did not come across as quite so bold as their British counterparts. Perhaps a lot of women feel better off without having to rely on their men folk to hold them up. Or maybe we have bought it on ourselves; modern feminism seems to have made men feel redundant to some extent. They don't have to financially provide, don't have to hold doors open or walk us home at night anymore. Or maybe we really are a nation of crazy folk; only mad dogs and Englishmen certain seems to apply to the lasses too these days.

Trying to negotiate my way out of Exeter with a hangover was a formidable task. It did cheer me though, (as ever) to be able to cruise with ease down the inside of a row of stationary cars, all stuck in a long queue at the lights. But when a blue metro pulled over to the left and blocked my path, prompting me to slam the emergency anchors on, I thought this must be someone's idea of a joke, and let forth a tirade of abuse at the driver. If I had wanted to be a good ambassador for cyclists, I should have kept my mouth shut. The old women in the passengers seat wound down the window, gingerly holding out some money in the direction of my collection tin, with only an after thought as to enquire what the charity I was collecting for actually was. Humbled and embarrassed, I thanked them profusely.

Today I was back with my old friend, more often my enemy, the good old A30. At least now it had filtered down to the standard and more manageable one lane in either direction road. I had felt duty bound to warn Andrew, my South African Chef, that if he intended to cycle in one day from Exeter to Plymouth, then the one thing he should do was NOT go via Dartmoor National Park. But he had waved my advice away by saying it would be no problem, as the previous day he had made it along the very hilly A30 and so had had plenty of practise. 'Watch out,' he had warned me, 'It's one killer of a road.'

I now looked out over what I would have called a pretty flat road by comparison to the previous few days, and my heart went out to Andrew. If he thought this was hilly, he was in for one hell of a shock across Dartmoor. I still would love to know if he made it.

Back on the A30, it struck me that a lot of people also appeared to be on move, although I was the only one to be carrying all my gear on a bicycle. I was frequently passed by loaded up cars, trucks and trailers, many of who read my charity bib as they passed and cheerily tooted their car horns in support…a beep for a bib, thought I. At one petrol station, where I would often stop to fill up my water bottles, a young man watched me, or should I say my Lycra clad legs, for a while before coming over to give me a charity donation. All these people did not know it, but they helped to keep my spirits raised that dispiriting day. I pedalled on all afternoon with a growing pounding headache and feeling immensely tired. There was something slightly strange I noted about cycling on whilst still feeling a little tipsy from the night before, something slightly entrancing and hypnotic that allowed me to push on without really feeling any pain. Unfortunately, the constant wet from the consistent rain eventually ruined the trance. I had water pouring off every inch of my saturated body, and by now I felt so tired that I could have nodded off whilst still pedalling. A couple of times I experimentally closed my eyes for a few seconds, but sensed the traffic coming dangerously close.

I seemed to be living in a very wet and watery world that first week, something I termed an 'aqua-cycle' experience. I mused that I wouldn't be at all surprised to wake up in the morning and find I had sprouted gills. The skin on my hands and feet were permanently wrinkled like old prunes, and I thought ahead to the forthcoming rigmarole I had to go through every time I found a campsite.

1. Struggle to put up an already saturated tent in the howling wind and driven rain.

2. Head for campsite shower block and begin peeling off sodden clothes.

3. Stand in shower with temperature up as hot as I could bear for at least half an hour, this was usually the time it took to warm my body right through.

4. Return to tent and find ingenious ways to dry out clothes in the limited space of my home. And finally,

5. Wake next morning to find it was still raining and my clothes were still not dry!!

Despite the disadvantages of handling tents in wet conditions, i.e. heavier to carry and impossible to fold/unravel without getting soaked myself, I had at least solved one problem, by devising a method where by I could take the inner skin down first, and pitch the outer shell up first of an evening too, thus keeping the most important part of my mobile house dry. My 'Litchfield Viper 2' tent luckily was designed in a way that enabled me to do this. And for a reasonably priced tent, it stood up to all the elements, even the high winds of Northern Scotland. I had gone for this tent, partly because it only weighed 2.5kg, but also it was deemed as a 1.5/2 person tent. That meant it was more than big enough for me with my multitude of panniers, and could accommodate a second person sharing when needs be.

Another ten watery miles passed in a nonsensical blur. I remember stopping to photograph a spectacularly flooded river. As I hung over the side watching a swirling torrent of muddied water pass under me, I thought, it's no good, Glastonbury, the next place on my 'must see' list would have to wait until tomorrow. After stopping off at a trucker's road side café to devour veggie burger and chips, (where I sat eating with exclamations of 'ooh aren't you brave' from big burly truckers ringing in my ears) I made one last ditch effort to reach the long awaited campsite just outside of Honiton. My last atom of energy was spent. I wheeled into the campsite and skidded to a soggy halt at reception. The warden appeared, as if by magic, and grinned at my exclusive impression of a drowned rat. 'Oh deary me, lets get you sorted' he muttered kindly.

I hadn't even finished my nightly struggle with my voluminously flapping tent, when an old man appeared, as if on cue, to invite me in to the family caravan for a hot cuppa. I had a nice cup of tea and slice of cake with his wife, (as it turned out, the one who'd sent her husband out in the rain to fetch me in.) They were very nice, but during our chat, the women kept telling me how brave and courageous I was cycling all alone, to the point where I was beginning to feel a little embarrassed. All day long I had heard such compliments that usually would have been enough to make ones head swell, but in a way I felt in all honesty like a bit of a fraud. After all, all I was doing was embarking on a cycling holiday. So when they asked if I was afraid of attack or rape or whatever other gruesome images they held in their heads, I simply replied 'Well you're kind and safe and being nice to me, so why shouldn't the next Joe Bloggs?'

Now don't get me wrong, I know there are plenty of dodgy brothers and sisters out there, (and I was later to come across a few) but I refuse to let the mainstream media ruin my stance that most people in this world are good and kind and well meaning, with no dark psychotic motives under the surface. Perhaps if the daily morning toilet papers, (sorry newspapers) were to publish all the stories of good that go on in this world, instead of always the bad, I think the world could become a very different place. But bad news is always sensationalising and this appears, sadly, to be what sells. Personally I think there could be a darker reason to this trend, far darker than just newspapers making money. If we are all too scared to go out the front door, or talk to our neighbours…just stay at home and watch mainstream rubbish on the television, then there is not much chance we will ever use some of the inactive parts of our brain. We will never band together and work out that modern life is one big con; a conspiracy where a small handful of rich run the world for their own financial benefit, a system that feeds junk to our bellies, junk to our minds, and encourages us to continue with needless consumerism; a world run by they who like to make it seem as if technological advances towards a life with as little activity, thought or creativity as possible will be a happy existence…but please don't think I am paranoid in any way shape or form.

DAY 8   (wow; 58 miles!)

As consciousness slowly took a hold of my mind, I couldn't work it out, was it a dream or was it STILL raining? Finally too awake to put the pattering overhead down to a nightmare, I forced myself into the sitting position and reluctantly unzipped myself banana style from my warm cocoon of a sleeping bag. I certainly felt at peace this morning. Due to the severe overdose of spirits the night before last, exhaustion had finally taken over and I had fallen asleep the minute my head had hit the pillow. Not once since setting out on this trip, or come to think of it ever in the history of my camping days, had I had such a sound and undisturbed nights sleep in a tent. Perhaps at last my comfort-nursed body had finally got used to lumpy floors and draughty sleeping bags? Feeling revitalised I unzipped the door, gaily leaping out to greet the day…only to narrowly escape slipping head first into the small lake which had collected outside the tent door over night. Ho hum.

Packing up my equipment of a morning, especially in these weather conditions was fast becoming a daily headache. For no matter how hard I tried to stay organised, a scattered mess of pannier bags, saucepans, clothes and tent pegs would prevail the surrounding area, whilst I would mutter and crawl around, flapping like a headless chicken, swearing because I couldn't find this or couldn't locate that. Professional certainly didn't come into this morning ritual. But despite my frustrations, even I have to admit that once everything was packed up and loaded correctly, I couldn't help but stand back in admiration at how it was possible to travel and live self sufficiently, and all out of four small bags that fitted neatly on to the humble bicycle. I felt proud of my minimalist lifestyle. (Just why did tatting down for the off take me so damn long?) This morning was no exception. It took a bewildering two and a half whole hours to get moving. Though admittedly, stopping off for another two cups of tea with Mr and Mrs Nice, and an hour spent browsing around the food shops of Honiton probably didn't help a great deal either.

I had only been in Somerset a day and it was already winning me over. The land features of Cornwall and Devon had been quaint, and due to its hilly features the horizon had never been too far away. My mind had been constantly occupied by my own small world of pushing up the next winding, grinding hill in front of me. But now all that was to change. Somerset's chief features, I noted for my diary later…'lots of flat bits.' I felt a new sense of freedom now I was over the lung bursting hills of previous days and my mind and eyes were free to wander over the rural idyll before me. This, I sighed happily to myself, was what it was all about.

I had been hoping to head directly north through a pancake flat area known as the Somerset Plains, but my new sense of freedom was disappointingly brought to an abrupt halt when round a corner I almost ploughed into a police notice which read 'Road closed due to flooding.' Sighing I realised that flat landscapes presented their own sets of problems.

I stopped two young boys coming the other way on their mountain bikes to ask them just how bad the flooding actually was. They muttered something about it not being too bad though in some parts it was bad, so actually they told me nothing of any use. Straddling my bike I pulled out my map. It was four miles to Langport this way, the way I wanted to go. Or another twelve mile detour. I stood for a while watching car after car turning back. Stubbornly I didn't want to detour and thought, why should I let a bit of water stop me? Its not as if I could get any wetter, and I didn't have to worry about my engine breaking down like all these big softy car drivers had to.

Carefully I began stripping off Lucy's panniers and pilling them onto the handlebars out of harms way before cautiously wading into the murky waters that was once a road, feeling proud that bicycle and rider could go where car could not.
But only half a mile on I quickly began to regret my decision. The muddy water began swirling up around my thighs, and it got to the point where I could no longer tell if I was still walking on the road or whether I had wondered off piste and into the adjoining fields. I couldn't see me keeping this up for another four miles, so mainly out of respect for my bicycle I aborted the mission and about turned. Setting off again on the twelve-mile detour, my cycling song for the day became the one about

Noah's Ark...'The animals came in two by two, hurrah, hurrah...'

Luckily I was still reeling with energy from a decent nights sleep, (at long last) and what would normally have been a dispiriting twelve-mile detour, actually turned out to be a very pleasurable spin. And within a flash of bike tyre and a few arks of rainwater I was soon back on track, taking a leisurely five minutes in the town of Langport. Langport was not what I would have called particularly touristy, or famous, in fact I may even dare to say it was all rather ordinary. I certainly had never heard of it before. I wondered then if this was why the place seemed friendlier than most places I had stopped at up to now? When people weren't smiling hello, they would look at me sat with bike propped on a bench in an inquisitive friendly sort of way. This came as such a relief, as up to now, I had had to deal with looks that seemed to say I was out of place, had made me feel self conscious, even unwelcome. And funnily enough they had all come about in touristy areas. They seemed to say, 'you're not a regular, 2.4 children family, holidaying with air polluting car, and kitchen sink in tow. Get out of our comfort zone girly, your face doesn't fit and you're making us feel uncomfortable by being so different.'

There seemed to be a bit of a pattern forming here. In heavily touristy areas I was gawped at in a manner usually reserved for the most bizarre animals in the zoo, (come back anteaters and armadillos all is forgiven!) But in areas that were not used to a huge daily influx of visitors, I was made to feel more than welcome. As if to prove my point, a group of locals out for an afternoon stroll stopped for a chat, and each made a donation before bidding me farewell. I thought about this as I sat resting my legs for a wee while. People seemed to be donating charity money, not out of pity or guilt, as I am sure often happens, but motivated by the determination of someone else's actions, surely one of the best reasons for giving freely. I felt proud of being a part of this country. What a charitable kind nation the "Brits" can be.

The hot topic on everybody's lips right now was, of course the weather. It had got to the stage when you didn't have to say a word with those you exchanged pleasantries with; you simply looked heavenwards to get people to tut and shake their heads. It turned out I had crossed the West Country in one of the wettest summers recorded in fifty years. This I could believe. I also discovered through reading other cyclists stories, that this was not an uncommon occurrence. It would appear that once you have set off cycle touring, no matter what part of the globe you were aiming for, Mother Nature will endeavour to deliver the hottest weekend since World War One, or maybe the worst blizzard since Christ was born, or even the longest drought since Tutankhamun. I think other global citizens find this great British obsession rather strange. (I'm talking about the one with the weather, not drinking tea...nor am I talking about our infamous habit of making jokes about anything toilet related!) But back to the weather, according to an article I read, if two Brits were to bump into each other in, say Outer Mongolia, it is statistically likely that within the first few minutes, one of them will have mentioned the weather. But I say, 'To hell with the critics.' What could be nicer than the observance of Mother Nature and sweet conversations about the one element in life that links us all? In modern life there is sadly a diminishing lack of connection with the natural world. People step from air-conditioned office, to motorised car and back to centrally heated homes. And they fixate on television and consumerism, rather than the world around. But for those who still work the land, make their homes for natural materials, or have been struck by the forces of nature, it is not so easy to forget we are in fact, all fallible. And it would be wrong for us to think we are mightier than the natural order of nature's chain.

Twice in my life, I have been sent a frightening reminder of just how powerful nature can be. Once in Thailand I was trying to cross a river with some other travellers, only to be swept away by currents whose strength took me totally by surprise. I distinctly remember just how frightening it felt to be swept away against your will by a force so incredibly strong, you are utterly powerless to beat it, no matter how hard you try. Luckily for me, and to the relief of my older sister, some local villagers fished me out further on down stream. But it was a lesson never to forget.

The second experience was when cycling a lonely mountain road across the Cullin Mountains on the Isle of Skye. The weather forecast had been pretty decent for February, cold but clear. How wrong it was. By the time the weather had taken a turn for the worse, I had no option but to carry on towards my destination, as to turn back would have been further to go. But as I struggled forwards, the wind became so strong, that even when I got off to push, I was still being blown backwards. At one stage I was bowled completely over, and as I found myself on my back staring at the sky, I witnessed my bicycle also being picked up by the wind and, despite the weight with all the panniers, it sailed off the ground, straight over the top of me too. Miles from anywhere, face red raw from the hail stones slamming into me, I felt increasingly powerless and lost. I thought I was in a nightmare, where no matter how much my legs pushed on; I was still no closer to getting to where I was heading. I would be stuck on this lonely mountain road forever until hypothermia and then death took me. I was just a tiny speck of insignificance against the almighty Mother Nature, moving amongst huge towering mountains that went on and on forever. I was caught in their trap. The sheep carcasses that lined the road, recently dead from exposure seemed to mock me as I struggled past. Luckily as I was on the brink of hypothermia, a girl whom I'd met the previous night in the youth hostel passed me in her Combi van and stopped. Rider and mount were rescued in the nick of time. Later when safely tucked up in bed at the youth hostel, as I closed my eyes to sleep, the whole experience came back to hit me, the vastness of that wilderness and the fright of being so helpless against it. I remembered the tears of frustration at the wind and how close I had come to perishing. As I dozed off, the fear and danger of the situation finally hit me.

Back in Somerset the weather couldn't have been more different to my memories. The rain had ceased and the sun was even daring to make an appearance. I felt strangely at home as I crossed King Sedges Moor by way of a network of deliciously traffic free minor roads. To one side lay farmland and on the other were hills reminiscent of the South Downs in Sussex where I am from. A cornucopia of birdlife appeared in the skies above. I spotted Sparrowhawks and Jays, and listened whilst Skylarks sang their song above, trying to draw my attention away from their nests, which they make on the ground. Hoverflies chased my fluorescent cycling bib down the road in the sunshine. Unfortunately the irritating common fly was everywhere too; I suspected this was due to the area being full of dairy farms, so there where plenty of cows for the flies to happily contend with…not to mention all the cowpats…it must have been fly heaven!

Last night my left knee had begun to ache, so I had slapped on enough Tiger Balm to stink the entire campsite out, and luckily it had done the trick. Now though, as I was fast approaching my sixtieth mile, by far the furthest I had ever cycled in one day, both knee joints began to voice their complaints at me. Not to mention all the various insect bites I had, that now began to itch with maddening vigour. So it was with much elation that I finally homed in on the campsite just outside of Glastonbury town. I couldn't wait to crawl into my tent and escape all the ailments that had made my life uncomfortable that day: damp, hunger and flies. I went to pay my levy at the reception desk...only to be told that the camping field was under two feet of water. I knew I shouldn't have packed that snorkel away just yet!!

DAY 9 (14 miles)

I was stunned when I switched on the radio to find it was already 9.30am. I had slept for almost fourteen hours and it felt great. To fall asleep from physical exhaustion and without the aid of medication or alcohol surely has to be one of the most satisfying sleeps a person can have. Unfortunately I think the majority of people rarely reach such a state. Western culture seems hell bent on making peoples lives as sedentary as possible, as if this will somehow make their lives more fulfilled; motorcars, drive-thrus, home delivery, microwave meals and escalators, to name just a few. I myself found there were people who even reacted with abject horror at the thought of using a bicycle as the preferred means of transport. And these were usually the same folk who could not even walk a short distance to the shops say, always taking the car instead. But what they failed to see was what they were depriving themselves of: not only a healthier way of life and all the benefits physical fitness has to offer. But also what I can describe as a real wholesome and feel good factor that comes from getting around using one's own energy. It is a feeling that is liberating and uplifting to both body and soul, and I believe the secret to an altogether happier life. All those lethargic insomniacs take heed...the more energy you use, the more you will have and the better you will sleep.

At half past nine in the morning, the day was already scorching. It was such a pleasant change after the deluge I'd woken up to almost every day so far. The only things to spoil it were the flies. They did that thing they were put on this earth to do; buzz around my face as I tried to eat breakfast and get on my nerves. But nothing could spoil the sweet feeling of a hot summer's day and it was with a happy grin on my face that I cycled up towards Glastonbury Tor.

On the road below the Tor the local council had thoughtfully provided cycle racks for Tor visiting cyclists. Why though, I would like to ask the council of Somerset, were they positioned on the other side of a high fence, accessed only by a locked gate? Luckily for my back, (and Lucy's paintwork,) a kind passer-by and a bus driver who'd stopped for a fag, saw my predicament and gallantly came to my rescue. (Don't you just love men sometimes!) And between the three of us, we managed to hoist Lucy with all the panniers safely over the barricade.

Glastonbury Tor is a bizarre 518ft rise in the middle of the Somerset Plains, (Tor, logically means hill in Celtic.) It is a natural formation made up of layers of clay, blue limestone, and capped by hardy sandstone. The tower on the top is sadly all that is left of the medieval church of St Michael that once stood here, but the Tor seems to have had a very dark history, and was once long ago the scene of many a hanging, drawing and quartering. Nice. But it has also been thought of as a most magical place, and in fact still is to the masses. For example, it is said that the medieval terraces, which run along the edges of its hillside, actually form part of a giant 3D maze, whilst others believe the Tor may in fact be hollow. (I sincerely hoped not as I stood on top.) But the superstition that really captured my imagination though, had to be the one that says the Tor is in fact a gateway to the underworld, spooky or what!

I dutifully followed the footpath that led up to the top of the Tor, where I was greeted by an impressive, if slightly hazy view of the surrounding county. What seemed even hazier though, were the minds of some rather curious characters that strewed the top. Various rather befuddled hippies sat about in various states of nirvana, smoking or chanting, whilst another group of friends stood in a circle at the base of the tower holding hands with eyes closed. As I watched and listened, they seemed convinced that they could feel themselves flying up towards the top of the tower...'Hey wow man!'

After half an hour sat drinking in such scenes of cosmic delights, I began to feel disappointed that the ground did not look as though it would open up any time soon. I darkly imagined tourists, cyclists, hippies and all, dropping like a brick through into the dark clutches of the underworld below, never to be seen again. O.k. actually I was quite glad it didn't happen, not on a sunny day like today. Instead I went off on a quest of my own to find the location of a wasp's nest that provided the Tor with a liberal yellow smattering.

Glastonbury town itself was not what I had been expecting at all. I guess I had thought Somerset would still be alive with 'olde worlde' folk, who once a year get swamped by alternative types during festival time. Not so. As I sat on a bench stuffing my face with my organic bananas and strawberry flavoured Soya-made milkshake, purchased from one of the many wholefood shops on the high street, I contemplated the dreadlocked heads tooing and frooing. It reminded me somewhat of Brighton where I had previously lived. There was definitely a full on alternative scene going on down here too which I was thoroughly enjoying and even mused as to what it would be like to reside in these parts. The folk of Glastonbury certainly seemed contented, living out the wildest of their hippy dreams beneath the shadow of the Tor, and it helped to remind me of who I really was before my true self was swallowed up by the grind of daily life. Which I suppose in a way was one of the things I was hoping to gain from this trip.

Despite the long sleep I was still a bit physically worn out after yesterday's marathon, (two and a quarter marathons to be precise) so I decided to be gentle on myself, and took up the reins again in the direction of Wells. It was only six miles and not too hilly, but the hot and humid wind did nothing to help my progress, (is there any such thing as perfect cycling weather?) My plan was to visit the Wookey Caves before pressing on to Chester for the night. But plans took an unexpected twist when outside of Wells Cathedral I bumped into Les.

Les was 39, half 'Kiwi', mountain bike mad and was also cycling Lands End to John O Groats, only to put a more interesting spin on things, he was pedalling via the twenty four cathedral cities. And as if that wasn't enough, he was also diverting to the three peaks, where he would down bike for the day to scale each one. But more importantly, he was raising money for the British Red Cross landmines clearance appeal. Within minutes of this extraordinary meeting, we both agreed to call a day on our cycling plans and go celebrate our progress so far and compare notes. An enjoyable tour of the cathedral and the pubs of Wells ensued, finishing off in a rather nice curry house.

Les was an ex squaddie and exuded the air of someone so exceedingly well organised that it almost put me to shame. He was obviously very wealthy, coming from a high-class background, and was more than keen to take me on a grand tour of all his latest high-tec equipment. It was indeed very impressive, with an impressively high price tag to match no doubt. My 'high-tec' equipment on the other hand consisted of hand made bike panniers, a draughty sleeping bag, an excruciatingly uncomfortable carry mat, and my non-waterproof waterproof coat that stayed shamefully hidden in my panniers.

I couldn't help but like Les for his energy and enthusiasm for life. And he certainly had the self-confidence to go with it, (he managed to chuck in his life story over a few beers.) He was a rich successful businessman, had been a high ranking army officer, and had spent years living in New Zealand making a success of himself there too. He was all geared up to meeting Princess Di after this escapade and next he wanted to be an M.P. (He also mentioned that his sister had bags of energy and had once cycled across several continents with a couple of guys who wrote a book about their expedition. A few years later I coincidentally happened upon this book...his sister it seemed, was a moody nightmare and the bane of the other two lad's life and in the end they were glad when she gave up and went home.)

However, I was glad we weren't travelling companions, because I knew this almost hyperactive mentality would have got on my nerves before long, and I wasn't the only one either. In the course of just one evening, Les managed to run into dispute with several different people, and his highly strung nature ensured he got very worked up about the tiniest little thing someone might say to rebuke him, which perfect strangers seemed to do on an alarmingly regular basis. I put this down to his overly loud voice, with its BBC English intonations and his sometimes overly confident male manner. These combined qualities seemed a sure fire way to get folks backs up. To be fair to the poor chap, I must admit I quite liked him (albeit in small doses.) He was humorous, interesting and intelligent, and it was refreshing to meet someone who didn't have so many of the usual right wing views other Tory voting, financial advisors I'd ever met had had. But by letting him pay for absolutely everything that evening, I suppose one could say I was just cashing in on his wealth and very generous nature. I was thoroughly ashamed off myself...yeah right!!

DAY 10 (44 miles)

9am; and another roasting, sticky hot day awaited. Wookey Hole, on the other hand was dark, damp and wonderfully chilly, (they remain at

11 degrees Celsius). I wasn't too happy at being charged nearly seven pounds for a quick tour, particularly as our guide spent the majority of the time cracking pathetic jokes that only a six year old would find funny. But nothing could ruin the natural wonder of the underground taverns. I had always naively believed that stalagmites (which might one day reach the ceiling) and stalactites (which hold on tightly to the roof) would be thin shards, maybe icicle type formations, but these were more like great pillars. The name stalagmite comes from the Greek word 'stalagma' meaning drop or drip, which surprise surprise, is exactly how the stalagmites are formed; by mineral solutions and calcium carbonate dripping through the ceiling on to the cave floor below. The stalactite name comes from the Greek word 'stalaktite' meaning, that which drips, and is made up of the same sort of stuff. Their growth can be as slow as 1 millimetre a year...phew, that's nearly as slow growing as my savings account.

The cave tour is all based around the telling of witch-based legends... well, who else would you expect to find living in a cave? The story goes that that an old woman lived alone in the caves with her dog and her goats. She was, surprise surprise, blamed by the local villagers for anything that went wrong in their lives and they long suspected she was constantly up to no good; boiling cauldrons, casting spells, that sort of thing. The locals turned to the Abbot of Glastonbury for help, who in turn sent a monk, (delegation, delegation, delegation,) Father Bernard, to exorcise the witch's spirit. The brave monk went into the caves where a long chase ensued, and ended with him turning her to stone. Neat! As it turns out there could actually have been something to this story, because in 1912 an archaeologist found the almost complete skeletal remains of an old woman, some goat bones and an old dagger.

After the cave experience, I was delighted to then be taken on a tour of the paper making mills of Wookey, which I didn't even realise, existed. It is one of the few places left in the country that still makes paper by hand, but not just any old paper. Produced here was thick parchment paper used in courts or for long living legal documents. During the 19th century, the paper was made of old rags, and as much as 35,000 sheets were turned out every week. These days it is made by cotton imported from the United States, but apart from that the process for making it remains unchanged. I was delighted when the opportunity arose to make my very own piece of paper, and I lined up with all the rest of the under eights, and prepared to 'get gooey.' Proudly I smoothed out my finished work of art, which is then placed between two pieces of Hessian cloth to dry. Unfortunately I was unable to take my 'master piece' home with me as all sheets of handmade paper take up to three days to dry out, but I would like to think that somewhere in the world, maybe in the European Court of Human Rights, some important international agreement has been carefully signed on my very own hand crafted piece of paper.

In the adjoining souvenir shop I came across an amusing poster, which I simply had to buy. It went as follows:

RAGS MAKE PAPER,
PAPER MAKES MONEY,
MONEY MAKES BANKS,
BANKS MAKE LOANS,
LOANS MAKE BEGGARS,
BEGGARS MAKE RAGS.
Annon. 18th Century

A story not entirely dissimilar to myself!

By the time I came out it was one o'clock and the sun was at its harshest. But after a week of persistent rain, I certainly was not one to complain. As I pedalled on towards Cheddar village in temperatures reaching 25 degrees Celsius, I marvelled at the brightness of the world and I was pleasantly surprised to find the 'A' road deliciously free of traffic save for the odd car…and me of course. Despite being a 'cheese-aholic' I managed to stay out of the dozens of tourist shops in the village of Cheddar, and instead made for a phone box to ring home. I had considered arranging to meet my parents in Cheddar tomorrow, but decided against it, partly because it was already swarming with tourists, but mainly because I still had oodles of energy and felt very keen to put a few more miles under my wheels. After a quick chat to my mother we decided to rendezvous in Bath. Feeling happy I replaced the receiver and made my way back out into the heat wave.

After topping up my water bottles, I picked up Lucy, and on the hottest day of the year so far, I set off on the long and arduous climb out of Cheddar. The road wound its way up over the gorge and into the hills beyond. Cheddar Gorge is a natural phenomenon made by the moving of the Earths tectonic plates, millions of years ago, and standing at 700ft is Britain's largest. The whole area is a site of special scientific interest, and the Calcareous grasslands are home to Peregrine Falcons and Horseshoe bats, whilst grazing Soay sheep keep the scrubland in check.

I found it a little disconcerting that as I set off along the road, folk coming the other way not only stared, as they were prone to do, but were actually shaking their heads at me as I passed! I guessed they thought I must be barking mad, but care I did not, and retorted to their doubting minds by flashing a sweet smile. As a matter of fact, the climb wasn't that bad after all. The first half a mile was probably the worst, rising at a rate of 1 in 3, but after that the road makers must have calmed down and the rise became a far gentler, if arduously long, climb. As I toiled upwards for another four and a half miles I tried to look out for the rare bats, birds of prey or Soay Sheep that may have wondered into my path, but the sweat dripping in my eyes meant I was virtual blind for the duration of the ascent. It was with relief I finally reached the summit and noted the fact that the road now ran almost flat across the top of the Mendip Hills. I stopped to catch breath, and decided to

follow a bumpy track that ran across the fields and into the cool and privacy of thorn thickets. There I was able to remove a great deal of my sweat-saturated clothes and enjoy the cool breeze on my bare chest and back. After several litres of water and a rest I felt revived enough to photograph a spectacular view of the valley below, of which, I proudly noted, I had traversed under my own steam.

Cycling across the Mendips felt to me like cycling across the top of the world; the flat road made it an almost effortless pleasure, the temperature was cooler than the heat hazed roads in the valley below, and the 360-degree views were spectacular. I spied a number of gypsy camps along the side of the road, many of them advertising 'Real Romany fortunes told here.' After passing a few I was seriously considering giving one a go when I realised that yet again I had managed to get lost…well I say lost, I just wasn't where I had expected to be on my map, which I suppose is kind of the same thing! What was even more puzzling about this latest set back was that I had thought this route was just a case of staying on the same road all of the way over the hills. Puzzled as to how I could have gone so far wrong, I doubt even a fortune teller could have worked that one out.

Luckily a more appropriate type of good fortune rolled up…literally. Another psycho tourist called Martin. I explained my predicament, and together we studied both my map and his, and he pointed out why I kept going wrong. Because I was using photocopies of a map it meant without the aid of colour it was sometimes impossible to tell when the route I was following was just a bend or whether it had forked off and become a new road. Relieved it wasn't just me being stupid I let him show me exactly where I was, and then as a double dose of serendipity he also topped up my diminishing water supply with his own. It was an act of kindness that only someone stuck out on their own in the middle of nowhere, without the supposed free energy of a motorcar could appreciate. It took me back to a pledge I had made after nearly perishing in Scotland that I would always look after other cyclists. (As it happened I had the opportunity the very day after my near death experience. I had been whizzing around Skye in a combi van with Sarah, my saviour from the day before. As we sat in the warm admiring the view of the Cullin Mountains, my attention was drawn towards a lone speck struggling up the hill towards us. As Sarah put the kettle on, I went out to hail the approaching cyclist and invite him over for a cup of tea which he gratefully accepted.)

After bidding Martin farewell the road began its descent off the Mendips. After my earlier five-mile struggle against gravity, this was the reward I had been longing for. With the wind through my hair and the sun on my back I swooped and fell down that scenic road without a care in the world and a smile on my face, happier than I would be if I had just won the lottery. Alas it was all over too soon, only taking around fifteen minutes in total.

Somewhere nearing the bottom of the hill, my attention was drawn away from an impatient Volvo that had almost turned me into 'people pate' and towards a man who was stepping from his car and waving frantically at me to stop. 'Hello' said I hopefully. He had seen my charity bib as he had passed and had desperately wanted to make a donation. He told me his son had been in Cambodia for two years and they knew all about the horrors of landmines. I was so touched by his donation and the praise he had bestowed upon me that I kicked myself afterwards for not asking him more about his story before he left.

The older I get, the more curious about things I become, and the more my thirst for knowledge grows. But in a way I've had to teach myself to always ask plenty of questions when the opportunity for learning from someone arises. It seems odd now thinking back to school life, I don't ever recall being all that keen to learn the things we were taught. Now though I almost wish I could do it all again. I'd love to be reminded of all those ancient battles, the pollination cycles of plants, how to say in French 'You have sexy eyes,' and just what the hell was chemistry all about? I am glad I never decided to pursue the avenue of becoming a school teacher…trying to get a load of T.V obsessed kids to take an interest in what you are talking about. And yet I have read many times, that children in a lot of third world countries would be only too happy to get a chance at school and to better themselves.

Maybe it is just human nature to not appreciate what you have in the first place. What is the point in parents saying to their kids, 'I have worked hard all my life to give you the things I never had.' Of course they won't appreciate this because they weren't the ones who went without in the first place. Surely it is better for the young to learn by example, and god knows there is a shortage of decent role models these days. I have always looked to my parents to show me how it is done. Now there are two people who have never been particularly wealthy but who have always found work come what may, even (as in the case of my father) if it meant working for poor wages, (having been a child during the second world war and left school with no qualifications.) To them there is no other way out, no handouts and no easy options; you just went out and got a job. I know of families whose kids are now the third generation of dole claimants, and no wonder. Because their parents never went off, worked their butts off, and bought back prizes to the kitchen table, the children never got to see the benefits of hard work and bettering yourself. So when the children grew up they sat at home and accepted the situation of having little and relying on state benefit and acting as though working for a living was some alien concept that might even hurt them. They have had no good role models to teach them how to drag themselves out of the poverty trap, no one to teach them that life can be different, you just have to go out into the world and work at it, show you're worth something and opportunities will come your way. It's called a life of self-respect.

For some strange reason, I had visualized that once over the Mendip Hills the final road into Bath would be a flat one. I couldn't have been more wrong if I had tried. The road was disappointingly very up and down, and what was worse, it was composed of short sharp ups and downs. In plain English this meant that the downs weren't sufficiently long enough to regain breath and stop heart palpitations before hitting the next up. And before long the familiar sensation of water pouring off my body returned, only now it was sweat and not rain. God it was hot. I tried forcing my tired limbs onwards, trying to take encouragement from a sign that said Bath was only another eight miles away, but eight miles at the end of a long day may as well have been eighty. It was no use; I needed to rest…now!

Halfway down the next hill I spotted the perfect place, a grassy lay-by complete with a tree-shaded bench. But for some reason I will never understand, I decided I did not want to share my space with a young man who had also stopped there, stood leaning on his car staring out across the fields into the distance. It was a nervous reaction to a stranger I had never experienced before. I struggled on but only made it as far as around the next bend before I collapsed on to the grassy verge. I had to lie motionless for several minutes before I could summon up the energy to get up, dust myself off and drink the warm dregs from my plastic water bottle.

As I did so, I noticed a car pull over and the driver jump out. I was half expecting to hear a request for directions, when I recognised the driver as the young man from around the corner, and heard the words,

'Excuse me, do you fancy a shag?' I stood there dumb founded; a sweaty, smelly cyclist in a silly sun hat trying to study my map...did I really look as though I did? Momentarily in shock, the only words I could summon up were...'Sorry?' The guy repeated his lurid offer, by which time I had managed to collect myself together enough to reply... 'No but I can bring my knee into sharp focus with your bollocks if you don't fuck off pronto.'

At the time I wasn't in the least bit afraid of this guy, it all seemed faintly ridiculous, and he certainly was. I just felt proud that some undiscovered sixth sense of mine had emerged just at the right time, and I made a mental note to listen to it more in the future.

Meanwhile it did occur to me that if this guy was weird enough to introduce himself to a perfect stranger in this manner, then exactly how deep did this weirdness go? I decided I most definitely did not want to find out. I picked up my bike and as hot and exhausted as I was, believe me I did not stop once all the way into Bath.

DAY 11 (1st day of rest)

I was rudely awoken by some inconsiderate git with a very large motorbike, (and probably small genitals to boot) who thought it would be fun at some unearthly hour on a Sunday morning to start his engine, (which just happened to be missing the silencer on the exhaust,) and rev it for a full five minutes before roaring away. This particular campsite had a field set aside for people without cars. Sadly they hadn't thought to ban all combustion engines from this area. And clearly I wasn't the only soul to share these sentiments, as tent zips began unzipping all around me and the air turned a shade of blue as folk were to be heard cursing this biker fool for waking them so inconsiderately.

But nothing could dampen my spirits that morning. I had just awoken from a fantastic nights sleep, again brought on by pure physical exhaustion. Yesterday night I had arrived at the campsite at the same time as a seventy year old man who claimed he had walked the same distance I had cycled that day, which rather put my efforts into the shade. Fair play to him. I had then spent a good half hour in the showers, much to the annoyance of other waiting folk who probably wouldn't have understood the novelty I was enjoying in taking a cooling down shower at days end rather than a warming up one. Next I discovered the on site restaurant where I dined on a sumptuous meal of veggie burger and chips, and did my best to sup a pint so cold that it numbed the back of my eye balls. But by then tiredness had taken such a hold I almost had to race back to my tent before I fell asleep on my feet. I fell into a contented coma listening to owls calling each other and the gurgling song of a nearby stream. It had been a state of paradise and happiness I am sure that would have surpassed the effect of any recreational drug.

Today was parents' day. They arrived in a sea of smiles together with my sister, who was still unexpectedly in the country, and after a quick discussion we all decided it would be the perfect weather for a day at the beach. Rock and roll!

It was my first visit to Weston-Super-Mare. The sheer size of its beach is an impressive sight for the eyes. Miles of windswept sand and boggy mud flats that with a bit of imagination had an almost fantasy adventure type of appeal. My mother sister and I decided to brave a paddle, this being low tide. But nearly twenty minutes of walking proved fruitless; the water still hadn't even covered our knees yet. It was the lowest tide I'd ever encountered; in fact it can get out to as far away as a mile from the seafront. This trick of nature allows the beach to be used as an extra car park until the tides come creeping back in again. Signs are everywhere reminding folk what can happen if they don't return to their cars by a certain time, surely more effective than any threat of wheel clamping. We also learnt that a huge motorcycle rally is held on the beach once a year… I just hope they clean all the litter up before that tides come back in!

Back on shore I was revelling in the delight of not having to get anywhere for a change. As I lay on my back I slipped on my shades, staring up at a bright blue cloudless sky, it struck me this was the first time I'd been able to appreciate the full effects of the heatwave and the suns burning rays on my skin, as for once I had no cycling breeze to accompany me. We lunched in a pub; where I gorged myself silly on gargantuan pub grub meals and supped ice-cold pints of lager, only to complain not half an hour later that I was hungry again. My mother brought with her some much-appreciated supplies, including my old British Rail outdoor jacket, which I thought might be a tad more waterproof than the cagoule I was currently using. She also bought me a stack of mail, which I saved for later. My sister Rachael expressed horror at how little funds I'd collected for the charity; about twenty pound so far, (luckily I had around seven hundred promised in sponsorship from some of the folks back home.) She suggested standing around outside shops in the towns and cities I passed through along the way, and start jingling my collection tin under people's noses. It was a thoroughly enjoyable day out, and after they left late that evening I was left to my owls and my gurgling stream, silently saying my blessings for a loving and supportive family.

ROUTE MAP 2: THE MIDLANDS

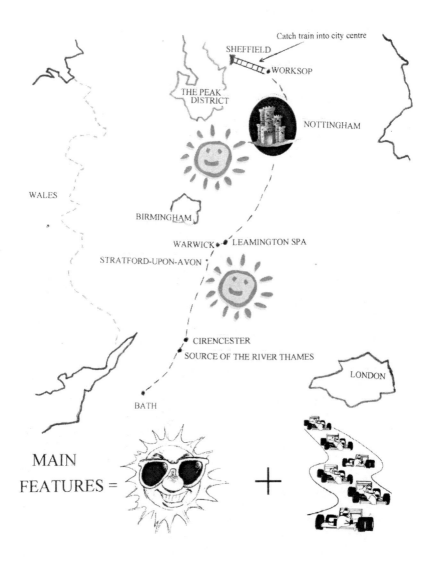

Catch train into city centre

SHEFFIELD

WORKSOP

THE PEAK DISTRICT

NOTTINGHAM

WALES

BIRMINGHAM

WARWICK   LEAMINGTON SPA

STRATFORD-UPON-AVON

CIRENCESTER

SOURCE OF THE RIVER THAMES

LONDON

BATH

MAIN FEATURES =   +

DAY 12 (45 miles)

By now the trouble I had experienced sleeping on my not so comfortable sleeping mat, was definitely a thing of the past. The morning got off to a good start; it was a pleasure to be able to buy breakfast from the on site restaurant, liberating me from the time consuming hassle of washing up afterwards. After a lot of baked beans and a few too many scrambled eggs I set out full but happy.

The city of Bath lay before my wheels; a maze of warm honey coloured buildings made from the famous Bath Stone that made it a World Heritage City. The streets were hot, but also relatively silent. Occasionally I would pass the odd person doing 'Sunday things;' washing their cars, walking the dog or strolling with the kids to the park. As we passed, they would all bid me a cheery good morning or nod or smile. Shops remained shut and cars were for the most part, left at home. It took me back to when I was a kid. In those days, Sundays felt different to the rest of the week. Whilst many of my young friends I went to school with would gripe about the boredom of Sundays, I loved them. It meant a ride out on a friend's horse in the morning, then home for my mothers Sunday roast beef, and a hot bath before bed. Sundays felt like Sundays. Now though in the urban south east of England things have very much changed. Shops and pubs are open all day, lots more people are therefore working and as a result, roads seem as busy as any other day of the week. As you would expect, gradual changes are hard to notice. In fact it was not until I spent time in Germany and observed the way the people and particularly the young adults spent their Sundays, that I became aware of the changes to my own culture. In the west of Germany where I stayed for many months, I spent my Sundays with my German friend visiting his family for a Sunday meal. Afterwards there would be no shops or bars open. Instead we would visit his friends who would go for a game of football or Frisbee in the park, or sit about having a jamming session with their instruments. They told me they liked to relax ready for the start of another week at school or college. It all seemed some how so much more innocent and almost old fashioned, even though it was in the west of Germany, a very modern western nation if ever there was one.

Back in Somerset, whilst expecting to find things very quiet in rural areas on a Sunday, I was also delighted to find this also applied in the city and it made my cycle tour through Bath and out the other side a most pleasant one. Everything I had seen of Somerset so far I had found very agreeable and it made me wonder, could this be the place for me to settle down and start a new life?

After the usual faffing about with poor maps and wrong turnings, I finally found my intended road out of Bath, a minor road that wound its way up over Banner Down. The road was as steep as it was long. The only way I found I could manage such a steep gradient was to cycle for a few minutes, and then stop to rest for a few minutes. This way I was able to regain my breath, intake a few mouthfuls of liquid and then try again. I also found it helpful, each time I stopped, to look over my shoulder at the view behind, which spectacularly improved as I gained height, and feel pleased with the progress I had made. I was sticky all over and tried distracting myself by becoming mesmerised by the way in which my sweat soaked arms and thighs glistened in the sunshine. I had slowly pedalled my way up on to the Cotswolds and once at the top, the road thankfully flattened out.

This particular flat straight minor road was known as the Fosse Way, a Roman Road that runs all the way from Exeter to Lincoln. It is special as it is the only Roman road in Britain to retain its' Latin name, the rest having been renamed by the Saxons once the Romans had gone. Along this pleasant partially shaded road I passed mainly farming land and an M.O.D sight with a miniature airfield, sinisterly guarded by armed police. I also passed into Wiltshire, my fourth county.

As usual my photocopied maps led me on a variation of my intended route, and I ended back on the A429 sooner than I had intended. But for once it didn't seem to matter because here too in Wiltshire, the Sunday traffic was very thin on the ground, leaving me to breeze along unthreatened by the presence of cars, and breathing easier without a constant stream of exhausts passing me by. I passed through a beautiful town named Malmesbury where part of the old Abbey church still remains. It was from this tower in c 1000AD, the flying monk Elmer leapt from, in his attempt to become the first man to fly! Luckily most of the residents these days seemed a lot saner by comparison, including a couple of local cycling lads who invited me to join them for a drink. But just in case there was some surviving inherent madness about the place, I declined and pressed on towards Cirencester instead.

By this time I was beginning to flag, (more like melt) in the summer heat, and rather worryingly I could hear sticky patches of tarmac squelching beneath my tyres. I felt pleased that despite the piss takings from friends, I had packed my floppy…worn on Bournemouth beach by old folk with socks pulled up to their knees …sunhat, that was now working a treat, not only at preventing me from squinting but also from suffering sun stroke. I stopped off further up the road to take shade under a glorious old oak, but had to jump up quickly when I found myself dozing off. I longed to escape the heat, and for extra protection pulled on my thin blue cotton shirt to protect the back of my neck, which I'm sure, was beginning to fry. Further along the A429, passing from Wiltshire into Gloucestershire, (three counties in one day…not bad eh?) I passed a curious sign. It informed me that the road beneath my wheels was in fact a recycled road construction. Now did this mean it was an old road, resurfaced using recycled materials? In which case it was a wonderful idea.

There was one particular must see spot on my trip today, just off the A429 near a place called Kemble. I kept a sharp eye out for the sign and finally spotted it half buried in a hedge; a footpath marker that read 'Source of the River Thames – 1 mile.' As I locked Lucy to a gate, a young couple were just returning from a walk along the same route. They saw me and came over. 'It's dry' they said.

'Sorry?' I asked.

'It's dry... the River Thames. There's nothing there.'

'O.K thanks' I replied, more curious than ever and set out along the path. Certainly the day I had left London for Cornwall, the mighty river running through our capital was as full as ever. But there I found it, the Source of the mighty River Thames, dry as a bone in a desert. This, the official source, comes from a natural underground spring called, rather logically, the Thameshead. After heavy rain the spring bubbles up and water begins to flow on its 215 miles journey to The North Sea. But during dry spells, like now, the water is too deep underground to bubble to the surface and the official riverbed is quite dry. An empty channel could clearly be seen, cut across the field where water should and often does flow. I walked along this dry ditch; well it's not everyone who can say they have walked along the bottom of the Thames! During these dryer spells, the shortage of water flow is boosted by Lyd Well, an old Roman well about a mile further east from Kemble, and from there on it swells with the addition of many tributaries along route until it becomes that almighty flowing torrent we see through London every day of the year.

At the end of a long hot day, wheeling into Cirencester, I slammed on the anchors at the first cash machine I spied. As I fiddled with my wallet and wandered if there was a tourist office nearby that might direct me to a campsite, I suddenly became aware that a group of teenage lads I had passed some minutes ago, had caught me up and were now hollering and pointing in my direction. 'Oh hell, here we go' thought I, expecting the usual aggression and cocky comments, so was taken aback when what I actually got was a genuine show of interest and a whole barrage of questions. 'How far is it?' they asked wide-eyed.

'You're cycling a thousand miles?'
'What with only one water bottle?'
'Why not drive a car?'
'Why have you come through Cirencester?'
'Are you a traveller?'
'You shouldn't wear those big boots for cycling you know.'

I tried to hide my giggles as I stayed to chat to the lads for a bit, glad of some entertaining company in my wearied state, but I also remembered I still had to find a place to sleep for the night, so asked the boys if they knew of anywhere. They did not, but took it upon themselves to charge across the road and hail down a police patrol car that just happened to be passing. I thought the coppers inside might have been furious, but here in small-town Gloustershire, they were not only very helpful but friendly and somewhat amused by me too. It was turning into one eye opener after the other. Round where I live in the southeast, teenagers don't chat to strangers. They bum cigarettes, gob on the floor, smash up the local bus stops and try to nick cheap cider from the local shop, and that is just in the villages. The PC and WPC in the patrol car began pulling out their loose change to fill my collection tin, and asked what charity it was for. When I told them, I once again heard, 'Oh Princess Di's thing.' (This could very soon start to irritate me.)

After this friendly interlude I waved good-bye to both teenagers and police constables and merrily cycled off in the direction they had pointed me in. As I cycled I hummed, and occasionally wiped the odd spot of rain from my face; there was one almighty storm brewing in the skies above and as clouds grew thicker, blanketing in the suppressing heat I began longing for the relief of rain. Alas, despite putting up my tent in super fast mode, the storm clouds passed that campsite by and I was left to a sticky airless night, spent thrashing around in a sweat soaked sleeping bag.

The campsite that night was the first and come to think of it, the only one I stayed at whose owners seemed to have a conscience about the environment. There were separate bins for recycling the different materials; whilst in the shower blocks great signs had been erected, telling people to conserve the earth's resources by turning off taps and light switches after use. This was a message that particularly struck a cord with me. Tourism already plays its part in environmental impact, and we certainly shouldn't forget that just because we are on holiday, we are exempt from continuing to care for the planet. At home I gather all tins, plastic and paper and then once a fortnight lug it all by hand down the road to the recycling centre. This somewhat monumental effort seems to me justification for the waste I produce in my life. For by choosing to do this the hard way, it serves to remind me of the waste my modern life style produces and that I need to take care of the planet by cutting down on unnecessary packaging and consuming, something I think people avoid thinking about when they just open the waste-bin, drop everything in and let someone else dispose of their rubbish.

It is sad but true that here in the west we think we can continue to use up the earths finite resources without ever putting it back. If every one could cut their consumption rate by even a third, think how much less strain we would put on our planet and the natural world. And how hard would this be…In my life I try not use the car, eat organic food, reuse and recycle everything and avoid meat, (the production puts a great strain on water resources and the environment.) I reckon my consumption must be at least fifty percent less than most other western citizens but I certainly do not lead a difficult, constrained or deprived existence, far from it in fact. It just feels to me like common sense. You cannot escape the adage that what goes around comes around. If you keep smashing up the earths eco systems and hacking away at nature without repairing the damage, how can you expect our planet to keep supporting us? Destroying that what keeps you alive is the most stupid thing to do in anyone's book.

What is even more frightening is the American attitude to this problem is to continue as they always have done and if the eco systems fail, just build an artificial one. The cost of doing what nature already does for us for free has been estimated at 35 trillion dollars…per year… ridiculous?

But back at home, I find that time and again I hear the ignoramuses telling me that environmental damage and climate change is just a myth.

If this is so, than can some one please explain to me why even in my short life span I can see the effects with my own eyes? If the modern farming practises which destroy habitats have no ill effects, then why when I look out of my window do I see so few garden birds anymore compared to the hundreds I used to see every day when growing up? If the hole in the ozone layer does not exist, then please explain to me why as a child, with far more delicate skin than I have now, was I able to stay out in the hot sun all day before I started to burn, where as now burning time can be as little as an hour?

The evidence is right there before our eyes and one doesn't need to be a scientist to know the truth. Either people are too stupid to see it, or more likely they go into ignorance mode and it is just easier not to care. Sometimes I have such a sad feeling that it is too late. Here in the west we are already so far removed from nature that we can no longer make the connection. And as we are so selfishly carrying on with our ways, then neither are we in a position to tell developing nations not to develop along the same lines as ourselves, and so the problems can only get worse.

* * *

Despite all the advantages of travelling alone, I was not immune to the odd twinge of loneliness, especially when everyone else appeared to be in a couple or playing happy families. Of an evening I ideally would like to party, or just settle down for a good old natter, but tonight I was getting neither. And what was worse was being pitched up right next door to an Italian family having a wonderful time, but at the same time shooting me looks similar to those I received in the 'oasis' on Bodmin moor. I tried not to notice, busying myself with dinner, radio listening and diary writing. But it was clear they thought me some sort of social retard. With these not very happy thoughts in mind, I retired early to my bed.

DAY 13 (48 exceedingly weary hungry miles)

I write this at the end of one of the most exhausting days so far, and I might add, exhausting for a most unexpected reason. When I set out this morning I set out without any breakfast...isn't that a lovely self-describing word; break (the overnight) fast. I wouldn't normally have done such a foolish thing, but I had made a terrible miscalculation and let my food stocks run dry. Never mind, thought I, I was bound to pass somewhere very soon: a village shop or general store on my route north that morning, somewhere I could stock up on much needed supplies. However, unbeknown to me up till that day, I was about to uncover a very new and worrying trend. A modernisation and an Americanisation that has inevitably arrived in this country.

The terrain that morning was pretty exhausting. All ups and downs... just what one needs with no breakfast inside them! But my reward for the discomfort was seclusion, as I cycled past acres of farmland and impressive woodlands I realised that since setting out, this was the first time I felt as though I was truly in the middle of nowhere. It was such a wonderfully and unexpected feeling on this wee, crowded island of ours, but a bit further on I began to see signs that the developers had been here also.

With a very urgent need to fill my belly I looked out eagerly for the number of villages marked on my route. I say villages, to all intents and purposes that is what they looked like on my map, but when I arrived I was disappointed to find nothing more than a housing estate of new homes. The people from these places were far from friendly. They eyeballed me suspiciously, usually from the shield of their car windscreen. At each new village I passed, I looked out eagerly for signs of civilisation as I knew it; shops, a post office, schools, a children's adventure playground with an ice cream van or a small tea stall for the mums. But I found none of these. All I found were soulless sterile places. There appeared to be no community spirit, no village centre, let alone a pub or local store. Just road upon road of identical characterless 'new builds'.

I wondered what the thinking was behind these new villages, and considered their location on the outskirts of the industrial midlands. Were they families transferred here under the promise of affordable housing and a new beginning in an attempt to ease the overcrowding in city suburbs? Or was it that they were city types who wanted to come home to something more rural after a hard day in the office. Folk whose livelihoods had nothing to do with the local countryside, and a scheme that would be likely to push up the housing prices for the locals who had grown up here and worked here and wished to remain near their families? Whoever they were, it seemed to be such a bizarre place to create for them. There were no local facilities whatsoever and certainly no bus stops as a sign of local public transport that I saw. These families would be forced to travel by car some twenty odd miles on a round trip just to reach any sizable town for the facilities most of us require on a day-to-day basis: shops, schools, entertainment etc. This is true to form of American style, and to me created nothing but a soulless depressing place. No wonder the locals weren't smiling. A message for travellers of this country should be…BEWARE OF VILLAGES WITHOUT SHOPS!!

Finally after many exhausting and hungry miles I reached Stow-on-the-Wold. It was the first 'real' town for nearly twenty miles, and I arrived literally shaking with hunger. Stow was a pretty town and the highest in Oxfordshire and indeed the Cotswolds, and had a magnificent range of shops. Well actually they were just a normal range of shops but having spent all morning in ghost-ville they were a sight for sore eyes and indeed a sight for empty stomachs. Choosing a health food shop I stocked up and was soon sat out in the sun devouring a vegetable curry pasty, Kendal mint cake and whole pot of yogurt.

I discovered that now I was back in a 'real' town, the people also became 'real' once more and I fell easily into conversation with the folk around me. First off came a lady from Blackpool who stopped for a natter, then an old hippy who was originally from Cornwall and now lived locally also sat down to pass the time of day. Both of them on hearing about my trip helped to make my collection tin a little heavier. But what made me happiest that day was when another local man approached. He told me he had passed me in the car some hours ago and had seen my charity bib and wanted to make a donation. He then proceeded to empty all the loose change from a number of pockets in his clothing and empty it all into the collection tin, about ten pounds in total. It was around this time in my trip that Princess Diana had been visiting the victims of land mines, and it had all been thoroughly televised. So whilst the annoying wise crack from people learning of my trip, usually…'Oh you must be Princes Di' ever increased, so too did the images of limbless children on the television and the more the donations began to flow forth. Friends in high places eh?

Eventually after a hearty scoff and a good hours rest I could feel the energy returning to my body, and was able to return to the open road without wobble or faintness. I found the geography of the main A429 road an agreeably gentle up and down, which given the afternoon heat was a major blessing. After a time I began to wonder if I soon would end my days on this Earth, just a melted mess stuck to the road like an ice cream dropped by a child. Luckily Comic relief was never too far away. I pulled over into a garage on a water stop and witnessed with amusement everyone dining in the adjacent Little Chef restaurant stop what he or she were doing and turn to stare in my direction. Lord only knows what they made of the bicycle and rider set up that made them stare so, but the cold British reserve does have a habit of making even inquisitive stares feel somewhat threatening. Luckily a friendlier face came to join me as I sat on a wall outside gulping cold water from my plastic bottle, a handsome biker in all his leathers. I like bikers; I find they are much more on my wavelength than a car driver ever could be. (O.k. so I am a little biased, I used to be one.) We shared a cigarette and talked of common concerns: weather, traffic volumes, etc. And before leaving he earned himself an extra gold star by popping a coin or two into my collection tin.

By the time I rolled into Warwickshire and Stratford-Upon-Avon, (the birthplace of Shakespeare) I was completely and utterly exhausted. By now though I was beginning to get the hang of this end of day lark. First port of call would be the tourist information centre, when there was one, to find out the whereabouts of the nearest campsite. This I discovered, (albeit painstakingly slowly) was by far a better option than cycling round and round the local area like a headless chicken, looking for campsites that had either shut, moved or had never existed at all. Next, and of equal importance was to plan my route from tourist centre to campsite via some sort of shop or handy store to stock up on supplies for dinner and breakfast. This saved a wasted trip back into town later when I was at my most tired. And then came the most satisfying part of the day…checking in at the campsite reception desk, giving myself a mental pat on the back and silently saying to myself, 'thank you I made it.' It should be noted though that after one or two mishaps later on, I'd wait until I heard the receptionist utter, 'yes we have room for you tonight' or words to that effect before I would breath my sigh of relief.

The elderly warden of tonight's campsite took down my particulars and confided in me that many years ago he had been extremely fond of a lady who shared my surname, a Stinton who had resided in Penzance. He asked if I thought I might be related to her, Stinton not being a very common name. But it wasn't until ages later chatting to my father it occurred to me that our family had indeed come from that same town, and he could well have been loved up on my very own granny...small world!

With tent up and kettle boiling for my ritual cup of tea, I was approached by a fellow cycling 'Brummie' lad who appeared somewhat lonely on his cycling tour and parked himself down for a very long chat, obviously mistaking me for another lonely person. He'd been pedalling his way around the Kent countryside and was now on his way back to Birmingham, which he hoped to reach tomorrow. Now this news was music to the ears...Birmingham already. Despite it only being in the Midlands, from where I started from, it felt a long way up north to me. Before this one could get too chummy, I made my excuses and fled on Lucy into town.

This was one night when I did not feel at all in the mood to prepare dinner, instead a glowing image of fast food was stuck fast in my brain, and like an itch that had to be scratched I sailed forth in keen search for the best veggie burger and chips in town. Ironically, despite 'town' being a mere mile away from base, I nearly never made it at all...as I pedalled the streets I alarmingly felt myself sliding fast into the 'Bonk.' Fellow cyclists will be more than familiar with this term, but for those who are not, let me explain, least you think I was heading for some kinky bicycle induced sexual experience. The bonk is used to describe your physical state when blood sugar levels suddenly nose dive, along with energy levels and a willingness to continue. This usually happens during a long cycle, where you may not even be aware of just how much energy you've been burning up and therefore have not replaced the calories in sufficient quantities. This is indeed a bugger because the onset is so fast that by the time you have noticed it, it is almost too late. And before you know where you are, your limbs are like jelly, you feel faint and your whole body is set to give up...and the cure? The trouble now is once you have hit this low it can be quite difficult to get back up again...Things that can help? A ten course meal, a full body massage or eight hours kip...all very good but as you can probably work out, not very practical if you just happen to be cycling miles from anywhere across the Gobi or Himalayas. My advice to any would be cyclists is to keep a whole array of tasty and calorie packed morsels in easy reach of one's mouth. The front panniers are often handy for this job. It's just a shame I didn't heed my own advice this morning, which seemed to have upset my blood sugar levels for the entire rest of the day. I could have saved myself from a most unpleasant experience. Luckily Stratford turned out to be littered with fast food joints and it was in no time at all I was wiping grease from my chops and brushing the crumbs of my rapidly consumed feast away.

As I stood carefully depositing litter into the bin, I glanced up and noticed a quaint looking public house next door that looked like it had the charm of a Shakespearean theatre. It was within these same few seconds I also realised just how dry my throat felt, and that there was an obvious cure. Breaking all rules about not venturing into pubs alone I found myself gingerly pushing open the heavy door. The inner revealed itself as a calm and safe environment with dark wooden floors and a polished bar, so I decided it was worth the risk. I ordered my pint and took my seat in the corner, not planning to stay too long, but it seems that the further north you go, the less chance you have of remaining anonymous and it wasn't long before folk began to show an interest in my presence.

First to take up the reins of interrogation was a husband and wife team. The man was aging with black teeth and a permanent cough that had me worried he was about to drop dead at any minute. He proceeded to spend the next hour of his life trying to arrange me a lift as far as Glasgow in the morning to save me from having to pedal, and when I would not accept he stormed out the pub in a blaze of fury. He just could not understand that I cycled for pleasure and I could not make him understand either.

The second encounter was thankfully far easier on the social skills. Jeff was a 28-year-old travelling salesman who was intrigued by my very southern accent and came over for a chat. He had recently spent a lot of time in southeast England where I reside, and was insistent that folk from these parts where some of the friendliest he had ever come across. This sparked an interesting debate because I myself found those same folk could be cold at best, and hostile or pretentious at worst, and I far preferred the more open attitudes of those residing up north. I guess this could be described as 'the grass being greener' phenomena.

Jeff turned out to be far from stupid, and accepting another pint the conversation inevitably turned more personal for a time. Thinking back now in that short conversation, he was the one person I came the closest to telling the real reason I was making this journey.

DAY 14   (40 miles)

Awoke with a familiar feeling, somewhere along the lines of 'I wish I hadn't had that last pint,' and scolded myself for breaking my own rules. Although I have to admit to being slightly perplexed, suffering so badly after such a moderate amount of alcohol. I wondered if it could be the start of something more serious. I sat outside the tent with tea in hand and sulked about the day's prospects…another hangover, another scorching day, and another forty miles. The three categories just didn't fit comfortably together whichever way I looked at it, huff, (another cup of tea and a further ten minutes of sulking ensue.) But there again, I began to muse, what did ever slot neatly into place in Sarah's world? Re a big jumble of mess and life experiences all thrown together higgledy-piggledy, and some how it always works in the end. I felt the corners of my mouth turn upwards at the silliness of it all. 'Come on girl, get your butt in gear and just get on with it.'

As I tatted down I came up with a fine plan of action…1) Cycle into town and take camera to chemist and get my finished roll of film developed. 2) Whilst awaiting pics to emerge, stand in high street with Lucy and get rattling my collection tin under people's noses. My sisters harsh but true words about the lack of fundraising had been nagging the back of my brain ever since. It was time to remind myself that as well as the mission to conquer the British Isles by bike; I was also supposed to be on a sub mission to rid the world of Landmines. And finally this would lead nicely on to 3) by this time, several hours would have passed, my hangover would be gone, and I'd be more than ready to tackle today's ride in the heat…good plan?

Who was I trying to kid? I often wondered if maybe I just looked fit for nothing that morning, as I stood trying to smile sympathetically as person after person chose to walk on by. It sounds bizarre to anyone who has never been out collecting for charity, but it is kind of hard not to take it personally when folk appear to look right through you. I think that morning only three passers by stopped, it appeared they wanted to use me as a convenient place to rid themselves of loose change, not even caring what the charity was! Apart from this, the only people to take a genuine interest in me were a couple of old ladies, probably struggling to live off a state pension. By time the morning was over I think I'd collected a grand total of £6.47

Well at least I could now tell my sister I'd tried. It would be easy to think this mornings example gave the impression the British were an uncharitable lot. But not so, in 2006 we ranked the second most charitable nation in the West, and our citizens have set up a number of international charities to be proud of, Oxfam in 1942 and Amnesty International in London in July 1961, to name just two. But coming back to Stratford, well I guess that, just maybe the whole bicycle/rider expedition set up some how looked a lot more impressive on the move. I certainly seemed to attract more willing donors that way.

Feeling disappointed I made my way forlornly back to the chemist to pick up my snaps. To my delight they had turned out far better than I imagined. It seemed as though my camera had survived being dropped out of the Exeter Youth Hostel window whilst arsing about drunk, very nicely.

It was time for the off. Part 3 of my master plan was set to crash and burn too. Why had I thought waiting a couple of hours would make things easier? The clock struck twelve, the hottest part of the day, as I set out feeling extremely worse for wear after two days of physical over exertion in the heatwave that had enveloped our tiny island. And it looked set to continue. Feeling sick and dehydrated to boot, I groaned to myself that I could almost wish for the wet weather to return. I realised as I ground my way out of Stratford that I hadn't even bothered to visit the tourist delights of Shakespeare's birthplace. 'Cultural Oaf' thought I. But I knew I was in no mood for playing tourist on today of all days.

Warwick was the next stop off point I had carefully circled on my map, and I had read with keen interest that it was a beautiful medieval town sporting one of the best castles in England. Having spent the last few months traipsing around almost every cathedral I had stumbled upon in Europe I must admit to being, well, all 'cathedralled' out. But when it came to castles I could always sum up enthusiasm for some exploration: turrets and fortresses, drawbridges and keeps. I could spend ages exploring nooks and crannies, enviously admire huge inglenook fireplaces, check out the royal kitchens where feasts of hog and broth would be painstakingly prepared, and let my imagination run wild as I gazed upon dining halls that would have held a sumptuous banquet for dozens.

I pushed my way through the gathering crowds and up to the entrance gate, only to read with disappointment that entry to the castle would set me back £15. I 'ummed' and 'ahhed' over the issue of budget verses the holiday and finally concluded to save my scant funds for something a little more important. As it happens this 'something' turned up a lot sooner than predicted. Before I had time to analyse motives I found myself pushing through the door of a local cycle shop and heading to the counter, where I heard a voice that did not particularly sound like mine, squeak 'I'd like to buy a cycle helmet.'

Now here is another topic controversial in the cycling world and I have to say my views have always lain strictly in the 'against' camp. Let me explain. The fact is why should it be up to the cyclists to protect themselves against rogue drivers? It can almost be construed as saying, "cyclists need to protect themselves, because we, (along with the rest of society) must accept the fact that car drivers will always drive without due care and attention, breaking speed limits etc, and are far too pig headed to ever mend their ways or take responsibility. They even come out with some old claptrap that goes, 'people who break the rules of the road aren't real criminals,' thus slightly ignoring the fact that their actions kill far more innocent people than those of cold blooded murderers...So pad up cyclists, pedestrians, children and old grannies, and get ready for the impact!"

I really cringe when I hear talk of cycle helmets being made compulsory in the U.K. Good grief whatever next, the announcement that anyone stepping outside of their front door should do so only when wearing helmet and padding, least a reckless fool in a ton of painted metal drives into them. I can speak from personal experience on this one. I recall one afternoon strolling down the pavement somewhere in central London, when a black cab driver approaching from behind decided he was too impatient to wait for the car in front to turn right, tried to squeeze through the gap, found it a bit too small, ended up mounting the pavement and struck me from the side. As I hit the deck and at the same time watched as the taxi's wheels narrowly missed me, I could be forgiven for wondering if that had really just happened. The taxi driver, who must have felt the impact didn't stop or even turn his head and most people around just rushed on by in typical Londoner style. If it wasn't for the horror and concern on one lady's face, I could easily believe I'd just imagined the whole thing.

But back to Warwick, and a blue cycle helmet with the words 'Free Spirit' nicely emblazoned on the side was purchased. Why? I hear you cry after everything I have just ranted about. Well to tell you the truth, pressure. Make that pressure and scaremongering. My mother had been doing it for years along with various other friends and family members, but the final straw had come from Les whom I'd met in Wells. He told of a friend of his, who out cycling one day had been over taken by a lorry. The driver had not long passed his H.G.V test, and had overtaken too close. Next thing the side mirror had cracked him around the back of the head and very sadly he died in hospital later that day. Outside the cycle shop, with my new helmet in hand, I dithered. I put it on and took it off several times, despite it being the right size it felt odd and uncomfortable. Finally I attached it to my luggage on Lucy's back rack. I took solace in the fact that it was still my decision to whether I chose to wear one or not, but now at least I had one to hand if ever I felt the need to wander along very main roads. (The scary irony of this tale is that about a year later whilst chatting to a very knowledgeable cycling friend, I showed him my purchase and was informed that I had been sold nothing short of cheap tat and I would have been better off cycling with a watermelon on my head.)

Next destination encircled on my map was another pretty town known as Lemington Spa. Here too there were places aplenty with historic interest to explore, but sadly I saw not one of them. By now it was gone four in the afternoon, the air was still and clammy with the temperature somewhere up in the dizzy head figures. Freewheeling into the centre I spied a park and collapsing dramatically under the shade of ancient oaks, here I stayed for several hours sweating it out hoping for a magical change in climate. My lifeless eyes stared dead ahead ignoring all the passes-by who may have kept me amused. For something non technical to while away the time, I read and re-read the park signs in front of me 'Please put litter in the bin' and the more unusual 'No drinking alcoholic beverages in the park' (what is this America or something?) Occasionally I would trek the few yards to a nearby kiosk to purchase sandwiches and ice cold sugar filled pop that I hoped and prayed would help to bring the life back into my lifeless being. And then it was back to my sign reading.

Eventually after two hours of this, I had no choice but to pick myself up off the floor, limb by dead limb, haul Lucy to an upright position and suffer the final onslaught of six more miles to the campsite. How totally and utterly exasperatingly irksome could it be, that this long awaited campsite was to be found on the other side of a dual carriage way, a road which was split in two by an four foot barbed wire barrier and could only be reached by having to cycle nearly another two miles further up the road to a roundabout and then back down the other side. The language I chose that evening that would have made Beelzebub blush.

But the road gods must have decided to smile on me because when I finally arrived the old lady owner and her son ushered me in to their cool dark farmhouse kitchen, bringing me glass after glass of chilled home made lemon cordial until the thirst of an army would have been quenched. We chatted whilst I drank and I answered all the usual questions (yes I'm doing this for charity, no I'm not lonely or frightened etc.) It seems odd thinking back to that time, that as I answered the same questions on a daily basis I found I was bored of listening to myself saying the same things over and over again, and I guess I assumed everyone else would find it boring too. It wasn't until a long time later when a friend said she couldn't believe I never brought up what I had done in my conversations because it was so worth talking about, that I began to understand why people on route did take such an interest in me. After all, the sight of a young girl cycling alone and far from home, carrying all her worldly goods with her like a tortoise, was not something you saw very often in those days. But because I often read books about this type of travel adventure I guess it was easy to think this type of thing was an every day common occurrence.

This campsite was located on a smallholding that was an absolute delight, and save for the main road (which alas had arrived a long time after the farm was built) it was the place of my dreams. The farmhouse was a little run down but small and quaint, with paddocks and stables out the back. I was told to pitch up in a field out the back, which aside from the nutty ducks running around I had all to myself. Now this is what I call bliss I thought, after such a bitch day, this was my reward. The noise that emanated from my mouth went somewhere along these lines; breathe in and sigh…oh so contently…eeeee…ahhhhh…mmmmmm… ehhh?...grrrrr…ah crap!! All silence was broken as a ford escort wheel span into the field complete with boom box pumping up the jam, and skidding to a halt not far from my pitch, out sprang its two young male occupants.

After dinner and a shower I decided I might as well go and join them. It amused me greatly how they reminded me so much of two chaps I used to go to college with, and I soon had them nicknamed Tom and Barry. Tom was the dude of the two, wore casual clothing, liked his clubbing and probably fancied himself. Barry was more of a punk rocker; he looked a little ferocious but was really quite gentle on the inside. I wondered as with the real Tom and Barry, how two people so seemingly different had ended up such good friends. The pair worked as painter and decorators in nearby Rugby but found they could save a fortune by living in tents rather than staying in a B & B. I filled them in on my own reasons for being here at the site. When I mentioned I was travelling alone, Tom turned to Barry and said 'We've got a right one here,' and I was invited to sit with them. I enjoyed listening to some of Barry's travel tales, particularly the one about him and a girlfriend who in order to get to Australia for free signed up to work on a cargo ship. The epic voyage took almost eight months! I wanted to talk to him about coping for so long in a seemingly limitless ocean of thoughts and isolation from all that is normal. But by this time it was rather late in the evening and the super strength lager and smokes had taken a hold of his mind. It appeared this was how the pair of them coped with the discomfort of living in tiny tents for months on end. Still, I enjoyed my share of their offerings and once they'd both crawled into their tents and passed out, I happily made my way back to mine. I lay awake for a while, my mind a trail of intriguing thoughts that flicked from one subject to another so fast that eventually I lost track and had to give up. To my delight I found my old camping mat had been transformed and for tonight at least, I was sleeping on the world's most lavish mattress.

DAY 15 (36 miles)

A gentle patter of rain on the tarpaulin awoke me around 5am, but without any trouble I nodded straight back off to sleep before finally stirring at about 8. I was relieved to find the suppressing heat had finally cleared and I greatly looked forward to an altogether cooler ride. The lads had gone, forgetting their promise last night to give me a shout at 7 (not surprisingly after their intake) and when I was finally ready to go, the old dear who owned the place wouldn't hear of accepting payment for my pitch. Again I placed the cost of a nights camping into the collection tin myself.

Today it seemed I was destined to take on the role of a historian as I once again pedalled the Fosse Way which I'd been following on and off for a number of days now. Today I reached the point where it crossed with Watling Street, another ancient track. This one was first used by the Celts and later paved by those ingenious Romans. In our modern world it takes the form of the A5 from Wroxeter to London and the A2 from London to Dover. I'd been led to believe there was a memorial to one of the most important junctions in Britain's Roman Road network, but my search proved fruitless. Later I read there was once a sundial placed here as a marker but it had been struck by lightning, and all that remained now was a brick ruin. As I cycled this straight road with the horizon ever far away I tried to imagine what it might have been like for the many armies who had once marched this way. The Romans architects were certainly clever when it came to road building. Roman surveyors simply aligned their sighting marks from one high point to another, result…a straight line in between and all important cross roads occurring on high ground out of harms way.

Passing through a village named Brinklow, I was once again touched by the reception I received. The friendliness and generosity just kept on coming today. One local lady stopped to make a donation and I asked her to tell me some more of the history of The Fosse Way, which she was happy to do. Then as we chatted, an old boy on a motorbike who had spotted my charity bib stopped too to donate five pounds into the kitty. He had been a soldier in the war he informed me, and judging by his age along with his mannerisms this was plain to see. 'I used to cycle' he told me, up until a few years ago when his knee finally packed in and now he had no choice but to stick to a motorised form of two wheels. But what really made an impression on me was he was one of the few people along the way who insisted on checking I had not run out of the essentials, namely food and water, and that I would have a place to stay that night. He seemed aware that kindness can sometimes be as simple as offering the bare basics of life. I wondered if this was something he had learnt from his time in the army and in the horror that is war.

Freewheeling into the town of Hinckley I was so busy peering at an approaching garage, trying to decipher whether it could offer me the use of a public convenience that I almost didn't notice a man stood in the middle of the road. He had leapt from his car and was holding out three pounds for my collection tin. I almost mowed him down!

My route that afternoon followed the A447, before turning off on to the B585. I couldn't believe my luck. Here I was cycling through the industrial midlands; Birmingham, Coventry and Wolverhampton to my left; Northampton, Rugby and Leicester to my right, and yet barely a car was to be seen, and the air smelt good and fresh. When planning my route this section had taken a lot of patience...whilst there were a few cities I wouldn't mind visiting, I certainly had no intention of 5 solid days of conurbation that would surely leave me prematurely grey! Now though, it became clear my meticulous planning had won through and I pedalled happily on some of the quietest roads I found in England...the new cycle helmet was left unworn, still swinging from the back rack.

I watched grey clouds gathering overhead all afternoon, sky watching became one of my favourite pastimes whilst bouncing along in the saddle, particularly across the flatlands of the Midlands where there was always so much of it in view. Along one of these deliciously quiet back roads I was curious when a flash, open top car pulled over, sporting a man in tweed and a lady in an elegant head scarf, they were right out of a 60's Bond film, very elegant and very wealthy, and I'm happy to say the sum of their donation verified this fact. As I waved goodbye as they sped away I totted it up in my head; they were the seventh and eighth people that day to stop especially to make a donation. This trip was certainly challenging my rather cynical view of my fellow countryman.

Next to join me that day was another psycho tourist who was very old hat at this thing, explaining that he had already cycled the End to End twice. He approached rapidly from behind and decided to keep me company for a few miles. This would ordinarily have been a treat to cycle in company had he not been one of those obnoxious fellows who always thought he was right all the time, and pretty soon I was grunting one syllable answers to his equally obnoxious questions. Luckily I think he found cycling at my speed far too frustrating for such a pro, (I couldn't help notice that I had to pedal on the down hills just to keep up with him, whilst he was constantly breaking on the flat to stay level with me.) After another mile of this he waved and was gone.

My home for tonight would be a youth hostel bed in a place rather sweetly named Copt Oak. Low and behold, only two miles from my destination the heavens opened and out tipped the equivalent water volume that Lake Geneva bares. Marvellous! Within just five minutes I was pedalling through foot deep puddles, puddles that motorist seemed more than happy to drive through at 60mph, spray me in spectacular style and then turn their heads to check out the poor fool caught out cycling in such treacherous conditions. Similarly, as I cycled past houses I caught glimpses of curious faces peering though net curtains. Although I could not here them, I swear I could have lip read their words…'Oh do come and look George, you'll never guess what I've just seen, ha ha'… etc. Thinking back I wonder how I ever coped before my life enhancing, if expensive discovery of the Gortex coat.

Travelling at the speed of a car, one could easily have missed Copt Oak. It was only the advantage of my reduced pace that allowed me to spot the half broken off sign that was rusting away, buried in an over grown hedge. The village consisted of a tiny church, a closed and very derelict pub and precisely six houses, whilst any village store had sadly closed down. I feel it would be safe to say Copt Oak was now a bit of a 'has been' community.

I found the youth hostel next to the church and was dismayed to find it didn't open for another two hours yet. They had thoughtfully provided a 'wet weather shelter' for any early/late comers and it was here I retired, soaked to the bone, my loudly chattering teeth the only thing that scared the hundreds of creepy crawlies away from my face. Another hour dragged by, when to my delight I was joined by a rather dishy looking Australian back packer called Guy who burst in full of smiles. (Why do I always look my worst when I meet someone I fancied?) Guy had already spent the previous night at this particular establishment and during our chat he warned me about the man who ran the youth hostel. I believe Guy used words such as rude, abrupt and aggressive. When I finally met the man in question, he came across to me as a clever and interesting man with a typical rather dry British sense of humour. I forgave Guy for his harsh misjudgement of the manager's character; he had only just arrived in the U.K. and obviously had a lot to learn about us Brits. After all, he had told me he found Copt Oak a cultural extravaganza for heavens sake!

DAY 16   (37 grumpy miles)

It seemed to take me rather a long time to get on the road this morning. Oh o.k. I know I say that every day, what I mean is, staying in the youth hostel I should have had the speedy advantage of not having a tent and camping gear to fart-arse around with, and it should just have been a case of; up, wash, dress, breakfast and go. But despite this it still took the usual number of hours, (a bit more than one, not quite two) to get on the road. I left Copt Oak, a place memorable only for its unmemorable qualities, feeling in the very highest of spirits. After a night of very heavy rain my olfactory senses were in for a treat as the morning sun began to heat up all that wet, fresh smelling foliage around me. The road steamed whilst the rain drops on the grass verges sparkled, and every grass blade, every flower every leaf could be smelt and enjoyed...it took around one hundred and eighty seconds for this stupendous natural high to be sucked away and leave me to the mercy of an altogether savagely difficult and frustrating day.

The first of my 'swear inducing' situations that day occurred as I cruised down the hill away from Copt Oak, where unbeknown to me one of the clips on my rear, right hand pannier had faltered. This fact only became apparent when I hit rather a large bump in the road, causing pannier and contents to fly off in spectacular style, an act which had the car behind (and the three behind him) slamming on their brakes to avoid squashing the offending article. By time I had bought Lucy to a halt, I was some way further on down the hill. Rather nicely I thought, the first car driver got out to retrieve my bag and bring it to where I had stopped, but his kind smiling face soon turned to thunder as I causally informed him what a good thing it was he had not run over the bag, the bag just happening to contain my highly flammable camping stove. Instead of a potential charity donation I instead found myself on the receiving end of a lecture that started off with my supposed irresponsible attitude to life, and ended with, and when was I going to get a job!!

Luckily I managed to rig up a make shift clip, (i.e. I tied the thing back on with string) and made it safely into Loughborough. I needed to ring Orbit Cycles in Sheffield (where Lucy had been made,) and see if I could arrange a free service that is promised to all Orbit cycle owners six months after purchase. O.k. so it had been over a year now, but I thought I may be able to sweet talk my way around this minor technicality, and in full optimistic mood I found a phone box and dialled the factory number. I chatted to a sweet sounding lady with a hardy Yorkshire accent, and when I explained my expedition she said that if I popped in Saturday morning she was sure they could fit me in 'Nay problem.' Beaming I left the phone box thinking, 'I love it when a plan comes together.' Shame then that I was so happy I failed to realise I had left the phone booth without my address book, and still didn't realise until twenty miles further on up the road. When I did finally realise, all the swear words in the world could not compensate for my dismay. All summer I had been on the road, making new friends, taking down contacts and promising to ring, write, visit etc. And now they were all gone in the blink of an eye. In my entire journey across the British Isles, I only lost three things. Unfortunately all three were very precious; a watch from a friend…damn, an exceedingly sharp and compact knife from my ex…damn, and now my address book filled with names of people who would think I had gone away and just forgotten about them…damn, damn, damn. O.k. so I could at least have a go at suppressing my dismay with swear words!

Pedalling the main 'A' route into Nottingham City I was astounded, but happy with just how empty the road was, the route I had chosen through the Midlands was turning into a whole collection of surprises. I am guessing the majority of traffic chose to take the quicker motorway route leaving me the freedom to breath and dream. Rounding a corner a small lake appeared to my left where the silhouette of a Heron stood poised and ready for action above the waters. It was such an opportune moment to see such a majestic bird against the back drop of a scenic view that I whipped my camera from my pocket. But the second the Heron spied me he flapped away. As I pedalled on I mused that so often I see wildlife that will run a mile when spotting a bicycle yet take not a blind bit of notice of the thousands of cars that zoom noisily on by… and guess which is more likely to lead to their demise.

Things took a dramatic turn however, as I hit the outskirts of Nottingham. The peace and tranquillity was replaced by the harsh realities of city suburbs, where over flowing bins and dog shit could be smelt at every corner, traffic approached from every angle and wailing sirens, screaming teenagers, drunken yobs, and impatient car horns bashed my ear drums succinctly. For the first time ever I found myself reaching for the cycle helmet as yet unworn on my back rack. It appeared Nottingham city council had made the effort to green their city by marking a number of cycle paths to various different locations. I decided to give it a go. Alas this idea just ended up with me getting lost, frustrated and further advancing my blasphemous vocabulary. What happened is I would spy a sign for the city centre and latch onto this route for a time, following as it twisted and turned; up alley ways, across parks and through housing estates, but after a time the sign posts for the city centre would peter out and be replaced by ones for more local sounding places, which not being local, I had never heard of and I would be left lost and directionless on some housing estate somewhere. So off I would blindly set until I hooked up with another cycle path sign pointing the way to the city centre, only for the same thing to happen all over again. After wasting nigh on two hours doing this, I finally saw sense and navigated my way back to the main road to take my chances with the traffic.

Whilst I applaud Nottingham city council for their green efforts there were some flaws in their plans, the first being a need for better sign posting so non-local cyclists could also benefit. But I also noticed that all efforts had been concentrated to the south side of the city only. When I tried to leave going north, it appeared the only option was the A60, a dual carriage way frequented by articulated Lorries, and I didn't once see hide nor hair of a single bike path. This wasn't the first time I have thought that whilst councils are going berserk putting in cycle paths around their cities, what is truly missing is safe passage between one town and another. And not some long winded route either (you know the ones; up hill and down dale, over gates and through the mud,) but a nice Dutch style one, where you see a nice smooth flat path running the quickest route to your destination. Well sign posted but separated from the roar of traffic by trees or a thick hedge. Now surely this kind of visible alternative to the motorcar would help to get people out of their automobiles and into the saddle.

I stopped for a sarnie outside of Nottingham castle, (which incidentally looks nothing like the place Kevin Costner and co. stormed in the film,) but looking was all I did. Nottingham was one of those cities I had looked forward to seeing but in reality, when I got there all I wanted to do was to leave. And leave I did, pedalling past notices glued to lampposts and closed down shop windows alike, all declaring 'tax the rich.' Maybe Robin Hood was still very much an icon in these parts.

It was somewhere in the northern city suburbs that I happened to glance down, something I am apt to do from time to time to reassure myself that both bicycle and bits are still with me and in one piece, when I noticed the back tyre looking a little flatter than it should have done. Passing a small green at the time, it was the perfect opportunity to pull over and examine any damage. I knelt down and gave the tyre a thorough pumping up whilst simultaneously trying to avoid the gaze of some weirdo that was taking far too much of an interest in me for my liking, and then continued on my way. But a few further miles on and another examination revealed the same problem…great, a slow puncture. Now I really had had enough for one day; sick of the heat, sick of the traffic, fed up because I'd lost my address book and now this, well I guess it would be enough to get any cookie down. At the first opportunity I turned off that nightmare road and made my way along the lanes towards a place named Calverton where my map promised a campsite. Ah, peace at last…or so I thought.

All silence was suddenly shattered when out of nowhere, three police cars appeared, lights flashing and sirens blaring. They appeared so quickly and at such speed, I barely had time to get out of their way as they shot passed far too close before disappearing from sight and sound as quickly as they had come, and left me spinning in their wake. How very curious, thought I, and then, oh well, at least they weren't after me! I pedalled on. I took a right at the next T-junction moving on to an even narrower twisting road. With only a mile and a half left I was lost in one of my favourite end of day fantasies about the impending campsite, (you know the sort of thing; deluxe showers, on-site bar, a lone hunky cyclist in the next tent.) It was then that I was rudely jolted back into reality by the same three cop cars still approaching speeds that made one think they were after Robin Hood himself! Not long after I finally rolled into Calverton itself and guess what three cars I found there waiting for me! Luckily before I got too paranoid that it was me they were hunting after all, the campsite owner let me in on the gossip. The police had been chasing armed robbers who had tried to make their escape across the fields. 'Wow the Merry Men have finally got themselves armed' I joked to the campsite proprietor, but he didn't seem to hear as he was too busy filling in the next arrivals with the same gossip. This was scandalous stuff for small town Nottinghamshire.

Once I was pitched and settled into the corner of the campsite, (a bare field with a chemical toilet…not quite the facilities I'd hoped for) I started up a conversation with my neighbour for the night, a motor biker by the name of Steve, (not quite the hunk I'd hoped for either).

He invited me to join him and as I plonked myself down in the shade of his rather large tent he promptly passed me a cold beer, and later even lent me his tools so I could pull a tiny sliver of glass from my back tyre. (O.k., I relented, he was probably much more useful than the hunk I'd had in mind.) After my puncture was fixed we decided to celebrate by heading off down to the local hostelry. I myself was probably on a mission to get smashed that night, after the frustrating day I'd had, and as it turned out Steve was just the man to accompany me. He wasn't backwards in going forwards to the bar for one, and every time I asked for a G & T he would make sure he came back with a double. The conversation flowed freely as if we had known each other for years, rather than only an hour, and I listened to his cheery tales of the rivalries between Yorkshire and Lancashire. According to Steve, the only reason the Lancastrians won the War of the Roses was because they hired a lot of Irish thugs to fight their battles for them. (Perhaps I should explain that Steve was a very proud Yorkshire man if you hadn't already guessed!)

By the end of the session I was feeling rather light headed, but also light hearted once more, as the alcohol had flushed away any thought of annoyances that had occurred that day. The two of us, giggling like school kids, staggered back down the road to the campsite. As I said good night to Steve, I thought I'd quickly check up on my puncture mending handy work before going to bed myself. And what did I find… the bloody tyre was flat again. ARRRRGGHHH!!

Above: Having a breather at the top of The Mendip Hills

Below: After sixteen days, the morning routine still hasn't
quite come together!

Above: Sherwood Forest…it's around here somewhere…

Below: …No this can't be it…

Above: …Here it is; the only bit left that hasn't had the chop…the saying goes that if Robin Hood were alive today, a group of school kids could track him down in half an hour!

Left: At 800 years old, The Major Oak now needs her Zimmer frame!

Above: Save the planet…Sheffield's newly working tram system

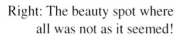

Right: The beauty spot where all was not as it seemed!

DAY 17 (30 miles)

Awoke from my slumber at 6am, determined to get cracking before the heat of the day started in earnest…finally got on the road at 10am. What the hell was wrong with me in the mornings? It seemed no matter how hard I tried to perform my morning rituals with speed and efficiency, as soon as my back was turned, some naughty little imp would fast wind the clock forward an hour or so, and then disappear to watch and laugh at me from a distance.

As I put the kettle on this morning it was tea for two. I couldn't believe Steve could get by without a cup to kick start the day, especially being a Yorkshire lad. But then he explained that he never had to travel on his motorbike for more than ten minutes to find one. I on the other hand may have to cycle nearly an hour at my pace and there was no way I could contemplate that. At the start of my tour I would always start the day with a thick black coffee, a small jar of instant being easier to carry around than a box of tea bags and a pint of milk. But after a while I began to suss out that more than one cup seemed to have a slowing effect on my athletic abilities, and so I began to go to the trouble of carrying around all the tea making paraphernalia. As it turned out it was so worth it, and one of my favourite parts of the day became the morning ritual of sitting in the entrance to my tent, swaddled in my sleeping bag with a steaming mug of tea in hand, slowly waking up and contemplating the day ahead.

I made the extravagant decision to use a brand new inner tube to mend my tyre, thus avoiding risk of cycling to the end of the road and getting another flat. As I had demonstrated last night, puncture mending was not my forte! And with all that complete, I shook Steve's hand and pedalled out to face another stifling day.

Back I pedalled through Calverton, and passed the pub and made for the A164 once again. I was briefly joined by the local post women who cycled along beside me, and put forward the best case I had ever heard for packing up my bicycle for good and going home.

'The A164…you're not planning to cycle along that road are you… what really…it's so dangerous…more people get killed on that road than the M25…just the other month there were some cyclists…yeah positively maimed they were…it's been voted the country's most dangerous road…especially in August when there are lots of visitors…

what month is it...oh it is August now...well you enjoy yourself...bye now...' Oh God, thought I. And what she didn't do either was to offer some local knowledge to a possible alternative. I tried to suss one out for myself but disappointingly there were none. With imminent death ringing in my ears, I reached the end of the road and turned right, out on to The Highway of Certain Death.

My reason for choosing this route was I wanted to see the famous Sherwood Forest for myself. Unfortunately it appeared that time for this was fast running out. As far back as one hundred years ago, somebody or another, (a then famous figure from Nottinghamshire) categorically said that if Robin Hood were alive today, there would only be enough wood left for him to hide out for about a week. In comparison, the saying these days is that a group of school children could track him down in just half an hour, which gives you a very clear but depressing idea of just how much of the forest has been axed. With two main roads cutting through its centre, it was indeed the drive-thru of forests. However determined to find something authentic to see I went on a tiring detour to visit, what is locally known as The Major Oak. It is place suspected to have been frequented by Robin and Co. on a fairly regular basis. Large trees were seen in those days as a medium of prophecy and knowledge, and in fact still are to the tree huggers among us. It was a very awe-inspiring sight. The oak is around eight hundred; yes that is EIGHT HUNDRED years old. But the poor old girl appeared to be struggling with her age and even had her own specially designed Zimmer frame, (i.e. her branches were now supported by specially made stilts.) The rest of what was left of the forest had been transferred into a thick soup of tourist titivation, which quite frankly left me uninspired and gagging.

Worksop was picked as tonight's destination, but despite only having covered thirty miles that day, I felt beaten. All day long I had suffered a complete lack of energy that didn't seem to correspond fairly with the ease of the flat terrain or my heightened levels of fitness, and I arrived in Worksop feeling a mixture of deflation, downheartedness and downright frustration.

And there was something else...this day had been the absolute height of the 'monkey in the zoo' stares and I was left utterly fuming. I guess by now I should have come to expect this in heavily tourist filled areas, but today it had made me growl and spit obscenities under my breath, and at one stage I even thought I had better brace myself ready to catch the banana someone would inevitably throw at me. O.k.; o.k. So I was an unusual sight but why couldn't they have just accompanied that stare with a smile too and it wouldn't have vexed me so. I know you'll think that if I just tried smiling at the spectator's it might make them much friendlier...but you'd be wrong. Today my usual rule of making eye contact and smiling at people seemed to make them look even more horrified than ever...they just couldn't cope; Young girl, travelling on her own, a fully loaded up bicycle, AND happy with it? That was too much for their tiny minds! So that day I just gave up on the niceties and walked with eyes starring stony faced ahead, but still I could feel every pair of eyes I passed boring straight into me. (The one and only thing to make me smile was the sound of a little boy asking...'Look mummy, why does that lady carry all her things on her bicycle?' I felt like telling him, 'Because I can!')

But as I sat in the high street of Worksop, The Little Road God of Travellers Fair must have decided to smile on me once again as he cast three, oh so subtle, magic spells. The first one I became aware of was when hunting through my panniers for a banana. I just happened to glance down and notice my milometer reading was 550 miles...Wow I was half way! The boost it gave to my confidence was like receiving a zap of energy through my entire body. Happily I sat back on the bench and began to munch, and people watch. The next magic spell was subtler; it slowly dawned on me that the people passing by were, well normal. No more threateningly cold stares, no more; 'Are you an alien?' looks. Just very pleasant everyday folks who would quite often smile and say good afternoon. After the aforementioned hell in Sherwood, this community of friendliness soothed my soul like nothing else could have. I often found throughout my expedition, that one of the best groups of people to get sensible conversation out of were usually men of a pensionable age. You could spot them a mile away. They'd catch site of my bicycle and silently watch, their minds could almost be seen to be working back to their youth when travel and transportation of things was more often than not done by the humble two wheels. Then they would notice me at the helm, look a little surprised for a second before engaging me in polite conversation, be it about the history of the area, how many gears I had on the bike, or even, what on earth did my mother think of all this.

In Worksop I found I had a dilemma on my hands. According to my map, the nearest campsite was twenty miles back the way I had came, (no thank you) or the far side of Sheffield, (too far to realistically cycle so late in the afternoon). The only other affordable accommodation

100

there appeared to be in this part of the world, was to catch a train from Worksop to a place some twenty miles out of my way where I knew there would be a youth hostel. I certainly wasn't keen on this idea either; forgoing all the aggro, I still had to get Lucy to Orbit Cycles in Sheffield tomorrow morning and this would be made a logistical nightmare if I followed this route. This was the first time on my trip I had encountered a problem finding affordable accommodation, and dealing with this when I was so exhausted turned a small hiccup into an utterly distressing situation. Finding tourist information I marched in to present my predicament to the lady behind the counter. After listening to all my far from perfect options she quite calmly said, 'Or you could just stay at the campsite here?' Here being a two-minute walk from the very spot we were stood in! Weak with relief I could have hugged her. Praise the road god for his third blessing of the afternoon.

I watched the comings and goings of the campsite from my tent door that evening whilst tucking into a Chinese takeaway. True to form of this area, everyone was terribly friendly; however I couldn't help think some of the caravanner's styles seemed just so extreme. They appeared to have brought the entire contents of their houses with them. I saw TV's in each room, video recorders, and computers, even exercise bikes! As I sat self sufficiently under my canvas: food, water, music and reading material, cooking, cleaning and bedding equipment, all portable enough to pack away into four bicycle panniers, the caravanners' style bewildered me. But I was left feeling very contented, knowing I could get by without all those unnecessary modern day gadgets and luxuries.

I thought of some alternative thinking people I knew (branded by the media as new age travellers), persecuted for wanting to live out an existence away from the modern world. They regularly found their way was blocked at every turn by prejudice, and fear from people who for some reason felt threatened by their desire to be non-conformist to the things they didn't believe in. One friend of mine I shall call Robbie was a horse drawn traveller, and another couple lived with their two children quite happily in a large caravan in a wood. What all of them had in common was a wish to find a network of places to be allowed for a small fee, to park up so they could move around to where the seasonal work is, and therefore not to have to rely on state hand outs. They are not terrorists, thieves nor are they scroungers. But will farmers, who are always bemoaning they can't survive on farming alone (and are themselves on state handouts), lease some land for these people. Yeah get real. And as for Joe Public who tar them all with the same brush, well isn't it ironic that these very same people could be seen here now, finding a sense of peace and relaxation living out the same lifestyle as those they condemn! Oh dear, is our entire world based on hypocrisy?

Chinese takeaway, half munched and half stored away for breakfast, I sat back contentedly and found myself casting a causal eye around the campsite on the off chance a friendly Yorkshire man on a big motorbike should arrive.

I thought of the day just gone by. Still the same question was thrown at me from almost everyone I came into contact with; be it hardened bikers, cyclists, Dutch backpackers or policeman. 'Why are you travelling on your own?' And this was more often than not closely followed by, 'you must be very brave/courageous' etc. How could I explain in simple terms? But I must admit, today despite having the utter hump with the sheer volume of traffic that raced passed my elbow far too close, threatening my safety and generally dominating the pace of life, I realised I actually felt superior whilst pedalling along. When you take yourself away from the realms of conformism, you can be whomever the hell you wish. A traveller, a hobo, an adventuress, an environmentalist, and human rights campaigner…the possibilities were endless. So far I had been regularly admired for my stamina and independence, envied for my freedom and even told I was an excellent role model for youngsters.

But you know what was best of all, feeling content from within. Whilst those around me where getting somewhere fast, they were cooped up in their artificial environments as if watching the world from a TV screen, whilst I felt free; the wind in my hair, really feeling the weather, smelling and hearing the sights and sounds. Knowing the land was what it was all about.

DAY 18 (23 miles)

I awoke to the cool of dawn and a sense of excitement at the first break in my routine for nearly three weeks. Scoffing the rest of my now cold Chinese takeaway, I packed up and made for Worksop station to find myself a train into Sheffield. I was more than happy to cycle this distance; it was only a mere eighteen miles, but on this occasion I was forced to choose practicalities over desire. My fear was getting into Sheffield late; the memory of suffocating traffic in Nottingham, the confusing road systems and cycle paths was still very much at the forefront of my mind. But worse than that, if the mechanics at the Orbit factory were busy and I had a long wait, or Lucy threw up a lot of time consuming problems, then the day would tick on by, and my worst nightmares about being stranded in a strange city with night fast approaching would become a reality. In all honesty, I would rather be out taking my chances with the bears and the wolves, than the snarling lurking perils of inner city life after dark.

As it was, I already knew Lucy was having a few problems. It was only yesterday I noticed a strange 'clunk clunk' noise, the source of which I couldn't pinpoint. To my mechanically unable mind it could have been anything; cranks, derailleur, chain sprockets…hell for all I knew, both wheels were about to fall off! But looking on the bright side, I guess I was lucky the problem had materialised now, the day before her service, rather than say, in the midst of the Highlands, which would probably have been more typical of the sod's law that can follow travellers around.

Down on the platform, awaiting the train to Sheffield turned out to be a curiously pleasurably experience, which is ironic as waiting for trains to turn up could never be said to be in anybody's top ten list of things to enjoy before you die. But here I suddenly found myself thrown back amongst crowds after a long period of solitude, and I found the atmosphere welcoming and safe, whilst the lack of pretentiousness in this part of the world seemed to make a mundane event almost a social occasion. The folk around me chattered happily and I was included too. It materialized that most folk were on their way into town to do a bit of Saturday morning shopping and they chattered excitedly, obviously enjoying the first day of the long awaited weekend. An old diesel train, just two coaches long pulled up and everyone clambered on.

On board I chatted to a couple about my parents' age. I learnt from them that there was in fact an old canal path from Worksop that I could have followed all the way into the city centre on my bike, safely away from the harm of traffic. Alas, one finds out these things too late. This wasn't my first trip to Sheffield and I had liked the place very much indeed. I asked my train companions what the employment situation was like here. They seemed adamant that even an unskilled worker could land a job very quickly. Sheffield received a mental tick for places to consider a new life in, in the future. On arrival at our destination I found the lifts to be out of order, so the couple helped me to carry Lucy up and over the footbridge and out the other side. This was fortuitous because as I may have already explained, the weight of a fully loaded touring bicycle is almost impossible to lift on ones own.

Now I had the challenge of trying to remember my way to the Orbit Cycles factory. From what I could remember it wasn't too far from the station and I set out hopefully, vaguely remembering roundabouts and road names. As it turned out my memory wasn't as bad as I thought and I was headed in the right direction at least, and with the help of a girl in the local petrol station I was right on course…Granville Road… just head up the longest, steepest road in the city and there it is, right up the very top!

Arriving at the Orbit factory was, for me, like arriving in my own personal Disney world. Everywhere I looked there were so many shiny new bikes that my tongue salivated as I oohed and ahhed at the many wonderful versions Lucy's brothers and sisters came in. As it happened I didn't have to wait more than twenty minutes for a mechanic to come to my aid. He clamped Lucy up in a vice at head height so the inspection could begin. I did my best to explain in layman's' terms the alarming clunking noise that had me worrying the day before, but typically, despite the mechanic twiddling bits and spinning wheels the noise refused to duplicate itself, and I could almost read the mechanics thoughts about how I must have imagined it.

'Perhaps it was your knee?' he suggested kindly. In utter desperation I took Lucy's front wheel in my own hand and spun it furiously. The fault sprung back into life…CLUNK, CLUNK, CLUNK, for the whole factory to hear, thank god for that! From this demonstration the mechanic was able to diagnose a problem with the front wheel bearings. He showed me too, they were dirty and corroded and one of them was missing. I thought back to when I dragged Lucy through the flooded roads of Somerset and felt extremely guilty.

With this problem fixed he lovingly tended (well I like to think it was lovingly) Lucy to a full service; gears and brakes adjusted, tyres checked and pumped and 'perfecto', all for no charge, and with a spare chain and two inner tubes thrown in for good measure. These last few freebies came after I had hung around to chat to the mechanic whilst he worked. He had confided in me that some of his recent customers had pissed him off somewhat; they obviously had money, along with that snobbish attitude that unfortunately sometimes comes with wealth. He said what a wonderful change it was to do business with someone 'ordinary' for a change. Hmmm, I guess it was meant as a compliment! Whilst he worked I watched on inspired and thinking I really ought to learn how to do some of this stuff myself, especially as he made it look so easy. It was a good idea in theory but in the real world I was perfectly aware I had a serious lack of patience with inanimate objects, and that any bike I tried to fix would end up in a far worse mess then before I began the butchering, this was at best. And at worse would end with said bike being deposited in the nearest garbage can. (In fact it was another ten years before I developed enough patience to even contemplate maintenance classes!)

With Lucy as good as new I was beaming with happiness and relief and was so blown away that he had done all this work for free that I thought I had better double check on this last point. 'What do I owe you?' I ventured, but the shadow that came across his face made me wish I had kept my mouth firmly shut.

'You don't owe me a thing' he replied looking almost angry. Oops, had I offended his generous warm northern nature by thinking that the power of wealth can be a substitute for good old human kindness, aka the snooty Orbit customers. I quickly changed the subject.

One of things I really like about Orbit Cycles is that they have a policy of donating 10% of their profits towards the building of cycle lanes. Huh, thought I, they can start with some decent ones in Nottingham. Funnily enough, whilst having a tour of the factory afterwards, I actually met some of these 'snooties.' They were stood having a conversation beside a touring bike, and I swear they were doing their utmost to ignore the scruffy creature in orange shorts and Doc Martin boots that appeared behind them. Sensing some fun I butted into their conversation. In my best ...'so put on I am obviously taking the piss'... BBC English accent I could muster, I barked,

'You know you really should try the Expedition bike' and pointed at Lucy. They just grunted and carried on their conversation. I wasn't finished yet.

'This one has just carried me from Lands End you know.' Ah ha, that got their attention and a few questions and slaps on the back were administered. Now was the time to go in for the kill.

'One is doing this for charity, yes Landmines Clearance International, hmm, oh yes that's right, Princess Di's thing.' I winked at the mechanic. Naughty me!

I headed north out of Sheffield and was relieved to find, not only was my route straightforward but the traffic was of modest levels too. I stopped to snap a photograph of the thing I thought might be responsible for this; Sheffield's newly working tram system. I loved it, the noise it made as it glided off, and that wonderful 'ding ding' of the bell bought back nostalgia of a once more sensible era before the car was king and public transport thought of as a poor alternative. In these days, when environmental issues are becoming a more, albeit slow dawning reality, trams are look set to become a revival in plenty of cities across the U.K. It is funny how things come full circle. I personally don't understand the logic behind binning them in the first place. In my many travels across Europe, from Warsaw in Poland to cosmopolitan Amsterdam I saw tram systems being utilised to the full.

It had occurred to me on several occasions that Britain seems some how cut off from her rightful place as a European country, hell bent on Americanisation instead. What exactly is it we are inheriting from The New World; fast roads, fast cars, fast cash, fast foods. Every thing is bigger and faster and more convenient when it comes from the states. There is less and less room for the small scale, homely or traditional, and even less respect for community spirit or the natural world and it's natural laws. I wonder about our special relationship with that superpower. Is it the history? The common tongue? Can we not say no to a fast buck and a gadget-filled life of unreality? Of course it would be utterly naive to think this doesn't happen everywhere, on my merry way around both western and Eastern Europe, I saw it too, and believe me I looked. But nowhere did I see the change coming as fast as it is in Britain. Nor did I see the desire to discard one's own culture so completely in favour of the American imports as here in Blighty... maybe we are the fifty first state after all!

I stopped for a break and watched fascinated at the trams coming and going. Maybe my father would have been less in awe of this scene than I as he would certainly remember them from first time around, but for me it was a totally new phenomenon. Sadly though I have read that the tram system has so far not been the success it could be, the reason being that instead of working in conjunction with the bus companies and setting fares accordingly or offering combined tickets, the whole of Sheffield's transport system has been turned into open competition and all sides were suffering as a consequence, aka Maggie's wonderful new Britain.

It wasn't much further up the road my belly began to get the better of me. Luckily providence was at hand; a baked potato shop appeared and the thought of all those dripping carbohydrates was too much to resist. Even here on the so-called rough outskirts of the city, I was still referred to by all and sundry as 'lovey' or 'pet.' And everyone wanted to know who I was, were I was from and what I was up to. (There was no disguising my foreign southern accent now.) As I pedalled on again, I mused over these great industrial cities of the north. Folk from the surrounding countryside had continually issued warnings as to the dangers of the rough inner cities. Now, I am sure trouble and strife goes on here same as it does anywhere. But I now realise there was no need to approach them with the fear that I had. And you know why? Because I could now see that these northern cities were no more dangerous than London, and I am certainly never nervous about a trip to the capital. In fact what I had learned beyond all doubt was they were a damn sight friendlier than London any day.

Pedalling away from the inner city I was lost in my own world, pondering house prices in the area, and slowly building up to my favourite 'Little House on the Prairie' daydream, when I rounded a corner and gasped. Sheffield was suddenly no more; instead the image that filled my head was one of gentle rolling hills covered with a patchwork of small green forests. After a day spent in 'civilisation,' the contrast hurt my eyes and flooded into my heart, I was back where I knew, and where I felt most alive. Rounding another corner, and not ten miles from the city centre, I found myself slap bang in the middle of the Peak District. Living on a farm in such beautiful surroundings and with a pleasant city like Sheffield just down the road…it was enough to fuel my daydreams for many miles to come. First Somerset, and now here…I was certainly discovering for myself some of England's hidden gems that I never knew existed.

There was however rather a down side to all this, the start of the Peak District signalled the start of a new struggle. Cyclist's red alert; when you see a sign declaring 'Scenic area ahead' read…HILLS! Fortunately for the time being I would be spared the sufferings as I didn't have much further to go that day. I was following the A616, which rose in a long but steady climb into the hilly distance. I watched as to my left the last of the houses and old industrial factories faded away leaving views of nothing but the empty moors far below, whilst on my right I was barricaded in by steep cliffs that seemed to stretch up to the sky. All this would have been fine if I hadn't been overcome by the desperate urge to empty my bladder. Cars whizzed past frequently and embankments both up and down were too steep to scale and offered no natural screening. Eventually just as I was about to reach bursting point I came across a natural gap cut into the cliff face by a flowing stream where lush green trees grew, and a viaduct beautifully framing the whole thing. It looked such a scene of serenity and almost too beautiful to use as a place in which to answer the call of nature, but I was desperate. I lay Lucy down and scrambled through the fence, which cut it off from the road.

At first I thought it was just the contrast from leaving the bright sunny road for the shaded area that caused me to shiver, but as I stood there and looked about the small clearing, I could feel every hair on my body standing on end...now I could see the clearing for what it was. I saw the rubbish that had been dumped there and the mosquitoes that whined over stale puddles, not to mention the stench. I could feel the bad atmosphere that prevailed the place, and I knew it wasn't just my imagination, but a sure fire sense that told me something very sinister had happened here. I could not bear to think of such bad things as murder, rape or torture, and I was sure someone was watching me. Cautiously I pulled down my trousers and squatted, but I couldn't empty my bladder fast enough. I was genuinely scared and all I wanted to do was to get back to the safety of the road. I pulled up my kecks and made a dash for the bright spot of sunshine through the trees. Bursting back out into the open I have never felt so relieved. I picked up my bicycle, but before heading off I glanced back at the clearing. Once again it looked picturesque and was back to a scene of serenity.

I arrived at the Langsett Youth Hostel with an hour to go before opening time. The village shop in this part of the world had so far survived the onslaught of multi-nationals and I came out with three huge cheese and mayo rolls and sat in the afternoon sun munching hungrily. However the after effects got me wondering if maybe dairy produce was responsible for my recent lack of energy in the same way I had found coffee was. As it turned out there may have been a grain of truth in this theory; a year later I read that the body needs energy to digest protein. So for someone completing a marathon a day it is best to stick with carbohydrates during the day and save protein for the evening meal instead.

The hostel was empty, bar me and the old couple who ran the show and I spent a very peaceful evening pouring over a stack of old Cyclists Touring Club magazines. My room for just four pounds a night (cheaper than most campsites,) was all mine. I camped on the top bunk so I was level with the window, and propped myself up on my elbow so I could gaze out at the view outside and watch the horses in the field next door, the isolation spoilt only by the roar of traffic from the road outside.

DAY 19 (2nd day of rest)

The lady running the hostel seemed horrified that my parents were driving all the way up from Sussex, just to spend one day here. My parents, when they arrived, seemed shocked by just how much I could now eat! I on the other hand, neither horrified nor shocked, couldn't have been happier, with a big grin on my face and a happy heart was delighted, both with my parents visit and food portions.

Off we went for our picnic in the peaks. In the back of the car, before we'd even got to our destination, I tucked into sandwiches, crisps, pasta, pies, cakes, desserts and fruit, and still had room for the veggie Sunday lunch I decided to have when we stopped for a pint a bit later on. After reading this you won't need me to tell you what cycling does to ones appetite, what surprised me more though was after I got home, I found I still needed to keep up this level of sustenance for almost a month afterwards.

I also got the chance to delve into the bag of goodies mum had bought with her, (other than the food that is): clean clothes, an extra water bottle, more shampoo and conditioner (which I needed to tackle the dreadlocks beginning to accumulate at the back of my head,) and a new reading book. There was also a stack of mail to read. Included I found a postcard from Les the financial advisor wishing me well, and a letter from my German beau. The contents were tinged with sadness about him not being able to contact me as he was in Russia for four weeks and I was on my odyssey across The British Isles. I didn't realise it immediately but I think that was when I first decided the relationship was going nowhere. Yes absence does make the heart grow fonder, up to a point. But I think that was when I decided on the futility of long distance relationships; after all if you're only seeing each other once every couple of months and you're quite happy to be without that person for all that time in between, maybe they don't really mean that much to you after all?

The Yorkshire Dales lay before our feet. It was my first visit and the beauty speaks for itself. Oddly I should have taken this rare sneak preview to prepare myself mentally for the coming few days, but somehow I was so taken in by scenery gazing at the incessantly steep hills, that I failed to make the connection between the beauty and the pain that was to come in both leg and lung. I guess I was looking at it from the easy position of the back seat of the car, where reality from the outside world can become distorted for the cyclist. How frighteningly quick it is to switch back to seeing the world from a motorists mentality. I discovered I wasn't the only cyclist doing this. The peak district was full of Sunday cyclists. They would drive out to convene at a car park, then set out on some supper slim, super light racer, go for a burn before dumping said bike back into the boot again. At one car park I walked amongst these 'men' as they slapped each other on the back, congratulating each other in overly load voices…'Oh I say, great run Charles.' They carried no luggage, no house on their backs, and they did not have to find food and shelter at the end of a hard day, nor, did I suspect, they venture out in bad weather.

It was a great day and we had plenty of fun sightseeing the area. We even stumbled unexpectedly across the village of Holmesfirth which unbeknown to us was also the film set for the BBC series 'Last if the Summer Wine.' Of course on this discovery my mother and I went into full tourist mode and took in tea at Sid's Café and posed for photos upon Nora Battey's steps, much to my dad's embarrassment. I had forgotten how nice it is to spend time with people who already knew me well, and not having to start from the very beginning every time I started a new conversation was a blessed relief too. They deposited me back at the youth hostel and stayed for a cup of tea, promising to come for longer next weekend; the august bank holiday…how the summer was racing on.

In the hostel that evening another psycho tourist on a charity ride of his own joined me. He was very decent and gave me plenty of useful tips as to my route up in the far north of Scotland as he had completed the trip himself the year before. When we reached what should have been a natural break in conversation (when all useful info had been exchanged) I made ready to leave the room. Alas this chap must have been on his own a while and did not seem to know when to stop yakking. I shifted very bored from one buttock to the other and stifled a few yawns, when eventually the lady who ran the hostel entered the room. I took this distraction to flee to the sanctuary of my private dorm. I lay on the top bunk and pushed the window wide open and watched as the horses in the next field played in that frisky manner equines do when they sense the electricity of an approaching storm. The air was humid and sticky as I wrote long over due postcards and I sweated as I lay there. Finally I felt the long awaited cool breeze blow in through the window as the wind picked up in a sudden gust, nature's way of warning you the rains are on their way. I switched off the light and lay in the dark listening to the thunder rolling overhead.

DAY 20   (37 miles from hell)

For once I was actually packed up and ready to go by 08.30...'God be praised, it's a miracle!' The small family of hostel goers had increased over night and we were joined downstairs by two middle aged men on a hiking tour of the Peak district who, for some reason, instantly gave me the cold shoulder in that horrid way other tourists frequently did. I tried not to feel upset; I had come to expect it in tourist areas, but not in a youth hostel that should welcome youngsters away from home on their adventures. These two wouldn't even return my smiles, that was, until the jolly women who ran the hostel told the men about my adventures in a tone of voice that made her sound like a parent bursting with pride discussing her own child. After this, their attitude towards me miraculously changed to one of great admiration, and they even donated money into the tin, which helped to put the smile back on my face.

The first twenty miles across the Peaks that morning were almost magical. I was protected from the fierce heat of the day by a light mist that shrouded the hills, keeping the temperature cool and bearable and casting the world about me into a picture postcard scene. I passed a sign that welcomed me to West Yorkshire; 'Working for Peace' it declared. Peace with whom? I wondered, Lancashire maybe? Freewheeling on down into the next valley I once again arrived in the village of Holmesfirth, this time pausing only to buy a loaf from the local bakers. Now a Monday morning this tiny village seemed, well almost ordinary again. The weekend tourists were long gone and along with it, its celebrity air, almost as if it were now disguising itself as the famous film set it was.

It was now half past ten and the day had become hot and bothering. Those steep valleys that yesterday had looked so beautiful as we'd driven through them, today were slowly killing me! It had been a valiant start to the day. Not sure exactly what awaited me, I had started out gamely, but by the third torturously steep uphill stretch of the morning, I think I had got the picture. My limbs were numb and each progressive gasp of breath caused the stabbing in my chest and lungs to worsen. I may have had 600 miles in which to get fit, but nothing could have prepared me for this!

The morning consisted of short bursts of struggling, either to cycle uphill in Lucy's easiest gear, or getting off to struggle equally as hard to push Lucy up. The hills were that steep that I would stand with all my weight pushing against the handlebars in a vain attempt to stop her rolling backwards to the bottom again, and very probably dragging me with her. I hope this gives you a clear outline of the Yorkshire Dales... pretty they may be, but hell they were also. Downhill was no fun either, I kid you not; they were almost vertical! Down I would ride trying desperately to keep my heavily laden bicycle as slow as I could, but even with brand new and perfectly functioning brakes, they still would not hold the load on these sheer gradients. I rode in terror of veering out of control, possibly even being jettisoned over the handlebars.

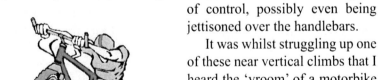

It was whilst struggling up one of these near vertical climbs that I heard the 'vroom' of a motorbike approaching six o'clock. It cruised nearer and nearer before coming right up behind me and tooted my rear. Leaping startled into the air, I momentarily lost concentration and grip, whereby both rider and cycle slid several yards back down the hill we'd just struggled up. I turned my head readying a tirade of abuse when I realised it was Steve from the Calverton armed robbery.

'I don't believe it' he said,

'I don't believe it' I said, and we both stood there for a second panting and sweating; me under my sunhat and shades and him in all his leathers, sat over the bikes boiling engine. I don't know who would have felt hotter?

We agreed we should find somewhere a little cooler to catch up on our travels, i.e. the nearest pub for one very cold lemonade. I set out first but had not gotton far when I heard Steve screaming my name. Alarmed I turned to find he had dropped his very large motorbike with all his heavy panniers over on its side. Oh dear, oh dear. As there was no way he could lift the thing without assistance, and me being the only person that might come along for hours, it left him in a very tight spot, and me in a very powerful position in which to bargain from. 'O.k. matey' I said, 'I'll help you if you help me and be my back up for the day?' What choice did he have? Ten minutes later, with all my heaviest items strapped on to Steve's realigned bike I was ready to do battle with the Yorkshire Dales. Without tent, sleeping bag, books, gas stove or tins of food, Lucy became magically lighter, as did my legs.

This particular stretch became a navigator's nightmare come true; a maze of winding back roads I had so confidentially route plotted pre trip, a route that was designed to steer me clear of Huddersfield's' busy centre…but in reality it was just a hopeless mess in which I spent most of the day lost and confused. Steve's help could not have come along at a more valuable hour. Despite him being Yorkshire born and bred, this was not his neck of the woods and he found it all as hellish as me. He though had the advantage of an engine so would go ahead to scout out the route, whilst I would wait his return in the shade before venturing further. This saved me so many incidences of screaming off down some steep old hill, only to realise I'd gone the wrong way and have to struggle back up the way I'd come.

Despite having the luxury of back up, the day was as painful as it was long, with searing heat and bodily pains as my constant companions. Even with Steve's help, I still got lost dozens of times. Looking back with hindsight and knowing far more about road layouts than I did then, I should just have braved the longer, busier main roads through Huddersfield; I guarantee you now, the hills would have been a damn site less brutal, (I have come to notice over the years main roads tend to be built around the worst of the hills, and not straight over them.) Not to mention far easier to navigate. It took me the rest of the entire day to cover a mere seventeen miles; that is an average of LESS than 5mph!! Talk about frustration; Steve must have had the patience of a saint. As bicycle and rider struggled across the Dales in the blistering heat, it was the one time on my journey that I really felt the cold despair creep into my heart. It was the one time I heard myself mumbling 'What am I doing this for?' It was a dark moment.

I had negotiated my way as far as the top of Sowerby Bridge where the humidity was temporarily relieved by a downpour that brought the rain down in sheets. As luck would have it, I myself had just pulled over to buy some sustenance and I got to watch the whole show from a shop doorway. As I munched on pasties and chocolate, I saw foot deep puddles appear in the road within seconds whilst thunder and lightening crashed overhead. But the whole pageant was not to last long. After just a few minutes, the deluge had slowed to a trickle, and before long it had disappeared completely. By time I had munched through my energy boosting food, the sun had burst forth once more and I was on my way in heat that was as hot as if the rains had never come. (When I met up with Steve just two miles further on up the road, he had asked 'what rain?')

The final run into Hebden Bridge came as a relief in more ways than one. Back on an A road, I found it to be the very road I had dreamt about all day. It was practically flat and I positively bowled along; the remaining five miles took only quarter of an hour; it was by far the fastest I had moved all day. The hell wasn't completely over though, consulting my map I discovered the campsite was two and a half miles outside the village and the road was a 1:4 gradient all the bastard way up. By now exhaustion had set in and cycling was no longer an option, my legs weren't even talking to the rest of my body and I was quite happy to walk this last bit and stretch off my aching limbs. Halfway up the hill I passed through the village of Heptonstall with its immaculately cobbled streets, all built on the same 1:4.

After the struggle I had faced today, I wondered who in their right minds would want to live up such a ridiculously steep hill, but as a dozen cars and then a bus passed by, where all occupants' eyes were on the poor sod with the push-bike, I had my own question answered; the age of the motorcar was here to stay. Rather than feeling sorry for myself, I instead thought of the working horses that once long ago would have pulled their carts up this very same road. I went into one of my self-hypnosis dreams to blot out the pain in my body. In the dream I was from a bygone era where four legged friends were king of the road and I was on my way back home after a long trip, but I was one of the more considerate owners who had got off the cart to walk with the horse up the steep hills. The buzz of the traffic around me faded out as I became enthralled in my own little world. I thought about the fairytale classic 'Black Beauty.' Not many people realise but the author Anne Sewell wrote the book for educational purposes, back in those days much cruelty went on, mainly in the hands of ignorance to a horses needs. And in fact it was thanks to her work that the cruel bearing reins were made illegal. I had recently watched the newly released black beauty film; needless to say I sobbed through most of it.

Back to the modern day and I found the campsite with 'nay' problem, although Steve's presents eluded me. I freewheeled into the campsite and collapsed on to the grass…no not from exhaustion, but from fits of laughter! Steve, (bless his heart) had 'attempted' to put up my rather complicated tent, but oh what a bodge job! It stood rather forlornly in the middle of the field; only half erected and ready to collapse at first sneeze. I put Lucy down and set about rescuing my little house, I found actually getting the guy ropes out of the bag was a definitely a good start! Steve finally reappeared at the campsite, he had been on a trip the local shop to pick up snacks and ten cans of beer…wow what a back up rider!

I seriously thought I may have died that day, fighting a loosing battle; my fitness and will power versus the hills and heat wave, but if this were true then at least I had now landed in my own personalised heaven. The campsite over looked a beautiful small valley, which, if you sat quietly you could hear the gurgling stream below and the sheep bleating on the hill opposite. I will always be able to picture that valley whenever I close my eyes, it all seemed so tailor made for me; so perfect. It felt as though this beautiful, amazing place had been sent here as a reward for having soldiered on all day when I felt so despondent about everything. I'm sure if I had given up the day earlier than planned, (or perish the thought accepted a lift on Steve's motorbike) than the place I would have spent the night would not be a patch on this little Eden. Nor would I be feeling the immense high I was feeling now.

We wondered into the pretty cobbled streets of Heptonstall for a few beers, but nowhere seemed to be selling what we were really after…a hearty meal, so we treated ourselves to a taxi back down into Hebden Bridge where I easily demolished two huge pub meals of pasta and chips. Later I sat cuddled in my sleeping bag in Steve's tent. The novelty of actually being able to sit upright was so welcome after twenty nights in my cramped little affair that I didn't actually make it back to mine. It was late but I chatted and laughed and listened to the bubbling stream below and then laughed some more, taking the piss out of Yorkshire man Steve and all his sheep...apparently that's why everyone is jealous of Yorkshire men, he explained...they have a wide choice of girlfriends.

I must have dozed off eventually because when I awoke it was the early hours of the morning, and my old friend 'dehydration' had taken a hold. I fumbled about until I found Steve's huge water bottle. I drunk gallons of water, otherwise I knew it would be curtains on the road for me if I didn't, but then I was cursed with bladder empting duties every half an hour. Each time I unzipped the door, the inside of Steve's' tent was turned into an icebox and I could hear him cursing me from the depths of his sleeping bag. It was in those early hours that I first noticed the change in nightly temperature from summer stickiness to autumn chill, and secretly it pleased me, as it was another sign of just how far north I'd come.

Not surprisingly we both awoke with major hangovers; despite all the water I had drunk, the gin had poisoned my system. I sat with a mug of tea in my hand; silently craving the huge fry up I knew would be the only medicine that could cure me of such ills. Last night I had tried to explain to Steve about this place being a close comparison to heaven. In hindsight and by the look in his face, I doubt very much he understood my philosophy of the struggle to get there and so forth, but in the end even he couldn't argue with the heaven theory when the women in the caravan next door offered to cook us a huge fry up for breakfast. Now that is what I call magic

DAY 21 (29 miles)

It was time for me to strike out alone and once more laden to the gills. I thanked Steve and left. He was due back to work in Skipton tomorrow; playing back up had waylaid him but I promised to stop off when I passed that way in a few days and buy him a pint to say thanks. I was really beginning to grow fond of these easygoing northerners.

It was fast approaching midday by the time I left. It was not the most sensible thing to do... leaving at the hottest part of the day, (and with a hangover to boot) but I think we established a long time ago that strict schedule keeping was not my forte. I pulled my sunhat down low over my thumping head in an attempt to keep the sun out of my eyes, rolling them in despair as I thought how I would be accompanied by the big three...hills, heat, hangover...I realised I was in no mood for heroics today given the circumstances, so after a quick glance at the map I decided to head via Colne to a place called Slaidburn where a bed in a comfy youth hostel awaited.

Compared to the maze of yesterday, today's route was mercifully very simple, just one road, winding its way across the Dales: hot, vast and empty. There was definitely something mystical about cycling across that wilderness where everything, including myself, was blurred into a heat haze, and I had nothing and no one to depend on except my own stamina. I paused to take a photograph. Now there was no cycling breeze to keep the heat at bay, it alarmed me somewhat just how strong the suns rays actually were. I looked out at the road ahead and saw nothing and no one, not even a sheep. I looked back and again saw nothing but the dry grass, the incessant hills, and a shimmering heat haze wavering above the tarmac. I suddenly became very aware just how much I wanted to flop into a ditch and sleep for the rest of the day, but the daily goal had already been set in my mind, and as I had learnt yesterday, to stop sooner than you mean to, reaps no rewards.

As I thought back over the course of my journey, I realised that I had mental gaps; it was as if I had got from Somerset to Yorkshire and nothing had existed in between, it was a blank. I puzzled over this some more as the sun tried it's hardest to frazzle my skin. I realised that this was meant to be the biggest mental challenge of my journey. Behind me lay more than half the trips mileage. In the first part, The West Country, I had got into a routine, built up my fitness, and learnt how to conquer a hill or two. Then there had been an easy interlude through the Midlands where it had been more about surviving the traffic than surviving the physical challenge. And now along Yorkshire had come, this was the struggle. On the other side was the Lake District and then easy cycling in Scotland, which felt to me like coming home; if only I could make it over these seemingly never ending, god forsaken bloody hills.

I was forced to give myself a twenty-minute respite from the heat. I sat in a farmer's field in the shade of an enormous oak and pulled from my pannier my long awaited prize, a large mango. It had been another thoughtful gift from my mother, which I'd carried around for a few days. I'd never eaten a mango before in my life, and it had been the source of all amusement that morning as I tried to convince Steve, as I had already convinced myself, that this would be my newfound magical cure for a hangover. But as I bit into its succulent flesh and felt its juices dribbling down my chin I realised, as delicious as it was, the only thing it would succeed in doing if I wasn't careful would be attracting the wasps.

Today I received one of the best pieces of local knowledge I was given on my entire trip. In a small hamlet named Roughlee, I showed my map to some old boy, and asked him where I could find the road in which I sought. Taking the map in his wrinkled hands, he studied it and then advised me to use a two-mile detour instead. This, he said, would save my legs toiling over an unnecessary hill. I thanked him and followed his words of wisdom. When I got around the other side and saw just what an enormously steep hill he had saved me from, in my mind I thanked the old man again. It was my second day struggling across the Peaks and I swore if I ever had children, I would never bring them here on a cycling holiday.

A little further on down the road I caught up with a young women who was out hiking alone. She pointed to a huge rise in the distance, and told me it was her favourite hill she was off to climb for the sixth time that year. It looked more like a mountain to me and I was seriously hoping the road bypassed this one! What I had troubled fathoming was, why she said she thought it strange that I would choose to cycle tour on my own when she herself was obviously happy and able to appreciate the benefits of hiking alone. It didn't make sense, I thought her of all people would appreciate the need for solitude on a journey.

From time to time I meet other women who are happy to strike out alone, and it always brings a strange kind of relief to discover I am far from alone. Take the women who cooked Steve and I our fry-up this morning. She had left city life to spend some time living on her own in the middle of nowhere, happy with just the occasional company from other passing campers. Whatever personal reasons drove her there I don't know, and even if she decides eventually to return to her former life, I believe she will always be able to draw strength from this time when she was brave enough to strike out alone. Then there is my friend Clara. Here was a woman who was left devastated when her husband ran off with another, taking everything they owned, including the kitchen sink. After the initial devastation period, she wiped away the tears, bought herself a combi-van, and four years on is still working and partying her way around Britain and Europe, enjoying, in her own words, the best years of her life.

'The best years of my life.' These words ran around my head for a time and despite the pain in my body, an unexpected smile came to my face. As it turned out there were some lingering truths to these sentiments I felt at the time. Twelve years on as I write this from the material I recorded in my cycle diary, I came to realise there are monumentally proud moments in my life where I have overcome difficulties or broken personal barriers. For example, the day in Devon where I realised that yes I could do this, I could cycle the length of the country, no matter how far it was, or how many hills I encountered. Or the time I jacked in my job and my flat, packed a bag and headed for the wild unknown lands of Eastern Europe.

I arrived off the night train in the Polish capital; tired, creased and bewildered. I tried to make sense of things, but it all conspired against me; I couldn't find any accommodation, no one spoke a word of English and trying to tackle the post-communist bureaucracy was like banging ones head against a brick wall; very hard. And all the while the hawkers and the perverts were circling, trying to grab my purse and backside respectively. Starting to freak out I cowardly jumped on the first train I could find back towards nice, safe (and very familiar) Germany. Unfortunately in my haste, I had boarded a train whose average speed was about 20mph, taking around fifteen hours and calling at every blade of grass on route, even the guard laughed when he realised my mistake. But those fifteen hours turned out to be extremely telling and one of the most revealing nights of my life.

I plucked up all the courage I could muster and in pidgin German I spent the journey communicating with the Poles in my carriage, who were very welcoming and friendly and were more than happy to share their food and water with me, (I had foolishly jumped on board with neither). This was a lovely surprise after the time I'd just had in Warsaw. But more was to come. Once they had gone I settled to sleep, when I was joined by a rowdy bunch of soldiers. After more pidgin communication, this time more with sign language and drawings than with words, this lot turned out to be Russian soldiers. I have to admit to feeling ever so slightly panicky… all alone with this lot for the night? My fears turned out to be unfounded and we had the time of our lives, laughing and joking despite no common language. They even managed to communicate that the short bald guy was the butt of all their jokes as he spent most of the time on the toilet and always used all the loo paper. As the evening wore on my eyes were streaming with laughter, and before they left they tore the badges from their uniforms to present to me. 'You…' they pointed at me, '…one girl travelling all alone…' They told me I was big, strong and brave. 'Bruno' they called me. That was when the final dregs of my timidness melted away and I can remember, even to this day, the freedom I felt it bring.

Through out this trip so far, I had many a time been met with people who said they would love to have the opportunity to do as I was 'Only not on my own,' they always added. Or if they were willing, they would admit to getting bored or lonely very quickly. BORED and LONELY? I cannot think of two words that least described this trip so far. I also find peoples fear of solitude a curiosity, this need to constantly surround themselves with the chattering masses; it just doesn't work like that for me. I often thought if I lived in a city with all that noise, I wouldn't be able to hear my own thoughts, and then I would end up feeling more lost, confused and ultimately lonelier.

Through a Lancashire village, (Steve would have been alarmed to know I'd moved into hostile territory,) I was stopped by some holidaymakers, who enthusiastically fired a whole barrage of questions at me. I was more than happy to chat with these friendly interesting folk and I was rewarded by a handsome sum into the charity box.

Feeling extremely cheery I dived into a café to refill my water bottles as I often do, so was totally thrown when the the proprietor refused my request point blank. It appeared that in this part of the world, the local authorities had forcibly put everyone on to water meters and they were now being billed according to how much aqua they used. I was astounded by this news. I know in the south where we have had the pleasure of maybe a few too many hot summers and dry winters, the government have been nattering about this possibility for ages now; but up here in the wet cold north? Were there any water shortages around here? I enquired, apparently not, so why the metering?

I did think he was a bit mean not to be able to donate just one small bottle of water to a thirsty charity cyclist, but I guessed he was feeling bitter about this newly imposed legislation. Rather unhelpfully he pointed behind me to a public convenience were he said I could fill my bottles up for nought. But I certainly wasn't going to back track and have to cycle up the same hill for a second time, (expedition rules,) so continued thirstily. As I cycled past houses I now found myself eyeballing people suspiciously as they watered their gardens or washed their cars.

As a keen environmentalist, I had always agreed in theory to the idea of water metering systems but this event made me think twice. Water is one of life's essentials, and I guess like fresh air it should be available free and unpolluted to all world citizens. By metering people, it could make them mean with one of life's essentials, and could even endanger the poorer families who cannot afford to pay through the nose for it. When you look at just how much water is wasted in industry, or lost through poorly maintained pipe systems, maybe these are the people who should be paying. After all, just one leak could waste a billion times more water than someone using a hosepipe to water their cabbages or because for once I choose to have a bath rather than a shower.

I was on the final seven mile run into Slaidburn and boy was it slow and painful. Luckily the oppressive heat of the day had finally subsided as a deliciously refreshing shower pattered down around me. I propped Lucy up against a gate and stood in the rain until goose bumps covered my entire body. On again to tackle the next hill, and as I made the top of this one I stopped and strained to catch sight of the much apprehended Slaidburn, but all I could see over the now mist covered land were more and more hills; not so much as a barn was in sight to signify civilisation.

It is at times like this that I play a mental game with myself. I turn my milometer upside down out of sight, and then say to myself, 'Right, the last signpost I passed said Slaidburn was still seven miles away' and then convince myself that I've done not many miles since then. I convince myself that I must have at least another five to go. Then what happens is, when I then come across another sign which tells me that, actually I've only got another two to go, I get an incredible rush of relief and it is usually enough to allow me to sail through what would otherwise have been the toughest few miles of the day…well it works for me anyway.

With a heightened sense of relief I finally landed on the doorstep of Slaidburn. It was a quaint old village, hidden like treasure in this beautiful valley, but by the way I was blanked in the local shop I got the impression it must be a much visited tourist affair.

Once I dumped all my stuff on my bed, I took a much-needed shower to wash away the sweat, grime and booze from the last day or so, it was heavenly. And then down I went to the kitchen to make myself what I term as a 'Youth Hostel Usual.' This translates as pasta and tomato sauce, (you watch the majority of folk in a youth hostel cooking,) and for my own luxury I grated in an entire packet of cheddar on top too. Delicious. In the kitchen I was spoilt for people to natter to. A boiler repairman from the south was able to tell exactly which county folk were from, just by listening to their accents, and on a few occasions he even guessed the exact town. (If you are wondering why I was so impressed then let me tell you how I am able to confuse an Irishman for a Canadian and a Welshman for a Norwegian…Accent identification is not my strong point!)

I found my fellow kitchen-goers smirking at the size of the portion on my plate and dropping comments about how far I must be cycling. Just as I was wandering how they knew, I was informed by a young Scottish lad that Slaidburn Youth Hostel is located on a most popular, and direct route from Lands End to John O'Groats, and that 'End to End' cyclists like myself often frequented the place. It turns out this Scottish informant was also on route, hoping to make John O'Groats in his two weeks summer holiday. (He had started out with a companion but he had quit only two days into the Cornish roads. On hearing this I found my head giving a knowing nod.) When I asked young Scotty how many miles he had covered so far I was amazed he'd only done around 400…I myself was sitting proud on 640. He told me about his format. Every day he had to complete between 60-80 miles in order to finish on time, this thought horrified me…80 miles of Cornish road; no wonder his companion had thrown in the towel. But what horrified me more was when the lad then said that since setting out he had not seen one single thing worth photographing. At first I thought maybe this was because being from Scotland he was rather biased, Scotland being so beautiful that anywhere else in the British Isles seemed dull and uninteresting by comparison. But then I began to realise the real reason. Pushed for time he was just getting his head down and covering the miles, and everyday would be no more than an endurance test. To hear this attitude, I felt sad for the guy. What a waste of such a fantastic opportunity, to see so much of the world from one of the best places to witness it; at the helm of a bicycle. I know I had deliberately set out to watch the world, (as much as it appeared to be watching me), added to which a lot of these places I knew I would never pass through again, nor meet the people I met ever again; it just seemed ludicrous not to take time out to smell the roses as it were. It reminded me of one of my favourite quotes from David Attenborough who said quite simply…'God help us, If we're not interested in the world around us, then what are we interested in?'

Moving up to my dormitory set for ten ladies, I found I was just one of two occupants. I settled down looking forward to a luxuriant evening: writing postcards, reading my book and wallowing between clean sheets. I was understandably disappointed to find this wouldn't be the case once I met the other mystery occupant. Right from the word go I didn't like her. I don't wish to be judgemental, but what sort of a person barges in and begins telling a perfect stranger all about the troubled relationship with her mother, IN GRAPHIC DETAIL, and about how she'd been kicked out of this particular hostel twice already for using drugs, returning each time using a different name. I don't condemn the taking of drugs, each to their own is my motto, but I feared this girl may have taken one drug too many and had clearly lost the plot.

Not wishing to appear rude, (in hindsight I should have told her where to go straight away) I tried to patiently chat with her, I even took up her challenge of a game of chess, but I was ill at ease. I could sense how unstable she was and it wasn't long before my nerves began to feel frayed. It was not my idea of fun after a hard day in the saddle, when all I had looked forward to all day was a quiet restful evening. It all ended abruptly when without warning, she snapped off the main light without even consulting me.

I had been writing my diary mid sentence but decided not to challenge the action. Wearily I put down my diary and politely called out into the darkness, 'Sleep well.' But it was met only by a stony silence. About five minutes later, on the verge of drifting off to sleep I was suddenly snapped fully conscious again by a hostile voice raging through the darkness.

'What did you mean by that?'

Unsure whether she was even talking to me or not, I chose to ignore her, but the voice came back alarmingly threatening.

'What the fucking hell did you say that like that for?'

123

Puzzled beyond belief how anybody could misinterpret such an innocent comment as 'sleep well' I adopted a gob smacked silence. But this crazy paranoid bitch was determined to get an answer out of me, and I was now receiving threats from her to 'give me a good hiding.' I heard her leap from her bunk and storm over to flick the light back on. I in the mean time sprang from my bunk also; I had no intention of being attacked in my bed. I couldn't believe what was happening.

I faced her trying to remain calm despite a racing pulse and rationally explain what I had meant when I had said 'sleep well.' Finally she seemed satisfied by my explanation and retreated back to her corner, though not without warning me to 'keep it shut.' I lay back down in the dark, heart beating fast and stupidly thought it was all over. I must have been too nervous to see what was coming next.

Two minutes later the light was on again and this time she was screaming at me for stealing her soap and toothpaste. Again I pacified her. But when the lights flicked on for a third time and she began rifling through my bags and threatening to 'lay me out' I couldn't take anymore. I stormed off down the main stairs and a few minutes later was banging on the hostel warden's door. Through a combination of anger and tears I relayed the commotion that had just occurred. He listened and didn't seem at all surprised.

'Stupid Cow,' he said. 'I cleared her toiletries up this morning after I told her not to leave them in the communal bathroom and she didn't listen.' So back up the stairs we both went.

Quick as I could I gathered up all my clothes and panniers, stopping only to shout some abuse back at this girl, now I had the warden as protection. (Later he told me he'd only felt brave enough to tackle her, as I'd been there to cover his back!) The old warden was full of kindness and took me back downstairs to another room where he poured me a shot of brandy to calm my nerves and help me sleep. He confessed to relying on a shot of it himself most nights. He had hoped coming to run a quiet youth hostel in a sleepy backwater would be good for his nerves that were growing progressively more frayed over the years. I giggled at the irony we had both just experienced. I had wandered alone through rough inner cities, and camped out alone in deserted places and had never even smelt a hint of trouble. I stay one night in what is thought to be a safe establishment with a family atmosphere in the Yorkshire Dales, and I had ended up meeting the biggest psycho going who had wanted to beat me to a pulp as I lay sleeping in my bed.

As we sat chatting we heard the mad women storm from the hostel, never to return, (heaven knows where she was headed this time of night.) But I don't know who breathed the biggest sigh of relief, the warden or myself!

ROUTE MAP 3: THE NORTH

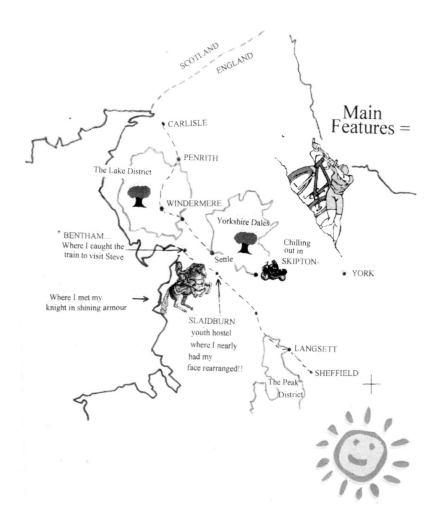

SCOTLAND
ENGLAND

Main
Features =

• CARLISLE

• PENRITH

The Lake District

WINDERMERE

Yorkshire Dales

* BENTHAM...
Where I caught the
train to visit Steve

Chilling
out in
SKIPTON

Settle

• YORK

Where I met my
knight in shining armour

SLAIDBURN
youth hostel
where I nearly
had my
face rearranged!!

• LANGSETT

• SHEFFIELD

The Peak
District

DAY 22 (16 miles)

During breakfast this morning, (left-over pasta,) I answered countless questions concerning the events of last night, news of which had spread like wildfire amongst the hostel goers. I didn't appreciate having to relive the events ten times over; although I did feel momentarily cheered when a little girl confided in me that she was glad the 'strange women' had gone, as she'd felt very frightened of her. That made two of us!

Whilst loading up my bicycle in the fresh morning air, some old 'git' seemed hell bent on worsening my mood, by patronising me with pointless questions that didn't even deserve an answer…

'You're a bit over-loaded aren't you, why don't you carry less?'

(I'm on a month's cycle and camping tour and am only carrying the bare essentials.)

'Why don't you get yourself a lighter tent, they're only two hundred pounds?'

(I don't have two hundred pounds to spare.)

'Your saddle's a bit low, you should be able to stretch out your leg and level your ankle bone with the pedal.'

(I can.)

'Your bicycle frame's too big for you…'

(It's not.)

'…Why don't you buy yourself a new one?'

This was the final straw. I was off, taking away with me very bad memories of Slaidburn. Before leaving, I had asked the warden if the road to Bentham was particularly hilly, and he had asked, if by hilly, had I meant very up and down? Yes, I had replied. To which he said, in that case no it wasn't hilly; it was just one long up, all the way. Great!

I set out on what was to be the third and final day struggling across the Yorkshire Dales. The weather, for the first time in ages was gloomy, but thankfully this also meant it had cooled. As I cycled that morning I slunk warily around the narrow lanes and kept a cautious eye out for any movement in the high hedgerows that lined the road, nervous that the nutty girl would be lying in wait, complete with chainsaw and axe in hand, screaming,

'I'm gonna get you for having me slung out of the youth hostel.'

After all, where the hell had she gone to in the middle of the night; stuck in the middle of nowhere, with no car and no public transport?

It struck me then, just how much my own imagination was scaring me. What surprised me even more though was how much this event was to effect me in times to come, how it would effect the way I handled meeting strangers and how it would be over a year before I stopped feeling automatically terrified of women more bolshy than myself. As it turned out, this shake-up in trust was to be tested far sooner than I had bargained for.

The warden had been right of course, for thirteen long miles I struggled up the steadily rising road. The route could, in another time and space, have been a pleasure. It cut clean through a beautifully deserted valley, where towering peaks fenced me in on either side, making me feel even smaller and more vulnerable than I already did that morning. There were no cars for half an hour at a time, and the drizzle hung low in the air adding to the ambience. This was true wilderness that people dream of; it felt even more remote than some of the Scottish Isles I've visited. I should have found pleasure from that scene; the eerie noise the wind made as it moaned through the rocky cliff faces of the hills, the green valley and the far off bleating of the sheep. But for me it held no enjoyment that day. The road was far steeper than it appeared to the eye and for some reason I couldn't ration with myself that this was why I sometimes had to get off to push; I felt like I was letting myself down, and that I was no longer capable of cycling my bicycle across England. And I wasn't sure anymore if my racing heart was from the physical exertion, or from adrenalin produced by the mind games my imagination was playing. Either way though, it was all thoroughly unpleasant and dispiriting. Finally, in one last desperate push, I made it panting to the top and looked out from what felt like the peak of all peaks at the valleys below. But there was barely time to marvel at this accomplishment as I spied in the distance a strange vision that made me rub my eyes in disbelief. There appeared to be a knight of the round table heading towards me on a beautiful black horse.

Introducing Sir Hellingwell and his gallant steed Oliver. Actually the knight's real name was David. The pair were on their way back from a tour of the castles of Cumbria, they'd had to cut the holiday short because both had been suffering in the recent heat wave. David explained that he slept in hedges or barns, whist Oliver was stabled and fed by the kindness of local farmers along the way. We chatted for a while and David admitted to being stuck in the thirteenth century. He asked if I too was a traveller, so I proudly introduced him to my 'mount' Lucy, and we exchanged tales of being on the road. He lowered his voice and speaking ever so softly, he confided in me that he believed he lived in a world all of his own and asked with all seriousness if did too. I ummed and ahhed and said, 'Well maybe just a little.'

To tell you the truth I was still in shell shock after the near attack on myself last night, and for the first time my usual faith and confidence I exude when greeting strangers was shattered. This extraordinary meeting with an unusual character in the middle of nowhere would normally have been a source of great excitement for me, but now I found I had to keep taking a step back to leave an unusually large space between the two of us. It was almost as if I was expecting him to bludgeon me over the head at any minute. I need not have worried though, David was perfectly safe, and if I am honest, probably one of the sanest people I met on my entire trip too. Being a horse lover and a hopeless romantic myself, I was actually quite envious of David's lifestyle, it is the sort of trip I dreamed of as a girl, and still do come to think of it. When David announced that his way was an objection to the motorcar and to modern life in general, I felt nothing short of admiration for him and I knew we were definitely on the same wavelength.

David let me have a ride on Oliver, (who looked thoroughly unimpressed when I tried to point him in the opposite direction to home.) They hailed from Sowerby Bridge, where I'd passed through in a torrential down pour a couple of days ago, and I was given an open invitation to visit any time. We shook hands and made eye contact. That contact that went between us seemed to make no words necessary, just a feeling of understanding that passed like lightning, backwards and forwards and it said it all; a sense of recognition...'I know you and I know your way. Good luck to you.'

Once I'd waved Sir Hellingwell and Oliver out of sight, I turned to face the valley before me. I felt (almost) literally on top of the world. I'd just completed the most difficult part of my journey, the Yorkshire Dales, I had met a wonderful character who had been sent by the hand of fate to reinstate my faith in people, and now all I had left to do was three glorious miles of downhill before being rewarded with a proper break, relaxing in the company of my new found friend Steve. I got myself comfortable in the saddle, let the breaks go, and shot off like lightening down into Bentham.

Studying the timetable, I once would have been dismayed to read I had a two and a half hour wait for the next train into Skipton; but not anymore. Comfortably settled into the new nomadic lifestyle I had forged for myself, I was able to see this wait more, as quality time to catch up on those oh so essential tasks; eating for example (more left over pasta.) I sat back and scoffed to my hearts content.

The sun burst forth from the clouds and I sat back contentedly on the bench wiping away the crumbs; now I had time to catch up on my diary which, recently with one thing and another (my parents, Steve and then that woman) had been rather neglected. I was about to make a start with pen poised over paper when out the corner of my eye I spied a character entering the otherwise deserted station. 'Oh God, who now?' thought I, nervously.

I watched the old bloke pootle about the station, clearing twigs and sweeping leaves. By these actions, one would make the assumption he was the gardener, but I know from my own employment history that railway companies use contactors to do these kinds of jobs. I felt as though the old man was watching me intently, which kept my nerves suitably on edge. I tried to ignore him and thought maybe he would just go away. No chance. The minute I tried to resume pen to paper, 'POUNCE' he was sat right next to me.

'Your not from round here are you?'

I have never been subjected to sit and listen to such an enormous pile of dross in all my life. After three quarters of an hour I even found myself praying for death to take me, when the conversation had progressed to how he thought the royal family had all had their bodies taken over by aliens. I looked at the station clock and sighed…oh god, still another hour and a half to go!! It appeared he wasn't the gardener at all, he just did it because there was no one to tell him not to. What better excuse could he have to be on the scene in a jiffy, to bore poor unsuspecting travellers to death? Thinking about it, he must have kept a regular watch on the station from his house, how else could he have appeared so quickly after my arrival.

What seemed like a lifetime later I arrived in Skipton. I looked at the clock and thought,

'Great, half an hour till Steve gets here. I'll just sit on this bench and finish my diary at last…'

…Another voice looms in my ear and another nosey parker plonks their arse next to mine…

'Your not from round here are you?'

Later on Steve giggled helplessly when I relayed all this to him and he explained,

'Oh the people from round here saw you writing and probably assumed you were a journalist!'

DAY 23 & 24   (zero mileage)

'Wow;' the novelty of not having to move a muscle for a couple of days was fabulous, well I did manage to move a little. After sleeping in until the afternoon, I would arise and be treated to one of Steve's northern style fry-ups. Then it was in to town or mooching about at Steve's getting odd jobs done. Steve ran his house pretty much like a bikers Bed and Breakfast gaff, so was used to having his home being taken over; it was just as well. I used his washing machine to clean every last item I had and then hung everything up to drip dry after, transforming his home into Chinese laundry. I used his phone to ring friends and family, I got my photos developed in town and helped myself to his bottle of his Baileys Irish Cream. I planned to leave on the Friday but Steve was out for the day, motorcycling with friends in the near by Lake District, and I was sweet talked into going on the back of his bike. All thoughts of Lucy were abandoned for another twenty-four hours.

But a hidden danger lurked along side all this comfort, luxury and friendship…I was not preparing myself mentally for the next stage of the trip.

DAY 25   (25 miles)

The morning was not a good one. For a start it was the first time in I don't know how long, that I had to get up extremely early (and against my will) and hurry, yes actually hurry, to Skipton station. I probably would never have made it had it not been for my amigo, come host, come back up driver; yelling at me from the other side of the bedroom door and threatening chilling threats to bring a bucket of icy water into my room pronto! I felt very sad too, I had become most attached to the charms and people in this small town of Yorkshire and now felt wrenched to leave them behind.

Now every turn of the pedals would take me further from this place and induce my brain to miss it all the more. Up to now, every day on my trip had been the same game; get from A to B. And the pleasure had always been in reaching my goal every night. Without realising it, in the space of two short days I had sub-consciously moved the goal posts, and instead had made my pleasures from making new friends, checking out a potential new home and generally getting comfortable. Not wise for someone who must not only tear themselves away, but still summon up the oomph and drive to cycle another six hundred odd miles; now was not the time for apathy.

Now here is a problem I myself have discovered can occur whilst away travelling for long periods at a time; you stumble on a great place to hang out and end up tempted to stay there for too long; and why not? You have found a comfortable place, made friends and everything you need, is on tap. This happened to me, and it took me a while to realise that this wasn't really travelling, because basically all I had done was settle in a place that became familiar and easy to be in; basically I'd tried to find a replica of home.

Travelling was never meant to be that easy, and isn't even necessarily fun all the time; I have experienced all sorts of emotions when out in the big wide world: boredom, loneliness, and even damn-right hard graft. But more than anything it is an education, and I have always returned home mentally, physically, spiritually and culturally satisfied.

The train I caught deposited me in Settle. This meant I had an extra five miles to cycle compared with if I had gone back to Bentham, but this way I was spared the final few gruelling miles of the Yorkshire hills. As I cycled it rained hard, adding to my misery, and when I stopped off in Kirby Lonsdale to eat the cheese and onion sarnies Steve had made for me that morning, I calculated it would be over a month before I would be able to return to this part of the world again.

I arrived at Kendal station in good time to meet my parents; I was relieved I had lost no fitness in the two days I spent slobbing about, and stood there, a miserable dripping wet soul, and waited over an hour for their arrival. I pulled the cord of my hood tight around my head, but the tale-tail wet patches on my back suggested that, once again my rain mac had already failed me. To distract myself from the wet I mused over Kendal; as a ticket office clerk at a railway station in South London for many years, I recalled the countless times I had sold people train tickets to the very spot I now stood in; tickets which were usual eighty quid a throw. It had always seemed like a faraway mystical place, and now here I stood, having cycled all this way here under my own steam. Even I was not too miserable to appreciate the sense of achievement it gave me.

Finally I spotted my parents pull up across the road. I wish I could have expressed better how pleased to see them I felt, but the cold had frozen my face in its' frown, and all I could muster was a weak smile. Lucy, along with all my panniers was unceremoniously dumped in the back of their estate car and off we drove in search of accommodation for the next few nights.

All my worst nightmares about mass tourism and the over-use of the motorcar came true that fateful bank holiday weekend. Every town and village was jammed solid with cars, whilst I had witnessed only a handful of people arriving by train, (but at eighty quid a person, who could be surprised!) The roads were filled with a constant stream of cars that we added to. It is sad that there is not better public transport on offer; surely having to drive so many cars to a beauty spot renders it less beautiful? I wondered why everyone appeared to be driving around in a seeming frenzy and very soon I knew why…and for the first time in my life I was almost glad I was not on my bicycle.

Finding somewhere to stay was nothing short of a nightmare. Bed and Breakfast establishments were out of the question, not unless you could afford to spend a fortune, (we couldn't) or were willing to be forced to stay a minimum of three nights, (we weren't.) We walked around every town and drove around the surrounding countryside, but to no avail. Everywhere we went, unscrupulous and scheming proprietors told us the same story. Feeling like Joseph and Mary arriving in Bethlehem, (I must have been the donkey!) we were given the same answer again and again; that there was no room at the inn.

Eventually my father and I managed the difficult task of persuading my 'no frills' nervous mother that camping may be the only option, her and me in the tent and my father in the car. WRONG, even the campsites were full to bursting. I stood outside the reception pleading with the young man that he must be able to find room for one teeny tiny tent. I tried every trick in the book and tried flashing him a winning smile; but he was having none of it. Now you can see why I was actually glad not to be in the saddle. If I had arrived here after forty hard miles pedalling, only to be turned away from every campsite in a thirty mile radius, I think I would have sat down and cried. The only site we found willing to take us could only offer a pitch in amongst the cow dung and a hole in the ground to piddle in. And for this the farmer wanted thirteen pounds per person per night for a minimum of three nights. It was obscene. I suddenly found myself back in my mother's camp; so to speak, camping was also out of the question.

Eventually we ended up driving an incredible twenty five miles, before tracking down a Bed and Breakfast in a place called Carnforth, (incidentally just outside of the official Lake District area.) We managed to hire a huge family room for just thirteen pounds per person, (the same price Farmer Dung Field had wanted.) In the pub that night over dinner, we joked; Carnforth appeared to be the kind of place you would never visit, not unless it was by accident (like us), or you had someone to visit near-by. But to be fair to the old girl, we were grateful to have found her all the same.

DAY 26 (27 miles)

The women who ran the B&B did her utmost to force-feed us as much fried food as we could manage that morning, beaming with delight when we accepted another sausage or one more tomato. It was what catering was all about. I quickly grew rather fond of this lady because when she learnt our reasons for coming to Carnforth and all about my trip, she swept aside her husbands' 'Ooh aren't you brave' comments, nodded her head and very calmly and sanely said that, I was just fine, that there was nothing wrong with me choosing to travel alone, and I should be proud of the fact that I was an independent young woman. To hear this after almost everyone I had met seemed intent on calling me peculiar, eccentric or even insane was a great comfort to the soul. We chatted to the only other man staying at the establishment and it seemed he was only there because he was visiting nearby friends. On hearing this we had to stifle a few sniggers; for this seemed to prove our theory about why you would end up here, right down to a tee.

Rather ridiculously, but the seemingly only way to get around the accommodation problem, we put Lucy in the car and drove back to Kendal where I was deposited in the exact spot I had been picked up. My destination this time was Penrith, and it involved a minor (!) detour over the Kirkstone Pass. The day was cloudy, humid and muggy, and the sun was having none of it, so I was relieved to reach the point where I could finally leave the busy main drag and relax in the comparative quiet of the back roads. But the geography gave me little respite. No sooner had I sighed relief at leaving the traffic behind, I passed a sign welcoming me to the Kirkstone Pass. '1500ft and winter conditions could be hazardous.' Eek; this was to be my first attempt at crossing a mountain pass on a bicycle.

Going up hill for a whole hour on end bought new and unexpected bodily sensations; and none of them were particularly pleasant.   I constantly panted and gasped for breath, (though I was proud to discover it never got so bad I had to get off to push.) My heart was a base drum; I could feel a red-hot pulse in my face and my cheeks burned. The one comfort was there was only about one car passing me roughly every five minutes, and due to the fact even motors struggled on this gradient, I could always hear their approach in plenty of time. This allowed me to use the entire width of the road to wobble on, and I was able to meander diagonally across it at the steepest bits to try to aid my ascent.

As I climbed and climbed and tried to loose myself in deep philosophical thought, I began to realise for the first time that, (and I know any non cyclists won't believe this) but the beating heart, the racing pulse, burning cheeks and struggle for breath was now not so much an uncomfortable sensation, more a sort of, well familiar friend. I swear! Today I was lucky, I was also aided by the fact that everything I usually carried, except for my water bottles, were all safely locked up back in the Carnforth B & B, and this made my first attempt at a mountain pass that much easier. I knew in my heart...I may always be a slow cyclist, but I was certainly, (for the most part,) a happy one. The one and only time I stopped on the way up was to pee, and finding a place I could do this in privacy became more of a challenge than the mountain itself. I found the low Cumbria stonewalls gave little screening and the one car every five minutes rule was always broken as I prepared to squat.

In under half the ETA I finally reached the peak and sat proudly outside the Kirkstone Inn, (said to be England's highest public house) and triumphantly gulped down a shandy thirstily; watching as other cyclists, mainly mountain bikers, happily conquered their mountainous challenge too. I then began to freeze. My parents, who had been off on their own adventures that morning were due to meet me here for a picnic, and I had foolishly said to them to give me at least two hours, misjudging my own fitness by miles. It was still in the days long before mobile phones and I had no choice but to sit and await their arrival. This would not usually have been a problem, as I'd discovered in Bentham, my nomad lifestyle had made me exceptionally good at filling in unexpected waiting time. But I was sat at 1500ft and the sweat was drying off me at a rate of knots. Teeth chattered and I rubbed my bare arms and legs, but the temperature drop, even in our petite mountain range showed no mercy. I tried to distract myself with the fantastic views and did a few star jumps for good measure, but by the time my parents arrived with the picnic, it had to be eaten in a heated car with me under two blankets. It was the first of only two chills I caught on my entire trip.

Like all patient and determined souls, you receive your reward in the end; and mine was to be the descent. I had to borrow a jumper from my mum before I left, and I decided to don the cycle helmet too; I predicted rather more rapid speeds on the way down, and I didn't even like to think of the consequences, should inadvertency befall me. I waved ta-ta to my parents and shot away into yonder. At first it was tempting to go full pelt, like a Tour de France cyclist on the home stretch, but it didn't take me long to discover the tarmac was a little too uneven for those kind of shenanigans, and only minutes later my heart momentarily stopped as I hit a bump so fast I swear I momentarily lost contact with Lucy altogether. Luckily I landed back in the saddle, Christ knows how, but after this, speed was modified to a much safer pace; the last thing I needed was to end my day flying over a Cumbrian wall with a follow up visit to the A & E.

The exhilaration was finally at an end; back on floor level the humidity now returned, and mum's jumper was securely tied around my waist. Now the main challenge was over I relaxed into easy cycling. I was rather enjoying the holiday atmosphere that prevailed the lakes that very warm afternoon; car drivers were considerate, people swam or sunbathed on the shores of the great lakes. I rather fancied a dip myself, but as I had no spare clothes to change out the wet ones I refrained, one thorough chilling was enough for me that day. Further along I saw a large extended Muslim family, all enjoying a feast that looked large enough to feed the entire Islamic faith…my mouth watered in envy.

I shared the road with lots of other cyclists; they all sallied forth in the opposite direction to me. I kind of got the impression the majority of them on this side of the mountain had hired bikes from Penrith for the day, and were enjoying the flat, easy to cycle road that ran around the lake; that was until they came around the corner and spied the Kirkstone Pass looming in the distance, and a look of horror befell what had up to now, been happy contented faces…

'Holy shit look at that hill,' I heard many a cyclist scream to their companions, or…

'No way am I cycling up there, I'm heading back, is anyone else coming?'

As I passed I would try to shout out some encouragement, but words such as…it's not as bad as it looks, or…It'll be worth it when you get to the top…fell flat against their resolute fear of physical hard work. Alas they had failed to see that this hill was in fact the best bit in disguise, for without the challenge of the hill, there would be no sense of achievement, no personal fulfilment that would stay with them forever. As indeed my many achievements on route have always stayed with me.

I rendezvoused with my parents at Penrith station, and they once again expressed their amazement at the speed of my progress, which gave my confidence a great boost and put a smile on my face. They seemed rather proud of the progress I was making and I was chuffed to bits. In Penrith we had the usual long family 'discussion' over where to have dinner before heading triumphant, if thoroughly chilled, back to Carnforth and a well deserved hot bath.

DAY 27   (20 miles)

It was the morning I had to say ta-ta to my parents, but before their long drive south, we spent a pleasurable few hours together, site seeing the areas we had not yet had the chance to see. One of the places I was eager to drive was 'Hardknott Pass' which I am told is the steepest road in England; and it didn't disappoint. Of course being a hardened cyclist I would rather have traversed the road on Lucy, (honest!) but my route (so unfortunately!) had taken me in a different direction. Halfway up the hillside I spied another cyclist who was taking down his tent where it appeared he had spent the night on the grass verge, and I realised I had not once since setting out, enjoyed the freedom of rough camping.

And so on to Penrith station where we said our goodbyes. There would be no more parents' day for me, by next weekend I would be well into Scotland and out of daily visit range. It was a sad moment.

The twenty miles from Penrith to Carlisle were a doddle. The road was as good as flat, and there was hardly a car to be seen. Well actually there were plenty of cars, but thankfully they were to be seen and not heard in the distance, all flying along the M6, which ran parallel to my A6, leaving it deliciously traffic free. The world around was flooded in beautiful afternoon sunshine and I was mesmerised by what I saw; to my left were the peaks of the Cumbrian mountains, to my right lay the Pennines in full view, and ahead of me loomed the hills and mountains of Scotland…yes, by tomorrow I would be over the border and into the land of heather, whisky and mountains. Just the thought of it made my heart dance happily.

Lost in a dream world as usual and enjoying the road that was empty apart from me, I jumped out of my skin when I suddenly heard a man's voice booming down my ear…

'So you're heading for John O'Groats too?'

It was a fellow cyclist who had crept up on me unawares. Like all other End to Enders I had met, (accept for John in Devon,) this guy was part of a team, assisted by motorised back up and staying at pre booked accommodation at a given target every night; and it goes without saying that he wasn't carrying any equipment himself.

'Why would I want to cycle with all that on my bike' he said casting his eyes over Lucy and trying to humour me. Indignantly I asked, had he ever considered that my way was far more exciting and adventurous, more satisfying and not to mention more environmentally friendly? But even as I spoke, one of the groups' many back up cars slowed to check he was o.k. which they did every five miles or so, and then sped on again. It all seemed rather flamboyant and unnecessary.

As there was no traffic to worry about, we cycled side-by-side chatting for several miles. As often happens when I meet other cyclists, I found I had to pedal at far more than my usual leisurely pace just to keep up, but it certainly helped the miles speed by, until signs signifying the outskirts of Carlisle loomed. I was given an invitation to stick with him to Lockerbie, the teams' destination for the day, but dismissed the idea after mulling it over for just a few seconds. As much as I enjoyed a bit of company, especially from fellow cyclists, I knew I couldn't bare to let someone else's journey steer mine, and at the next set of traffic lights I shot off right towards the city centre; yelling and waving goodbye. It was a relief to be back at my own pace again.

I had been a little concerned that my late afternoon start from Penrith might catch me out, for I was in desperate need of some local guidance; firstly on the whereabouts of a campsite for none were marked on my map, and secondly concerning the route ahead, so I was relieved to find the Carlisle tourist information office still open late into the evening. The women behind the desk smiled broadly as we chatted,

'Oh we're all a friendly lot up here.' She quipped. I'm not sure if this was just standard blabber they gave to all visitors or she genuinely wanted to reassure me; me coming across so southern and such a long way from home. Either way it had the desired effect as I walked about the pretty city centre in the warm evening sunshine. As I finished my supper on a bench in the main square, an elderly couple from Cornwall spotted my charity bib and came over for a chat and to donate a few pennies.

The last rays of the evening sunshine had now moved on behind the buildings and I set off for the campsite just three miles from the city centre, (and just a few miles to the Scottish border.) Anyone else in my position would have been jumping for joy, as I tried to toast my last evening in England with a cup of tea and a cigarette. But alas I found without the purposefulness of forward movement I sunk withered into the doldrums, and loneliness played a major part. I suddenly missed my parents very much, and as the sad thought-chain progressed, I remembered all the good times I had had amongst Steve and all his friends. But returning to the sanctuary of this regular companionship was months away also.

Above: My dad walks a tightrope in The Peak District

Below: My mother and I stop for tea at Sid's Café

Above: A much-needed down pour in Sowerby Bridge, West Yorkshire

Below: With Lancashire maybe?

Above: Steve, my back up for the day and me

Below: Sir Hellingwell…my knight in shinning armour, and his steed Oliver

Above: The Devils rock…call me superstitious but I was careful not to lean Lucy against it!

Below: My parents come to support me in The Lake District

Part2.Scotland

The Road.

DAY 28. Border Control.   (60 miles)

The light appeared rather dull that morning as I swung my leg over the crossbar; an everyday event accept today was very special. Glancing at the clock ticking loudly on the campsite toilet wall, I was amazed it was only 07.30am. Never, since starting out from Cornwall had I been this organised of a morning, but I guess sometimes you get this sense of just needing to get on with things. Ever since dawn the sky had been a deep red, and I found myself smirking as my memory recalled a book I had once giggled over. The book was titled, 'The old bastard's book of country lies.' It basically took the mickey out of all those old country proverbs, and right now a particular one came to mind...Red sky in the morning...the barn must be on fire.

Try as I might to remember more piss taking proverbs, thoughts of the day took a gentle hold instead. Nothing in particular; the road that lay before me, the sky with it's billowing off-white clouds that reflected the melancholy mood of the land it shadowed, and more than anything I was aware of a sprightly wind that had sprung up over night, and for once it was a tailwind. All this 'space' around me set the mood as I rolled into Gretna Green, my eyes searching for 'that' signpost and there it was...'Scotland Welcomes You'...I sincerely hoped so.

After snapping a quick photo of Lucy parked up against this sign, (and not for the first time wishing that there was someone to take the photo so I could be included in it for a change,) I stopped to reflect the situation. Here I sat breathing in my first lungful of Scottish air, and I wondered should I be dancing around whooping with joy, or maybe standing in silent contemplation? But as just the other day I learned the length of Scotland is in fact 56 miles longer than the length of England, I felt like doing neither. It is ironic that the further you travel, the less far you feel you have come!

'The Old Smithy' was a semi-interesting place, but the resident bagpiper, dressed in all his traditional tartan finery, looked bored out of his brains. It had dawned on me that there where folk in my life who would be more than impressed I had made it to Scotland by bicycle, so I sat on the wall outside and wrote a few postcards. As I wrote I sat proudly in my charity bib, convinced that anyone passing would notice me, come over for: chat, congratulations and to make a donation. But the visitors seemed only interested in the bagpiper and the bagpiper seemed interested only in going home. This was my queue to post my postcards and leave. As I pedalled away I thought to myself, 'Stupid town really. It was once the stuff of legends; where young lovers would runaway to wed in secret...now the waiting list to marry here was almost a year long.'

The route between here and Glasgow was the only section I had not pre planned before leaving the calm shores of home. The reason being, on first glance at a road map, it appeared every conceivable route running north was a potentially busy 'A' road; and these were not my favourite places. As planning an alternate route appeared mind numbingly complicated, I thought it best to wait until I got here, at least that way I could try to seek out more local, and probably more sensible advice than my own hapless gambling's. When I had ventured into Carlisle tourist information yesterday a fantastic idea had popped into my head when I spied some cycle maps. To be precise I found the 'Sustrans' Carlisle to Glasgow cycle route. Bingo. (Incidentally Sustrans is a leading cycle campaign group in Britain and stands for Sustainable Transport, and their long distance cycle networks are opening up all over the British Isles.) As I studied the accompanying map, I realised, if I followed this rather indirect route between the two said cities, I would be adding at least another one hundred miles on to my already wibbly wobbly route across the U.k. However, all this was put into perspective when the text accompanying the maps promised scenic rides and virtually traffic free routes; one hundred more miles seemed like a small price to pay in comparison. At the time, (and on my budget) I felt the cost of this map was not so small a price to pay; six pounds to be exact. But with this, a wonderfully detailed map was included so not even a buffoon like me could get lost, (famous last worlds.) I must also mention the fact that Sustrans is a charity and every penny goes back into their good work. I swallowed any doubts I had and let the till swallow my money.

And so Scotland lay before me, and I was very much looking forward to it all, the misty eyed beauty, the ever further impressive horizons I knew awaited me. I began the count...one, two, three...another ten minutes...eleven, twelve, thirteen. But alas, these were not the miles flying by, but the wholly dead and squashed animals that lined the road. I wondered if children ever get to see these once cute and furry animals that now lay with their guts spilt uncaringly across the road; I saw fox, rabbit, frog, even badger. I know if a domestic animal is run over, the local council have a duty to come and remove the corpse, but nobody seemed to care about the bunnies. I tried to keep a count, planning to use my newly discovered statistics for a positive purpose, but by about fifty something I gave up. The only thing I can say for it is…who needs to bother with fox hunting or spreading miximitosis…the road seemed to be doing a fine job of culling all on its' own.

The first forty miles that day did indeed whiz past, flying along the flat roads of Southern Scotland, my 'dim-wit' proof map took me through places such as Gretna, Annan, Ruthwell, Glencaple and on towards Dumfries. The meteorological conditions were cycling weather sent from heaven; the sunshine beamed down warming my back whilst the stiff breeze not only kept me at the right temperature on this very warm summer's day but pushed me along too. Sustrans hadn't lied when they stated 'traffic-free,' I barely saw a car all morning and the ones that did waved in greeting.

Passing through Ruthwell I came across a hidden gem. In 1810, Ruthwell's most famous resident, Dr Henry Duncan opened the world's first commercial savings bank. Here in this tiny remote location was the birthplace of what has now become an international, and probably most powerful of forces in the world. And yet by a sad twist of fate Ruthwell is not only devoid of a bank, but does not even house so much as a post office or local shop for its residents, forcing them to drive the ten miles into Dumfries for basic amenities…progress?

Inside, the museum curator pointed out to me the collection of home savings boxes, coins and bank notes from various parts of the world, and then turned her attention to a small model of the Ruthwell Cross. It is a miniature version of an eighteenth century cross; restored by Dr Duncan himself (he was also minister of the Parish). It is said to be one of the finest Anglo-Saxon crosses in Britain and now stands proudly in their local church. But back to the miniature model, the curator's eyes narrowed as she explained,

'It was stolen from me by the English.' There was unmistakable venom in her voice that made me feel she was holding me responsible for the entire English nation and I felt decidedly uncomfortable. She went on,

'It was held in Sevenoaks museum for years and years, but I knew I'd get it back eventually.'

I suppose I couldn't blame her for her resentment. If my village treasure had been held in a grotty middle class hole like Sevenoaks, I think I'd have the hump too. Just then a sparrow that had accidentally flown in through the museum door and was unable to find its' way out took her focus off of me. She and the other museum ladies were most concerned by the event and amid a chorus of Scottish accents flapping over what to do about the intruder; I found my own escape exit and fled.

I began to encounter more cars again as I neared the outskirts of Dumfries. The giant clock in the main square read a quarter past one, I had made good progress that morning so allowed myself time to take it easy. I bought a copy of the Big Issue from a local vendor, found a sunny spot in the main square and got comfortable. I read a contentious article on celebrities who earn ridiculous amounts of money (usually by doing seemingly very little,) and then use this status to try to get 'ordinary' people to give money to the said charity. The article asks why they don't just donate plump sums from their own excessive bank accounts, which is probably far more expendable and would probably amount to a damn sight more in the long run? This hot debate took me up to what I thought was lunchtime, and it was then I realised the town clock had been stuck on quarter past one for some time now. A passing shopper told me it had in fact gone three. I groaned loudly. If only I'd known, I would never have allowed myself to relax so much; but it was too late. My legs felt like lead and my brain (and will power) had nodded off in the afternoon sunshine. In truth I couldn't think of anything I would rather do less that afternoon, than cycle on for another twenty miles. It is one thing for the body to be fit enough to do the job, but the mind must also be willing; and if it isn't…then God help you!

According to the Sustrans guide, the next five miles were a gentle climb uphill to Lochfoot…gentle my arse! The climb finished me off and I had to keep getting off for short periods to walk and stretch my aching thighs and backside. As I made my snail like progress that afternoon, strange thoughts popped into my head to amuse myself, and I grew so fond of the name Lochfoot that I repeated it over and over to myself out loud, perfecting my Scottish accent. The gruelling five miles finally passed. Still another fifteen to go! It was somewhere not far from Lochfoot, that a lone car, travelling in the opposite direction passed by me slowly, it's occupants staring out. I could have sworn the driver was a famous actor I used to watch on Sunday night television as a kid.

The final joy of reaching the Castle Douglas campsite and my all time personal record of sixty miles in one day was suddenly soured, when I found out the cost for pitching one lousy tent for one even lousier night would set me back £8.10. The price, the women explained when my blood pressure had returned to normal, was based on the cost of up to four people sharing, (the lone traveller is kicked in the butt once again.) Some how she just couldn't see it as the rip off I did, (I guess she never has nor ever will travel alone) and even all my 'from the heart' pleas about being a charity cyclist wouldn't sway her miserliness. As there were no other campsites that I knew of for twenty miles I was cornered, and practically threw the money in her face. I just hoped this wouldn't turn out to be a typical rule of thumb in Scottish campsites or things could become very expensive north of the border!

That evening, the usual sets of eyes followed me around the campsite and I sighed wearily. Up until now, the being alone part had not bothered me all that much; in fact I had even tried to extol the virtues of solo travel. But being spoilt for company recently had been both a blessing and curse, for now I sat, surrounded by happy, (and some not so happy) couples and families and felt a distinct twinge of lonliness well up somewhere deep inside. I was very much looking forward to meeting my friend Sarah up in Inverness in a few weeks time.

It was with shock I came to realise that after thirteen previous visits to Scotland, for the first time ever, I had some apprehensions about the time I was to spend here. After the extremely friendly and very chatty Yorkshire and Cumbrian folk, the Scottish could easily be perceived as cold and distant by comparison, especially to the lone traveller. I have heard a lot of Scottish talk about their resentment towards us 'Sassenachs,' some of it in jest, some not. And although I would never doubt the genuine nature of this resentment, (I need no history lessons here) I do find complete bias from any sides difficult to understand. Still, a few people around the campsite smiled at me welcomingly, (although it didn't escape my attention they were holiday makers from the Midlands.)

Before I could find some energy to erect my tent, I plonked myself down using a pannier bag as a seat and lit my only cigarette of the day. It felt good; to take in a deep puff, sending the nicotine flowing and soothing around my tired body. It was a change to actually receive some physical reward at the end of an arduous day, and the icing on the cake was to top it all off by making myself a cup of hot sweet tea… heaven.

DAY 29. A right old day   (47 miles)

After cycling an exhausting sixty miles, one would have thought sleeping would come very easily, but alas things don't always work out the way you would hope and a fitful night prevailed. First off, my bladder did a wonderful job in keeping me up. I had consumed gallons of water in the heat of yesterday and it chose the night hours to re-emerge the other end; I woke up at least four of five times with a full to bursting bladder that screamed in agony, and I found myself sympathising with older folk. At least, I thought, I could take solace in the fact that excessive water drinking would not be a problem this coming day, not if the night-time weather was anything to go by! The wind blew with some gusto on the tent walls, which rather fancied themselves as a ships topsail, and heavy rain hit the tent above my head in an unending deluge. All these elements did a grand old job of upsetting my dreams and I lay awake a lot of the night praying the storm would move on by morning. But the only thing that appeared to have been blown away was my luck.

I emerged at 8am, a crumpled and bleary mess, and lay for a while trying to catch the radio above the noise of the gale. Around half past ten I was stood in the shelter of a red phone box, chatting with my mother giving her the thrice weekly report I had promised, whilst outside my sodden and loaded bicycle looked as though she too wanted to be inside. But the conversation could not go on forever. There were only so many ways I could describe Castle Douglas, the weather, and how wet I was about to get, before it was time for the inevitable replacement of the receiver and my exit back into the gloom. Huge drops of rain fell from heaven, (were they bigger in Scotland?) and found their way straight down the back of my coat, literally soaking me inside and out. Throwing a leg over the crossbar, I felt the stiffness after yesterday's excessive mileage in my limbs... Oh great! I made for the off with all the enthusiasm of the dead.

With sore legs and 'shite' weather conditions at the forefront of my mind, thoughts of leisurely meandering down leafy country lanes disappeared as fast as the only patch of slightly less grey to be seen in the sky. I abandoned the Sustrans cycle route and hit the directness of the main roads instead. The A713 cut straight up across the country heading for Ayr. Encouraged only by my northerly direction, I put wheel to tarmac and cycled. This re-routing however, turned out to be

150

rather a pleasant surprise; not only is this part of Scotland very sparsely populated compared to most of the rest of England, but is pretty devoid of tourists too, leaving me with the road all to myself, sometimes for many miles at a time.

It rained and it rained...and then just for good measure, it rained some more. Thank heavens the wind wasn't blowing directly into my face as once it had back in Dartmoor; but remained in the only place it is welcomed by a cyclist; directly behind me. The first twenty miles that day seemed to be taking an age. Ten minutes of pedalling, ten more minutes of getting soaked, and I would foolishly glance down at the milometer; and then frustrated, quickly look away again, wishing I hadn't bothered.

Oddly enough it seemed to be the road itself that made my morning drag so. This particular stretch was pretty much flat, and as the dull grey scenery rolled boringly past, I began to long for some hills to brighten the view and give me something to focus on. I cannot believe I could honestly mean this after such a painstaking struggle across Yorkshire, but yes it is true. Without a shadow of a doubt, I have learnt that it is hills that make a cyclist's day far more interesting. Without a hill to tackle there is no challenge, no push to the top. No doubts as you slowly struggle up and up, and then the elation of the final few yards as you realise you've almost made it. And then best of all will come the personal victory at the top that no one can take from you, and the thrill of the chase down the other side.

I was not used to feeling bored whilst cycling, so to try to battle against this worrying new problem I decided to try my hand at being philosophical.

Imagine if life was like this road... flat, dull and easy...monotonous and without challenges. No ups or downs, no pride to compare with a fall.

The boredom continued; the philosophy deepened...

Life, no matter how I try to avoid it, keeps coming back to the same principal; that all of us, everything in fact, is part of a giant revolution of principals that each and every one of us must adhere to. But for some inordinate reason, the human race always overlooks the simple premise that 'what goes around comes around.' The Earth turns, we orbit the sun; even the stars in heaven are slowly revolving. Nature too works on the same revolving basis. A tree grows its fruit and leaves. At the end of the season they die and drop to the ground where they rot away and help fertilise the earth, and this helps the tree to grow more leaves and fruit the next year. And the process repeats itself, round and round. You cannot fault it. I always feel that if you deliberately do something you know to be wrong, it's as if you leave a scar of bad intention behind. But because everything is rotating, you eventually come back to that scar and the wrongdoing is returned on you who left it.

Eventually the weather decided to give me a break and the rain ceased, however the skies remained leaden and threatening. Alas the break had come too late for me on this occasion; I was sodden to the bone, though come to think of it, it had only taken a record two miles to reach this state of total saturation. As I cycled I found myself longing for the very first time for some music to listen to, or the radio, or anything to bring to an end this unusual eerie silence I found in the Southern regions of Scotland. I debated for a time whether it was worth putting my portable radio in my jacket pocket and turning up the volume, but an experiment proved this was fruitless, I could hear nothing. Instead I returned to my usual way of passing the time when alone, and one I generally enjoyed; thinking.

Thinking…thinking…thinking. I thought about so many things and yet there were still an infinite number of things to think about, and I began to wonder how I had ever found the time to feel bored. As one would expect, these thoughts began to get more personalized as the days went on. These were some of the things I thought about as I cycled across the U.K at the age of twenty one. In my head I raged to an old friend about how she was destroying herself by constantly living in her own small self-pitiful world. I would definitely need to be cruel to be kind with that one. I spent a long time dissecting an old relationship; it had been my most important one so far. Now though I could see it all so clearly; when I'd first fallen for him, and more importantly, I could now pinpoint the exact moment when I realised that this particular candle had flickered out. And thankfully I realised it really wasn't worth trying to relight.

I remember with particular fondness a whole day I had spent on a beach in Thailand, a picture of crystal clear seas and white sands.

152

There was not a single other soul around and I had sat there for hours; not moving, not reading, just sitting and thinking as I stared through the clear waters. It was as if that piece of ocean floor held the answers to everything I needed to know about my life, and answers as clear as the ocean itself kept popping into my head; how I wanted to travel more, what I wanted to do with my future and who it was who had really touched my heart, (and I remember with shock it wasn't who I thought it was.)

I also trawled through the darker days of my life too, but not sadly as I once had, but with a mixture of pride and relief at having survived and come through them all. One by one I remembered it all; shaking out the memories, examining each piece and laying them down to rest out of harms way; closing the door on each one. I thought enough to last a life time. I had in fact thought my lifetime through.

It was the first lunch break (of many) that day; sat miserable and cold under the dripping wet trees on a village bench, when a brainwave struck home like a thunder bolt. I always make it policy on any cycling tour to keep a supply of plastic bags handy, just in case. So why not use these plastic bags on my feet as a pair of waterproof socks that would fit nicely underneath my boots and keep my feet dry. And dry feet meant warm feet…and hopefully warm feet would mean the rest of me would stay a lot warmer too…why didn't I think of this, 29 days ago? I sat on that miserable wet bench, cheerfully peeling off wet socks, rubbed both pruned and wrinkled feet vigorously with my towel until the circulation got going again. And then very carefully, I wrapped each one in a warm dry sock, secured it into a plastic bag and stuck them snugly back into my boots. It was only a few minutes before I could feel the warmth and comfort returning to my feet, a glow that stretched out to all extremities of my body. Oh the joy of warm feet. I couldn't help but feel excited, and my insides danced at the prospect…no more cold, wet feet.

It is funny how I came to appreciate everyday items that I'd never stopped to think about before. Take your average plastic bag. To most people, and indeed myself before my days of cycle touring, plastic bags are just a thing you pick up from the local shop to carry your tinned baked beans home in, that then gets shoved in a drawer with the mountains of others that you keep 'just in case' but never use…but not anymore. I now viewed a plastic bag as a vital part of my touring kit. I used them at every available opportunity, but they were best at keeping things dry: sleeping bag and carry mat (when there isn't enough room inside you panniers,) clothes, and in fact everything inside of my panniers too for that matter. And to put the icing on the cake, I now had the most sophisticated, cheapest pair of waterproof socks on the market. (That was, until it rained again, whence I discovered a hole in the plastic where my toe had poked through, and the plastic began letting in the damp once again.)

But the biggest surprise for me was that whilst on this tour, I did come to appreciate motorways...something I never, in my wildest environmentalist dreams, thought I'd ever hear myself say! Now I know only too well that cars are bad for the environment AND I know that more road building is not the answer to reducing traffic problems. I would hate to see anymore of the British countryside disappear under tarmac, and I am all in favour of improving cycle lanes and public transport too. BUT... I can accept that inevitably there will always be journeys made by car, and I just think that maybe it is best if it advances along the motorways, leaving the county lanes, town and village centres to be safely enjoyed by cyclists, pedestrians, dog walkers, families, children playing etc. I had noticed this rather startling change of heart within myself only recently, particularly when cycling into city centres and the outskirts of some towns. Carlisle particularly and Nottingham, (south side anyway) stood out as a good example. I remembered the virtually traffic-free road my wheels cruised along whilst watching all the traffic in the distance thundering the same way but on the motorway and out of harms way.

After lunch, the day (and my mood) began to brighten considerably. The sunshine showed its wee bonny face, which always has an intoxicating effect on my moods, whilst I got my wish, as the road began to leave its dull drab life on the flat and slowly and gently wind its way up and over the hills of Southern Scotland. I say hills, but I was later informed they were in fact mountains, and part of the Southern Upland range. For years I had been trying to find out, when does a hill officially become a moutain? But no one seemed to know. It wasn't until years later when I finally got connected to the internet, and after extensive research, did I find that a mountain is defined as; a rise that lies at least 1000ft above the surrounding topography, (and a hill is obviously anything less than that.)

The scenery was fantastic. The mountainsides paraded different shades of purples, greens and browns that I attributed to the different types of heather that no doubt grew there, carpeting the floors for only

the animals to tread. The pine forests grew in abundance as far as the eye could see, both below me in the valleys and above me on the mountain slopes. And wispy strays of cloud intermittently floated above them, giving the impression of dozens of smouldering forest fires all going on at once.

My reign of vision that day stretched so far that I had no trouble at all in spotting an approaching rain storm across the mountain tops, allowing me plenty of time to pull on my rain coat and silly blue hat, (which was now offering excellent multi functional use in keeping the odd bouts of driven rain out of my eyes.) Despite the frequent soakings that afternoon, it never took me long to dry out, not once the giant radiator in the sky had worked its magic. I simply powered along that day as the gusty wind that blew remained firmly behind me. It felt like Mother Nature was giving me a helping hand when I needed it most.

I was watched by hundreds of inquisitive cows that lined the fences as I cycled past, it appeared they rarely received such an interesting sight to stare at, and they certainly made the most of it. And I watched as dozens of tiny birds regularly flickered across the road in front of me. They seemed to be sheltering from the bad weather in the grassy banks that line the roads, and on several occasions I had to brake hard to miss them as they played games of suicidal dare. On one occasion I felt one brush my mud guard and I could only pray it had got away safely. Having seen the appalling result of so much road carnage I would hate to be responsible for this tiny creature's death.

The final four miles of the day were a fantastic decent to the bottom of the valley, closely following the way of a mountain stream that bubbled and sang as loudly as I did. The weather chose to be kind for my grand finale that day, and I was bathed in warmth and sunshine, as I swooped effortlessly away down the mountain road; just like my dream, long ago predicted.

In Hollybush, I stopped to buy myself my dinner (two cheese and onion pasties) from a petrol station come shop, the only retail place there appeared to be. Outside, a women stopped to chat, but the accent was so thick and strong I had no hope of deciphering what she had said, so I just nodded and smiled in embarrassment before making a quick get away. I found a small road sign for the campsite, which pointed me up and through a housing estate, and with the guidance of some local children I found it where the houses stopped and the fields began.

This campsite was fascinating to explore. It emerged as a sad relic from the 'has-been' days of British family holidays, and was full of dilapidated static caravans as far as the eye could see. The largest building in the centre was once the club house, holding nightly entertainment. But now, no bar nor disco was in operation; just the cobwebs remained, along with the dust and a strong musty smell. As I nosed around these derelict buildings, it was easy to imagine what it must have once been like; alive with holiday makers singing karaoke, whilst children would have competed in cutest kid contests, whilst tipsy parents cheered them on from the sidelines. I wondered if the old boy who appeared to run the place alone had let the place go because his wife had died, or whether he had simply gone out of business because no one appeared to holiday in these parts anymore. Cheap foreign holidays have all but taken over from the more traditional holidays in this country, whilst any keen visitors to Scotland tend to speed through this area and head straight for Edinburgh, Inverness and The Highlands, and what they see as the 'real Scotland.'

I had to pick my way past dozens of really cute semi-feral cats that appeared to be multiplying out of control around the neglected farm buildings. They dashed away when I first approached but slowly came creeping back in true 'curiosity killed the cat' style. I wondered if I had caught the owner in the middle of his supper, because he answered the door in a very abrupt manner. I could hear the theme tune to 'Neighbours' playing on the television in the background. He waved me hurriedly away with his hand, muttering the words 'pitch anywhere' before slamming the door in my face. I found the spot where I thought tents should go and set up in a sunny spot where I could watch the swallows swooping over the field, and keep an eye on some local children who were up to mischief with the water fountain. I hoped this place was okay and would be regarded as 'anywhere' as I certainly wasn't in the mood to move my tent again.

After spending nearly thirty evenings pitching a tent, I couldn't possibly come away and say I had learnt nothing, so here are a few basic guide lines I have put together that may come in handy, (provided you are given a choice of course.) Firstly pick as sheltered a spot as you can, especially if it's windy. Basically the less the tent's going to flap, the more sleep you're going to get…or remember to pack the ear plugs. Secondly, pitch near a fence, post or tree, or anything solid you can lock your bike to close by. This means you can then leave your panniers attached to the bike overnight, with any unwanted items stored in them. This will leave a hell of a lot more room for you in your tent, a particular concern when there are two of you camping. And finally, always try to pitch somewhere a little secluded and apart from other campers if you can. The reason being that if you have to crawl out in the middle of the night to pee and cannot be bothered to get dressed each time, you'll be able to do this safely without half the campsite seeing you…a particularly grave concern for a 'weak-bladdered someone' like me!

ROUTE MAP 4: SCOTLAND

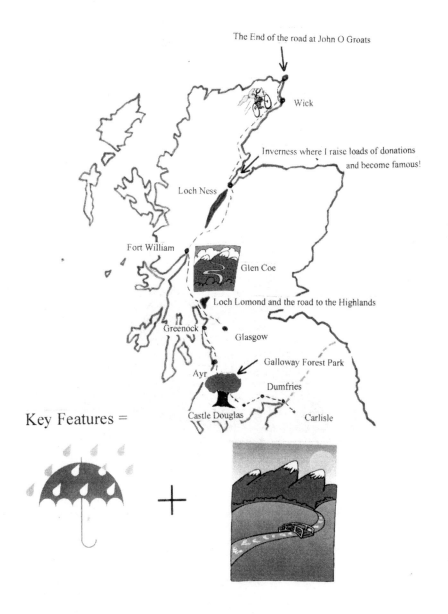

The End of the road at John O Groats

Wick

Inverness where I raise loads of donations and become famous!

Loch Ness

Fort William

Glen Coe

Loch Lomond and the road to the Highlands

Greenock

Glasgow

Galloway Forest Park

Ayr

Dumfries

Castle Douglas

Carlisle

Key Features =

+

DAY 30 & 31
Sealed with a Glasgow Welcome. (36 miles)

Late last night I was delighted when another lone female cyclist turned up at the campsite and pitched her tent not far from mine. She was the only other one I had encountered so far on this trip, and I was looking forward to enjoying a good old natter. But when we passed on my way back from the shower block, all I got was a grunt; not even a smile. I tried to swallow the disappointment at the lack of female comradeship, telling myself she'd probably just had a really rubbish day, with sixteen simultaneous punctures or something similar. Still, this morning as I was tatting down ready for the off, she stuck a sleepy head out of her tent and waved me goodbye, so I felt a little better.

Today the rain was making a notable and much welcomed attempt to hold off, and I set out for the eight miles to Ayr and hopefully breakfast. But it was more than just culinary interest that held my attention. A few years back I had decided to commit four years of my life studying at Ayr University for a degree in Environmental Protection. I was not only accepted but virtually had my bags packed as well when I suddenly had a last minute change of heart. I realised that student life was not for me and preferred to keep working instead, I don't know why; I just remember it felt the right thing to do at the time. It is so strange how life works out; I would find the path of my life had once again led me to Ayr, only this time for completely different reasons. As I stood in the main high street, I very much liked what I saw of the place. And if somewhere in a parallel universe, there was another me who did take the decision to go to Uni after all, I would like to think it would have been a very happy four years. Decisions...look what a vast difference they can make to your outcome!

Next on the list of 'must see' places was the urban jungle of Glasgow. I had the sense to pre book some accommodation at the backpacker's hostel, and with this worry taken care of, it left me plenty of time and breathing space that day in which to explore. I once again picked up the Sustrans cycle route and followed as it meandered through Western coastal towns such as Troon, where the spectacular beach must have been as long as it was wide. I sat on the breaker wall, squinting in the faint sunshine that was trying to burn its way through foreboding clouds, and marvelled at the yellow carpet that stretched away for miles into the distance. The beach front here at Troon was so beautiful, and yet was totally devoid of the usual swarms of tourists one would come to expect, along with the noise and litter they inevitably bring. It reminded me somewhat of the beauty of the beaches in North Wales during the winter when all the holiday makers had gone home. I wandered if Troon is somehow protected by its alias as 'just a suburb of Glasgow.' As I sat, I smelt the clean air and tasted the salt on my lips, whilst I gazed out to sea and saw on the horizon The Isle of Arran, floating on wave tops.

Along the road a bit further I conferred with 'Archie,' a local and a cyclist, who agreed with me that from time to time, the 'Sustrans' route seemed unnecessarily complicated. For example, it would detour off through a muddy field, (not somewhere you would want to cycle, particularly if, like me you are carrying a heavy load,) when there was a perfectly adequate and not too busy road running along side it. It became even more ridiculous when the field ran out, and you were routed back to the road anyway; you may just as well have stayed on it in the first place. Archie and I cycled along side by side for a few miles, chatting away about; yes you've guessed it, cycling...my favourite subject. He even made himself late for work so he could show me a better route to take than the one I was planning on, for which I felt most honoured. He'd just returned from a cycle tour himself, where he had cycled the Highlands self-sufficiently, and camped out wild every night. Whilst we agreed that the self-sufficient camping method was the best way to enjoy touring, he stressed concern that maybe wild camping alone was perhaps not so appropriate for a young lady. Scottish society appeared to be showing its' traditional values more often than England had. I waved goodbye to Archie at the next roundabout. I could deter him from work no longer, but it had been a pleasure to have met him. He was the first 'Scot' I had met that actually went cycle touring in his own country.

I stopped off in a petrol station in Preswick to grab a quick sandwich so I could recharge the depleted energy banks. As I sat outside on the wall, munching in the contented way only hard exercise can truly bring, a youngish couple appeared from around the corner and stopped for a lengthy chat.

I did do my best to understand them, really I did, but most of the next twenty-five minutes of my life consisted of them doing all the talking and I, sat nodding and smiling and hoping for the best. The trouble was, now I was on the outskirts of Glasgow, the accents were so thick and, well…'Glaswegiany', and I found it hard to follow at the best of times. But added to this, these last few days I had been suffering from blocked up ears, which had made hearing anyone difficult. But more than anything else, the reason for not understanding this conversation was that these two friendly locals were as drunk as skunks, and were slurring their words accordingly.

The women, whose name I managed to identify as Rachel, disappeared into the garage to buy some cigarettes, and when she re-emerged she'd bought me a Mars Bar as a thank you for 'looking after' her drunken husband, (listening to his drunken ramblings more like!) Some of the conversation I could understand and join in with was pretty much standard stuff.

'Ye' never cycled all this way alone? What d' y' parents think about it?' Rachel gave me their telephone number and said,

'Give us a wee tinkle when y' get there, let us know y' alright.' I was certainly meeting a whole host of friendly Scots today; drunk maybe, but certainly very friendly. I made ready to leave and they staggered off, supporting each other as they went. I picked up Lucy and continued on my way, none the wiser for the conversation I had just had.

The route I was following began to get more frustrating the longer the day went on, and I began to start wishing for the end of the day to come, not a very cycle friendly way to think, and it forced me to make a decision. Instead of heading into Glasgow, I would continue with my cycle north, up the coast until I was geographically level with the city center, and then catch the train into the city; cycling back out tomorrow. I found this a difficult but ultimately wise decision to make. I just couldn't face the urban jungle, the traffic, and the prospect of getting hideously lost amongst it all. And by continuing with my cycle north along the coast, I would not be missing out any miles either. There was also another worry I'd had with cycling into the city and it had been confirmed by Archie, who lets face it was a local and should know. Local cycle paths, in order to avoid main roads, instead detoured through back ways, and according to Archie were maybe not some of the most pleasant areas one would wish to traverse. This notion had already struck me whilst trying to negotiate my way into Nottingham, and so confirmed a need to stick to this new plan.

To tell you the truth, by the time I reached Greenock, I was more than happy to jump on the train and let it take the strain. I was, for want of a better word, utterly bored of the flat dull roads and dull unchanging scenery of the industrial outskirts of Glasgow; I just wanted to be there. I found the ticket office of the local station and dutifully paid for my fare into Glasgow, and then made a mad dash for a train that was just coming in…not an easy thing to do when the correct platform is up and over the footbridge and your bicycle and luggage are a combined weight of about six stone. It was only when the guard came round, I realised in my haste I had left my ticket at the office window…oops. I began my plea of innocence with, 'You're never going to believe this but…' It worked a treat, and I was thankfully left to ride ticketless into Glasgow. As the train chugged along, I gazed transfixed out of the window at a never-ending sea of housing estates, roads, factories, not to mention the stark formation of hundreds of tower blocks in every direction, and I went cold at the thought of trying to cycle through all that lot. I tried to work out where, for example, Paisley ended and Glasgow began, but like London, it was just one thick conurbation, from one end to another.

Over the years I had heard many a tall tale about the violent nature of Glasgow, and despite being proved at almost every turn of this journey that supposed 'rougher' areas are rarely as bad as you envisage, it did not stop me feeling overtly nervous as I stepped from the train station into the sprawling metropolis for the first time; I felt like a new inmate arriving on the wing. I pushed out towards the city centre and headed for tourist information, keeping my head down and making eye contact with no one. My imagination ran wild; I saw knives in pockets, and threatening looks on the faces of the people I passed…so had the wind totally taken from my sails when I entered tourist information and met Gordon.

'Welcome to Glasgow' he beamed at me from behind the desk, instantly relaxing my every muscle… Glasgow tourist board certainly picked its people well. All around me I could hear other visitors to the city desperately searching for accommodation, and failing miserably. Apparently there were a lot of business conferences going on in the city this week, and I felt both smug and relieved to have had the foresight to book ahead. I picked up my city map, recited the directions I'd been given by Gordon until I knew them word perfect, donned cycle helmet and crossed my fingers. Off I set, out on to the streets of Scottish mayhem.

There were many surprises lurking in store for me as I pedaled across Glasgow, luckily all of them nice ones. First off I was surprised at just how little traffic there appeared to be, well for a major city anyway; it being the largest city in Scotland and the third largest in the U.K; traffic levels were nothing compared to that of, say London. The architecture also came as a terrific surprise. Although there is very little left of medieval Glasgow, the city is full of impressive Victorian architecture, not to mention all the red and blonde sandstone buildings everywhere. As ignorant as it sounds, I had half expected grey tower blocks and dark gloomy streets, oozing poverty and an air of hopelessness. Instead I was delighted to find the main thoroughfares were wide and spacious with pavements to match, giving the place an almost European feel and certainly a much less claustrophobic air then the other city centres I had ventured into up to now. The whole place had a cosmopolitan and business like feel to it.

As I pulled up at a set of traffic lights, two men in a white transit van, (having spied the collection tin on my handlebars,) wound down their window and yelled across to me...

'What y' collecting for?' ... (Thick Glaswegian accents)...

'Is this y' first night in Glasgow?'...

'Oh the youth hostel? Left here and left again at the next set of traffic lights.'

Up a little further I suddenly panicked, thinking I'd gone the wrong way and pulled over to drag my map out. As I sat astride Lucy and studied intensely, a double decker bus approaching six o'clock, tooted his horn, drew up along side me and opened the doors so the driver could ask if I needed any help with directions.

'Oh the youth hostel, turn left just up here, y' can't miss it.'

Had I been in London, stopped in front of a double decker, I think I would have simply been mown down. Once again, I was finding nowhere to be quite as unfriendly, quite so pompous and stand-offish as the south east of England.

It had been a fabulous introduction to the city. I wondered if maybe Glasgow's violent reputation wasn't as bad as it once was, (either that or I was just lucky), but I am sure it is possible for a city to mellow too. Still, all this didn't stop me from feeling nervous as all hell when I went out to do a bit of shopping later that afternoon. And as if on cue, I spied a newspaper headline which read...'Attacks on English grow.' That was it; from then on I kept my mouth firmly shut; avoiding all conversations with people. And should anyone speak to me, I would give my bog standard response of...'Aye'...the only piece of Scottish

I could confidently mimic without sounding as though I was taking the piss, something I worried would land me in even more hot water!

The backpackers hostel stood firm in the West End of the city, where huge Victorian terraced town houses, with living rooms large enough to house a couple of double decker buses, sat grandiose style in perfect cream coloured crescents. The hostel itself was a converted student hall of residence for the summer months and was cool, light, airy and welcoming, and within five minutes of my arrival I felt very much at home. Later that evening, I jumped at the chance to accompany a group of backpackers, (mainly from Australia and New Zealand,) to a few local hot spots. It was the perfect opportunity to sample what I'd heard said was some of the countries most exciting night life, in the company of some fun and friendly travellers. And to top it all, their southern hemisphere accents would drown out my own English one.

We found ourselves in a late night bar, come disco that played alternative music, and I relaxed into the unthreatening atmosphere of the place. It did amuse me somewhat to watch the camaraderie of the Scottish male youth. They would spy a, (predominantly female) group of newcomers (read... new meat) in town, and after a while come sidling over and begin throwing out some well worn lines, (What's your name and where'd you come from?) It always made me smile, cause if any ventured near me, they would hear my English accent, look mortally disappointed, before hurriedly moving on to one of my more exotic female companions. I think my self-esteem could take it, and I spent a very enjoyable night chatting to one of the only male members of the group, a New Zealander by the name of Matt Hall, who gave me a very interesting lesson in the differences between the 'Kiwis' and the 'Ozzies.' I had become intrigued by New Zealand ever since I had met Les back in Wells, and he had told me (all!) his stories from four years of living there, and some very interesting history of the country too. I began to notice some vast differences between the two Southern hemisphere races, and I have to say that, no disrespect to the Ozzies, I actually preferred the company, the humour and the culture of the Kiwis any day. That night, despite my rather tipsy state, and my companion's obvious interest in me, I did a good job in making sure the confines of the evening stayed purely conversational and wholly un-physical.

The next on my list of 'must see' was Loch Lomond and Glen Coe, but when I awoke next morning and gazed from the hostel window out across the city, all I saw staring back at me where the heavy grey clouds and misty rain. I knew I'd be seeing none of the much desired, magical views in this weather, and certainly any breathtaking scenery would be firmly hidden from my sight, so I decided to stay put for another day and a night. This, I mused, was what was so wonderful about this journey. I could come and go whenever I pleased, stay where I liked and talk with whom ever I wanted. There was no one to dictate what time I got up in the mornings, how far I should be cycling in a day, or how I filled my time. Just before I had come away on this trip, an ex boyfriend I was still friends with had tried to persuade me to let him come along too. Thinking back now, I had definitely made the right choice to stick to my guns and go alone, despite the consequences it had on our friendship. I can't begin to imagine the sort of trip I would have had, had I agreed to let him come too; one of much arguing and misery no doubt!

Do you remember when you were younger and still very much under the control of your parents. And do you often remember grumbling that you couldn't wait to be older so you could do what ever you liked and there would be no one to tell you what to do anymore? But do you also remember the shock of waking up one day, years into your adulthood, and suddenly realising with a terrifying shock that there really is no one to tell you what to do for the best anymore, that even the hardest of decisions are down to you, right or wrong, for better or for worse.

I have an interesting line of thought for anyone who really struggles to make decisions in their life…I truly believe that there is no way you can ever make the wrong choice…think about it. Whatever you choose, life will carry on after the decision, and you will never even know how life may have turned out had you gone the other way, you can only speculate, and it just isn't worth worrying about. Even if bad things happen because of your decision, who's to say they wouldn't have been even worse had you taken that other path. Just make your decision based on what is right at the time and everything else will sort itself out eventually…with me?

I paid for another night's accommodation by spending two hours cleaning the hostel toilets and showers, which I set to with some gusto, even impressing the manager with my gleaming taps and spotless floors; I guessed they hadn't been done properly for quite some time. A fresh group of New Zealand travellers had arrived and I spent the evening in the hostel in their company. They would definitely be my favourite travel companions if I had to choose; witty, charming and very friendly. I watched as Matt, who was stationed on reception for the night, swigged 'Wild Turkey' whisky in between answering phone calls, getting more drunk by the minute and getting paid four pounds an hour for the privilege.

'This is my dream job' he slurred at one point. We chatted for a bit, but when his comments began to turn sexual, I escaped off to bed myself and slept like a baby.

Day 32. Margery (51 miles)

At 8am I stirred, still feeling tired and cold. Casting an eye around the room, I saw the rest of the dormitory occupants slept on, and so, I decided, would I. The next time I opened my eyes, the clock read ten and everyone else had gone. I cannot tell you how marvellous it felt to be able to drop back off to sleep in this way. Back in the world of employment ties, where spare time was regimented, I was never capable of this type of relaxation. It was; once awake, stay awake, as the nagging feeling that time was precious was forever engrained in the back of my head. But now, even the other dormitory girls packing up and leaving had not disturbed me.

Out of the dormitory window, a thin blue line of sky stretched far away across the city, and the decision was made in my head to move on once more. I packed up my panniers and made my breakfast whilst humming the tune to 'The Littlest Hobo' (remembered from my childhood.) Downstairs I hugged Matt, (looking hung over and sorry for himself) goodbye, and he gallantly carried Lucy and all her panniers down the grand hostel steps. Quite a gathering had appeared outside to see me off. Ironically, I didn't know it then but the next time I met someone named Matt Hall, I'd end up marrying him.

The sprawl of Glasgow lasted a very ugly ten miles, as I pedalled north out of the city. Luckily it was Saturday and this kept traffic lighter, for a time. But then the A82 opened out into a dual carriage way, which is apparently license for traffic to increase their speed by two hunded percent, and I spent the rest of those miles fearful and anxious for my life. Finally I reached Dumbarton, where I'd been told a cycle path would take me safely to the shores of Loch Lomond. Phew.

As I said my good byes to Glasgow disappearing over my shoulder, I couldn't help but hope I had left civilisation behind for a time, at least to Fort William, maybe even Inverness. And whilst this prospect filled me with excitement, it did make me wonder how on earth I would find a suitable supply of vegetarian food for the next week or so, especially the glutinous amounts a hungry cyclist can get through. I had a feeling I would be relying on a (hopefully) never ending supply of cheese and onion pasties, the one veggie food you can be sure to find in most shops in the British Isles. From experience I know that your average Highland settlement is a far cry from what you would come to expect in England. Any English village worth its salt will provide a public house, offering shelter and sustenance, and if you are very lucky, the village shop will have survived too. Not in Scotland. Hotels tend to replace homely pubs and, probably owing to the vast distances between settlements, there is usually a petrol station too, and this is the place to head for snacks and, I hoped, my much needed pasties.

In readiness for this anticipated time of culinary blandness, I had decided to treat myself by paying one last visit to a health food shop in Glasgow and stocking up to the gills on tasty and varied vegetarian snack food to cycle on. Unfortunately for me, these goodies, stuffed as they were into my front panniers were fast becoming a serious distraction from the pursuit of cycling. Usually I will only eat when hungry, or when I detect energy levels running low, but now though, I could think of nothing but the tasty morsels that lay tantalisingly within inches of my nose. I had earlier decided I would take my lunch on the banks of Loch Lomond, as a kind of celebration on how far I had come, but my taste buds drooled so badly I was in danger of drowning, and after running the list of edibles in my panniers through my mind for the forty ninth time, the will power gave out. I sat on a convenient stone seat and scoffed.

The A82 ran flat as an ironing board around the side of Loch Lomond. For weeks now, I had been dreaming of this moment; entering the majestic Highlands,

(…'I'll take the high road and you take the low road'…)

I'd pictured myself cycling on roads that wound on forever, twisting their way across the Scottish landscape; a romantic mountainous vision, interspersed with glens and lochs,

(…'And I'll be in Scotland before you.'…)

I could only feign disappointment at the dull flat road that seemed to stretch on for an age, with the cars racing past, just inches from my elbow, at speeds far in excess of the limit. It made me feel as if I had never even left the city,

(…'To the bonny bonny banks of Loch Lomond.') That long anticipated dream was nowhere to be found.

Bonny just wasn't the word I would use to describe my time in Scotland thus far. In all honesty I was beginning to feel a little peeved that my fragmented memories of the place, and dreams of romance with the landscape were nothing short of a stupid whim. Also since crossing the border, not one penny had been donated to my collection tin, and the majority of people I had come across had that staring syndrome that drove me to near insanity.

Added to all this, I noticed with dismay, the car drivers were becoming more arsey by the second. At one roundabout, an extremely obnoxious driver tried to wave me out of the way as I moved over into the correct lane, and many others tooted me, not in greeting, but as if to display disapproval at the use of the bicycle as a mode of transport in general. Many did it as they passed far closer than was safe. I lost count of the expletives I used that afternoon. Every nerve inside my fragile body felt grated and scraped, and my even more fragile temper was lost on several occasions. Honestly, you would think a cyclist has no rights on the road at all the way this lot carried on, but I knew. Having driven

all sorts of vehicles, I knew the rules of the road and I was sticking to my guns. Many a time I have been a passenger in someone else's car and have been witness to the strange, almost psychotic reaction they have when encountering a cyclist on the road. It usually goes something like this;

'Oh bloody hell it's a cyclist…. quick lets just squeeze through straight after the car in front…oh damn too late, something's coming the other way, now

I'm going to have to brake, such an inconvenience having to move my right foot downwards a whole two inches…. come on, come on, you shouldn't even be on the road, holding me up like this…sod it, I'll just rev my engine pointlessly, that'll show em who I think has all the rights here…and now I'll just squeeze past, quick…Now...' And with that, they then proceed to run the cyclist into the ditch.

A little further down the road I was passed by a white transit van; there was a pause, before a strawberry milkshake landed in my lap; the splash back dribbling down my face. I accordingly stuck two fingers up at the offending arseholes, but deep inside I felt very bruised. Was this the final symbol that the cyclist really is the underdog of the road? In our society today, a piece of pricey polished metal is fast becoming the be all and end all of social status. There are people who would rather lose their homes then be without their swanky cars for goodness sake. There are men who think they can use them to display their sexual prowess, whilst many juveniles believe owning a car is the surest way to enter adulthood and gain respect. And all this time, the clever marketing world try to have people believe, that the ability to sit on your arse and press your foot a couple of inches down on a pedal and get your machine to go fast, will some how be the biggest achievement of your life! How very, very sad. What about real talent or achievements: learning to speak another language, writing a beautiful song, climbing a mountain, challenging a government? And meanwhile we are all slowly choking on the exhaust fumes. I once heard that if you were able to bring a prehistoric caveman into our modern day world, it is likely he would be unable to survive more than a few minutes, the air in which we consider normal would choke him.

The road before me split in two at Tarbet. I took up the trail of the right hand fork, and thankfully it appeared most of the traffic took the left. This road was so much narrower and quieter. As I cycled, I felt a wave of calm wash over me, just as the waves on the Loch washed gently over its surface, quietly lapping to rest on the beach. The air began to cool off in the gently fading light, as the evening sunshine disappeared from the Glen. Surrounded by all this, how could I ever have doubted Scotland's magic?

Considering I hadn't left Glasgow until after midday, I totally amazed myself with just how far and fast I had progressed that day. I put it down to the magic ingredient in the geography of the Highland roads; they (well the more main ones anyway) went between the highest mountains, unlike Yorkshire or Cornwall, where the roads took you up and over every single last hill. This realisation was quite an inspiring one, and along with the breath taking surroundings, I cycled cheerfully on that afternoon towards my place of rest. In my head I hummed one of my favourite ditties, a song by Dire Straits called 'Brothers in arms.' I know it is not about, but I always think of it as, a song about the Highland Clearances. The sad and melancholy tune along with the fitting words have always made me think this for some reason, but I suppose that is the beauty of music; songs can mean whatever you want them to. As dusk began to set in I had to pull on my jumper. It was the first evening in ages I had had to cycle in anything more than just a T-shirt, and it was another proud reminder of just how far north I had cycled on this trip.

Arriving at the campsite in Ardleui, I felt rather peeved at the amount of noisy kids that ran amok the place, crushing the silent beauty around me, whilst the equally noisy parents hollered a lot but did nothing to effectively control their broods. They seemed to have little regard for discipline, nor did they respect other people's right to a bit of peace and quiet. It didn't take me long to set up my own system of defence against these marauding tribes. As soon as any of the brats came screaming and misbehaving near me, my tent or my bicycle, I would hiss and growl at them, a bit like a swan protecting her nest, and laugh as I watched them scatter. During some of the long and lonely hours of camping, I found myself focusing time and again on the prospect of motherhood. Like most young women, I have often thought I would one day like to have a family of my own (should I ever meet a decent enough fella) and I have even on occasion felt broody. But it was at campsites like this, and indeed in many before, I had bare witness to so many harassed mothers; running around after the family, holding it all together, doing for the most part all the worrying themselves, and never looking as though they were totally relaxed or enjoying themselves.

As I struggled to put up my tent in the stiff breeze, an oldish women parked next to me in her old battered Landrover, came over to ask if I would like to join her for supper. As she served lashings of tasty hot pasta, she told me her name was Margery. I had noticed her when I had first arrived and thought from her accent she was a very well spoken English women; this turned out to be most inaccurate. She was in fact originally from Melbourne, Australia, though her accent had mellowed with her travels, and what travels they turned out to be! As we talked

I realised she was an amazing women who had not wasted a single second of her life. She had lived in many amazing different places around the world; she had completed a long spell in the army, and was at present, travelling around the British Isles, exploring and living out the back of her Landrover at the grand old age of seventy. She told me she went by the philosophy that it was far more important to see the world than to make money from it.

When she spoke I was transfixed. One didn't need to search her words for hidden wisdom, just by the way she spoke it was there for all to see; wisdom that radiated out comfortingly like a bright lantern on a foggy night. Oh it felt so good, after all the dumb, (however well meant) questions, to speak with, and more importantly, listen to someone so unquestionably frank, wise and honest, and especially for that someone to be another woman. The majority of the folk that had approached me on this trip so far had all been men, which is a great shame as I am sure there are many more women out there, (maybe hidden behind their bullish husbands, brothers, work colleagues etc) that have some hidden gems of wisdom to share.

I was comforted by Margery's words. Although I hadn't exactly been short of people congratulating me on what I was doing, they generally had to go and ruin it all by asking me, why? Margery understood though, no questions asked. Apart from Sir Hellingwell, and maybe John too back in Dartmoor, she was the only one to understand the need to make a journey; to know that to test one's self is a right of passage, and not necessarily just for the young either; journeying on until one finds themselves and knows who they truly are.

Margery and I chatted easily, late into the evening. At last I had met an elder who could guide me. She was a women of substance; I wonder who had been her guide? I would liked to have chatted on, but the sudden drop in night temperature in the Highlands came as a bit of a shock to the system, and despite wearing every stitch of clothing I had, I still shivered uncontrollably. I bid Margery good night before diving into the depths of my sleeping bag to stay warm. (I found a fiver stuck in my collection tin from her next morning.) As I lay in the dark, I heard a sudden excited scream from the camp children, who had sited bats up in the tree tops above. But alas, despite loving these fascinating creatures, by this stage I was too stiff with the cold to dare venture outside again that night.

Day 33. R.T.A's   (64 miles)

Poking a frozen hand out of bed to switch on the radio for my early morning time check, I listened intently as the commentator's jumbled words slowly became clear,

'...And I am sure the nation will be shocked and saddened by the death of Princess Di...'

I wasn't aware it was April fools day already, cripes, how long had I been asleep? I struggled out of bed and pulled on my coat, which was cold to the lining and waited for it to warm through.

But as I listened further it finally dawned on me that this was no sick joke, and I listened to the full horror of the story of the paparazzi car chase in France, and the fatal crash that ensued. I have to admit that my instinctive thoughts were ones of conspiracy theories, after all, her recent popularity and dilly-dallying with other rich and famous men could be construed as an embarrassment to the royal family. But one cannot go about making such accusations, although in the years that followed many would try. And so the women who first brought the horror of landmines to the attention of the mainstream media was now dead. Les from Wells would never get his big chance to meet her now. I wondered if the night's events would have any bearing on my charity ride? I pushed all thoughts aside and began the morning drill.

I'd noticed that a young Dutch backpacker pitched up next door, who had been doing his damnedest to ignore me up to this point, suddenly and unexpectedly tried to strike up a conversation as I was making myself a brew. He explained that he was stoveless, and not being one to kick start the morning without a caffeine fix, I politely offered him a cuppa, which he gladly accepted. As we sat drinking we chatted, or rather I chatted and he tried his hardest to patronise me. Comments such as,

'Oh but you're a bit young for all this,' (he was only twenty three himself) ensured I did not offer him a second cup. After saying a fond farewell to Margery, I was glad to get under way, if only to warm up again.

The road started off pretty much as it had done yesterday, running flat and curving its way gently around the lochs. And in the meantime, the heavens let loose a light drizzle that was to last all day; the type of rain that doesn't feel particularly heavy, but soon has you soaked to the bone in no time at all. I powered along, refreshed by the cool morning air. I felt as fit as a fiddle, my thighs were powerful and the cycling effortless. The wind had been blowing behind me ever since I had arrived in Scotland and today was no exception. Even as the road eventually left the lochside and began winding it's way up and over the mountains I barely noticed, I simply changed down a few gears and was able to continue at the same steady pace without wearing myself out. The scenery was fantastic; the mist, far from hindering the views, simply added to the eerie, mystical look of the land around me, and only the occasional car that splashed past broke the isolation.

I was highly surprised to hit a sign that lay by the roadside, proclaiming I was now at the peak of Rannoch Moor, 1145ft above sea level. I'd barely even noticed the climb! I stopped to brush the wet hair from my eyes and gaze out across the moor known as the most inhospitable, wildest terrain of all the British Isles; a mine of peat bogs where one could be horrifically swallowed up, never to be seen again. The moor stretches for 50 square  miles and there are very few signs of the hand of man to be seen, save for the railway line; an amazing feat of engineering considering the terrain it had to traverse. But before the building of the railway could even begin, it had to be crossed by foot and this daunting task fell to seven gentlemen. In January of 1889, the men, a group of contractors and civil engineers set out from Spean Bridge in suits, tall hats and umbrellas, to walk the twenty three miles in order to find a suitable path for the proposed railway. Needless to say they nearly died; maybe something to do with the fact they had set out in the depths of winter and had tried to cross the biggest expanse of wild and uninhabited land in the British Isles, totally unprepared. But the story has a happy ending, they all survived and these days, if the mud and rain are not for you, you can catch a train safely across the moor.

173

As I stood on the road, for the first time ever on my trip, I had the urge to go walking and to be a part of this landscape. I longed to wander across it, with the wet ground beneath my feet and the smell of heather and peat in my nose. I had been fascinated with the place, ever since I'd read a book about a guy who traversed Rannoch Moor with his two horses. But at the same time, these thoughts of being at one with the wilderness filled me with a fear, and rightly or wrongly, I felt scared of the true wildness of the place. I guess being stuck out here, alone with only a bicycle and my own energy to get me through, I could sense that this wilderness commanded a great respect that maybe a person in a motorcar could not comprehend. Even from my position of safety on the road, I suddenly felt very lonely; standing on that narrow slither of tarmac that man made, in attempt to claim a hold on such a vast expanse of wilderness. I pedalled on with reverence.

Despite the marvellous scenery, my effortless progress and the sullen romantic atmosphere of the landscape, cycling along for hours on end when you are soaked to the bone, complete with a swimming pool in each boot, (the plastic bags had once again failed me) was, believe it or not, rather unpleasant. I found myself trying desperately hard to trick my mind into not thinking about those freezing pools of water in my boots, and not thinking about why the hell was I out here? I tried hard to avoid that nagging thought in the back of my head that said, 'you could be looking at these beautiful views through the window of a warm bar,' just incase I should come to feel at all downhearted by my chosen predicament.

Sometimes when the isolation and seclusion out here began to get me down, when there seemed to be no other beings for miles, other than the odd tin-pot car from another world, splashing by, that may or may not contain human life forms; when I was bored of talking to myself, and thinking just seemed to go round and round in circles; it was at times like these that I relied on singing to keep my spirits lifted. I made a whole line up of songs in my head and sang them all, one by one. Trying to get my croaky vocals to fit into the varying harmonies of the different songs was not easy. Some of my more memorable cycling tunes included Lou Reeds 'Perfect Day,' most of the songs by The Beautiful South, Roxette, 'It must have been love,' and a song that had recently started playing on the radio, with a women claiming 'You're free to do what you want to do.' I also regularly sung the entire album of Simon and Garfunkle's greatest hits. I knew this one particularly well, because as a child there seemed never to be a time when we went anywhere in the car as a family, and it wasn't played...usually followed by Abba's greatest hits and my mothers own vocals accompanying the lot.

Further along the unending road, I spied a minibus parked in a lay by and suddenly felt very conscious that all it's occupants were staring at me. As I neared, through misted up windows, a van full of young Scots peered out. I decided to act the entertaining part they were obviously hoping for, and stopped to ask for the time. To be honest I didn't really care to know, in a way I just needed to hear another human voice. When I revealed I was heading for Fort William that night, I promptly wished I had kept my mouth shut as I was bombarded by a string of smart-alec comments.

'You'll never make it there tonight.'

'It's one big long uphill all the way.'

'The best thing you can do is to turn around and head back to where you came from.'

As if! Good old 'Jocks', right there with a bit of comic relief when you needed it the most. I was handed a hot cup of tea through the passenger window and stood out in the rain drinking, as looks of admiration and a chorus of, 'you must be mad' came from the shelter of their van. I have long since come to the conclusion that this is a common prank played by the natives of Scotland; they seem to enjoy telling us poor unsuspecting cyclists that the place we are headed for is via a few mountain ranges, or twice as far as you originally thought. I think that living and having to cope with these difficult, harsh and remote areas on a daily basis, leads them to the conclusion that anyone who voluntarily comes cycling here must have a few screws missing, and therefore deserve all the ribbing and wind-ups they get.

Not far from this spot, I passed another important mile marker of my trip; a sign which read, 'F'aite don Gha'idhealtachd.' Or in English, 'Welcome to the Highlands.' I looked at my map and then the milometer several times, not the best way of making the miles go quicker, but I found my brain trying to make up some bullshit about working out what time I would arrive in Fort William. Oh hell, it all seemed such a terrible waste; here I finally was, cycling in one of my favourite and most stunning places in the U.k, and all I could think about was getting to where I was going and longing for the day to be over. I just couldn't help myself, I was feeling so overcome by negative emotions, and try as I might, I couldn't control them. I was getting just a little bit sick of being constantly soaked to the bone, and just as sick with the boredom of pushing the pedals round and round. I longed for a hot shower; longed to be dry and most of all, I longed to be free of having to make my feet go round and round.

But just as I was beginning to feel tearful with all these negative emotions, I was sent relief by the hand of fate, and a reminder to appreciate how lucky I was to be where I was; fifteen glorious miles of downhill. That was fifteen miles where I could sit back and watch the gorgeous views; the craggy cliff tops and rocky peninsulas rolling effortlessly past. I flew by roaring waterfalls thundering down the mountains, and fifteen miles where I didn't have to pedal once. Down and down I went, spiralling forever downwards, through thick banks of low cloud where I couldn't see where I was going, before bursting out for a few seconds to catch the beauty of Glen Coe, before hitting another cloud again. It felt for all the world as though I was falling into the arms of Fort William.

By the time I had to pedal again, I had reached the front door of Ballachulish, where a welcoming sign told me Fort William was only fourteen miles away. I found a phone box and made a call to the backpacker's hostel, securing a nights accommodation with my debit card...I wanted that longed for shower guaranteed. I stayed in the phone box a little longer to shelter from the wind and the rain for five minutes and munch on a cheese and onion pasty. I watched as cars appeared out of the mist, having come from the direction of Glen Coe and the very same road I had just traversed, and wondered if they had enjoyed their journey. I wondered if they had ventured from their cars at all, and maybe gone for a walk and really experienced what it was like to be in the Highlands on a day like today. Ballachulish was an eerily quiet place, stuck between the two major tourist attractions of Glen Coe and Ben Nevis, it seemed to have escaped a decorative glossing over for the sake of attracting tourists. Two young boys played happily in a puddle outside of my phone box, whilst a rather old run down tea shop offered hot drinks and cream buns. But I passed on the opportunity, and instead took up the reins, (or should that have been rains) of the final leg of the day.

It was heartening to find that my legs were still in fine working order, even after sixty miles on the road, unfortunately the same could not be said for my backside. I think it was something to do with not having the correct sized saddle for my bottom. My seat-bones wrongly hung over the edge, as opposed to being supported by the saddle, and this was sending reoccurring pain waves to my brain, so much so that I was beginning to feel physically sick and had to resort to getting off to push Lucy for several miles at a time…not the quickest way to get through the last few miles of the day. I could see many a car driver staring at me through their windscreens as they overtook, probably wondering if I had a puncture or something, although not one of them stopped to ask if I was o.k., a completely different attitude to the one I have experienced in the Lake District, where it is almost mandatory to check travellers are not in trouble. To while away the time I came up with amusing one-liners over the state of my current affairs, and I decided that if by any miracle someone did stop to ask what the problem was, I would reply that 'my backside had had an argument with my bike saddle.'

Fort William was a lot bigger than I expected; a built up town with modern shops, numerous hotels, restaurants and car parks, all built beside the lapping shores of the Loch and over-shadowed by the mighty Ben Nevis, which standing at 4408ft was the highest mountain in the British Isles. It all came as quite a shock after the tranquility of the mountains and moors that day, but there was no denying, I have never felt so relieved to have reached the warmth of the modest but comfortable backpackers hostel; to close the door on the elements that had whipped and punished me all day, and climb into that much anticipated hot shower and stand there until I had thawed out, right down to the last toenail and strand of hair. And just as an extra treat, I moved on down to the backpacker's lounge where I could sit with my hair wrapped in a towel, boots drying by the roaring fire and sip complimentary tea and nibble biscuits. Once again I found the greatest joys in the simplest things were always at the end of the hardest days.

Later that evening, I had gone into town to find an off-license, complete with booze orders from half the hostel goers, (goodness knows how I got suckered into that one.) On my way back I found a phone box and rang to have a chat with my mum and amaze her with my speedy northerly progress since last we met. As we chatted, I failed at first to notice a tragic drama unfold opposite the very phone box I was in. A wee lad of about six had been knocked off his bicycle by a car and lay quite still in the road. The ambulance had luckily just arrived on the scene and were in the process of checking the casualty over. I was unsure if the boy was still alive, I reckoned so as I believe they cover a dead body over quite quickly, but I moved on all the same, spectators were the last things the family needed.

Despite the elation I had felt at completing the day, a wave of sadness caught me around the throat and dragged me back down. The day had started and ended with an R.T.A…a road traffic accident; one of them an internationally famous person, the other an unknown local lad, but both of them equally as tragic for the families concerned.

DAY 34. Home and Dry (35 miles)

My map collection, now that I was so much nearer the top of the country was getting lighter by the day. Before leaving, I had taken my parents' large and very detailed road atlas, photocopied the relevant pages and marked my route upon them. Then, as I cycled and completed the route on each page, I was able to throw it out. This meant not only was my load getting lighter as I progressed, but I also had the satisfaction of discarding that which I did not need; like clearing out unwanted junk from the cupboards at home…always good for the soul. I have heard some cyclists use the Ordnance Survey 'Landranger' maps, but I actually found these were too detailed and small scale, and at a fiver a throw, they just weren't worth it; I would have cycled the width of the map in just a couple of hours. Being new to this game, learning what works best when touring had been a bit if a hit and miss affair, but the discardable maps idea was definitely one that got the thumbs up, and was one I adopted in my cycling adventures around the globe forever after.

After the marathon of yesterday, I had no intention of putting pressure on myself to do it again so soon, and as I cheerily left Fort William that morning, I passed an encouraging sign that read 'Inverness 66 miles.' Just for a split second I did think, could I do this in the one day? But after just five minutes with bum in saddle, I knew I could not. In keeping with the fort theme, I was headed for a campsite, this time at Fort Augustus, 35 miles down the road. As I cycled, I fidgeted and shifted my weight constantly around in the saddle every few minutes, but trying to settle an already saddle sore bum into a bearable position was not easy. My latest cycling fantasy became one of a twenty year old, well worn ladies Brooks' leather saddle. You're probably wondering why I didn't buy myself a new and better saddle, but some how at this late stage of the trip, I didn't want to risk it; didn't want to go through the rigmarole of trying to wear in a new saddle, only to find it was worse than the old one.

I pedalled the A82 out of Fort William. Regularly I would study the skies above, the outlook, thank goodness, looked more and more hopeful. Perhaps the rain would finally give me the break I thought I deserved? My socks squelched inside boots that still hadn't dried from yesterday, but I hoped just one rain free day would sort all that out. One thing though was for sure, thank heavens I wasn't walking...wet boots would have been agony if I had been. This main road was a busy one; taking the traffic to Inverness, it follows a glen that cuts its way across the entire width of the country, stretching from south west to north east, like a razor sharp dart, fired across the land. It is natural phenomenon that was created by the moving of the Earth's tectonic plates many ice ages ago, and is now filled with a vast expanse of water; better known to you and me as Loch Ness and the home of the elusive Nessy.

As the cars passed in a constant stream, I found myself wearing my cycle helmet for the third day in a row. Actually, once I got used to wearing it, it wasn't as bad as I first thought. Ironically I had my one and only near miss of the trip on this day, but I guess considering the mileage I had covered, maybe I was extraordinarily lucky to have survived thus far without one.

I was making slow progress along the winding, undulating road towards Fort Augustus. I had almost become immune to the roar of cars racing past, but the distant sound of a lorry rumbling up behind me did make my ears stand to attention. It was a big'en by the sound of things; struggling and groaning its way up through the gears in an effort to get some speed up along the steep winding road. Unfortunately for me, by the time it had caught me up, I too was slowly struggling up a very steep incline and halfway around a blind bend. I heard the terrifying screech of brakes right behind me as I must have suddenly come into the driver's sight. I remember making an ungainly leap for the grass verge, Lucy toppling one way, and me the other. 'Thud.' Startled and dazed I landed in a heap on the side of the road, and looked about me for some reassurance of my continuing mortal place on this Earth, and found it; a blooded scratch on my thigh where the handlebars had caught my leg. Phew. The relief that I was still alive whipped me into action and I leapt to my feet…where I was rather taken aback to discover that the lorry in question had actually ground to a halt not nearly as close as it had first sounded, the driver was obviously far more clued up on air-brake systems then me. He gave me a quizzical stare before pulling around me and moving on his way. Hurriedly I rescued Lucy from where she'd fallen in the middle of the road before the twenty car tailback ran her over, and I went in search of a place to calm my nerves.

By a small loch reserved for fishing, I calmed my thumping heart with a cigarette and a sandwich, and surveyed the mess around me. A few days ago on the radio, I had heard that Coca-Cola was now the biggest selling soft drink in every country in the world, (a rather depressing statistic,) except that is for Scotland. Standing out like a beacon of light, it's citizens prefer the nationally brewed tipple, 'Iron-Bru.' Cycling around at a pace slow enough to observe the often litter ridden gutters, I could confirm this at least appeared to be true.

Time and again, it couldn't escape my attention that cycling was becoming more and more philosophical, and could so easily be compared to life. Unfortunately, when you have spent the last thirty-four days struggling to the peak of each hill you encounter, (and believe me there are an awful lot of them in the U.K) only to nose-dive back down the other side again, you seriously begin to wonder, (and hope) that life is not the same. But on a much more optimistic note, I also found another similarity which I still adhere to, even to this day.

It has come from the amount of times over the last thirty-four days I have driven myself on in the hope of finding the perfect place to; rest, eat, camp, pee etc, and have always eventually found them, simply by believing they are there to be found. Belief really is a powerful thing. And from this example, I can then go on and use this belief in every aspect of my life. Take for example the time I arrived in Brighton with no money, no job and nowhere to live, save for a mates floor. Despite all the jobs and flat shares I chased, each time coming away disappointed when they turned out to be highly unsuitable, I never once lost faith. The image of the right kind of job, and the perfect flat were firmly ingrained into my mind, and within a month I had found them both, simply by believing they were there to be found. I even like to imagine this is how I eventually found a suitable Mr. Right…I am sure some people will be thinking I had been spending too much time alone recently!

It was a very slow thirty-five miles to Fort Augustus that day. I kind of got the feeling that the Orbit Expedition bike was not exactly the fastest bicycle on the planet, but this is another reason I think we were beautifully matched, and to be honest, even if I had a racing bike, it still wouldn't change my over-all speed. Slow and steady, that's me, whether it be cycling, walking or working. It is amazing how attached one gets to a bicycle. During one break, when I was forced to take time out to rest my sore bottom, I gazed at Lucy, leaning up against the fence. I took in the angles and geometry of the bike frame, in the same way a horse dealer would look at the lines and curves of an animal. She had carried me and all my heavy panniers so well for so long I was almost bursting with pride. Yes I know Lucy is just an inanimate object, but as a friend once said to me; it is almost as if all your thoughts and dreams and observations whilst cycling, make up part of the frame itself, and some how you become so attached, almost as if your bicycle was a second skin or a third leg.

I watched eager eyed today, as the milometer ticked on to the thousand miles mark. One thousand down...how many more to go?

I was thoroughly impressesed with the campsite that night. Situated just two miles outside Fort Augustus, it was a beautiful spot with flat ground to pitch the tent, and hot showers that were included in the very reasonable price of just three pounds. But best of all I was pitched up next to a picnic bench, which doesn't sound like anything to get excited about, but it allowed me to perform all of my evening rituals of cooking, eating and diary writing off of the floor, and it made a wonderful change. Regularly I would make a visual sweep of the campsite to see if anyone interesting was arriving, and I noticed another loner, sat in his tent, car parked next to him, doing the very same.

After a shower and dinner, I lingered around the pay phone thinking of Steve. Should I or shouldn't I give him a call? It sounds daft, but I was suddenly very worried I might be giving him the wrong impression, and I suddenly had to ask myself whether I wanted to give him 'that' kind of impression. I felt very confused by my inner feelings. In the end I thought, sod it what have I got to loose, and dialled his number. I chatted happily with Steve for a good twenty minutes, and as usual we had plenty to say and lots to laugh about, but when the phone call was over I realised I just felt worse because I missed him all the more. Honestly, this was so typical of me. I can often spend months on end with a guy who is nothing more than a good mate, and think no more of it. But once either them or I have moved away, I suddenly start missing them and panic that maybe I've just missed out on getting together with someone who could have been very special. It was stupid really, as this time, along with almost every other time, turned out to be just another false alarm.

Day 35. Coming Home   (35 miles)

In my mind, the route was clearly laid out before me; into Fort Augustus, take the right-hand fork in the road and follow the B862 as it wound it's way up and into the Monadhliath Mountains. From there I would enjoy the ease of the road, as it ran almost flat across the mountain tops, before I would be rewarded by a five mile descent all the way into Inverness, the capital of the Highlands and what I have always thought of as my second home. On leaving Inverness, I would then take the one road heading north, swapping the Highlands for the relative flatness of Sunderland and Caithness, where I would stick with the A9, all the way to John O'Groats. The way seemed so simple and the end so close, I almost expected to see it around the next bend...

I breathed hard against the steep road, even having to admit defeat on several occasions, getting off to push. But this time, my desire to reach the top was also fuelled by the knowledge that this would be absolutely the last of the steep hills I would face on my journey, and with that carrot dangling in front of me, it was enough to draw me upwards, despite my lungs bursting from the sheer steepness of this gradient... Had I realised that my memories of the far north being almost flat were completely inaccurate, I don't think I would have tackled that hill with quite so much vigour.

But for now I was as happy as a lark, up here in the Monadhliath Mountains, cycling along 'my' road. These mountains and lochs were as familiar to me as my own back yard, as over the years I had been back to explore them, both on bicycle and on horseback. I had escaped into their beauty, slept by the lochs and had even dreamed of their existence, and I always knew how it would feel when I returned. The Monadhliath Mountains were always black to me, but not dully so. Dull is brown or grey, but these were crisp black, particularly with the bright sun behind them. There was no sun today however, but they still looked crisp and

enticing. I had first visited the area when I was sixteen, on holiday with my parents. Despite me trying to fight the last of the parental ties and pretty much making everyone's life a misery for two weeks, none of us could miss the charm of the landscape, as it lifted our spirits in a way no amount of family bonding ever could.

But Inverness beckoned. Inverness was the place that would normally take all night to reach by train, and I had cycled here...all the way. Could it really be possible that I had done it, I found myself wondering? Strangely enough it didn't really seem so, because if I tried to cast my mind back over the last thirty-five days; at the places I had seen, and the miles I had come...it just didn't add up. For some reason, the last place I can clearly remember was Yorkshire; remember far more vividly than even yesterday. I remember Somerset too with the same clarity, but what had happened in between just didn't seem to connect, how had I got from there to here? But Inverness was coming, the home of my dreams, and for some reason, the dream of the end; a dream I would reach Inverness and freewheel from there to John O'Groats. I was so caught up in the excitement and momentum of my pace that I failed to hear the quiet voice in the back of my head, desperately trying to remind me I still had two hundred miles to go.

For six miles now, I had been fighting to keep my balance along the mountain top road, as near storm-force winds whipped me mercilessly from the back and sides. A welcome break appeared in the form of a refreshments van parked in a lay-by, and whilst I stopped to sip on a piping hot tea with the other holiday-makers, my gaze fixated on an extraordinary sight coming the other way. A man on a bicycle was being battered and fighting head-on the same wind that, through most of Scotland had pushed me along. He was single handedly trying to fight the forces of nature , and I didn't envy his challenge one little bit.

Luckily this was one part of the world where there is no need to pretend not to see other people, and without invitation, he joined me at the snack bar for a cuppa and a chat. I had been trying without success to smoke a cigarette, but any enjoyment I might have received was lost as the wind took my breath away far more than any smoke could. Michael looked on a little disapprovingly at my bad habit, whilst he fought to get his breath back; declaring himself as an official 'End to Ender.' He'd completed his journey yesterday and was now cycling back to his home in Glasgow. I tried to sound sympathetic about the terrible headwind, but I'm sure I just sounded relieved that I was going the other way. But Michael, in true 'blokey' style made out as if it were nothing, so instead I changed the conversation from one of sympathy to one of charity, and pressed him for a donation. He tried to press me for one for his cause. I gave him a girly smile and won the day, and he dropped a fifty pence piece into my tin. I thanked him and made ready to go, leaving him to his 'easy headwind' when I heard a whistle from the snack-van proprietor. He had been listening to our conversation with, I might add, some amusement, and now held out the same fifty pence I had paid for my tea, dropping it into my collection tin. I thanked him and shot off along the road; jet-propelled by the wind for easy cycling.

At a junction further along the road, I felt a great pull to go and search for one of my favourite places in the world. A four mile detour, down narrow roads and minor tracks would bring me to a small but perfectly rounded loch, enclosed by hilltops and hidden away from sight, except to those who knew it. One could speak ones name, or play a flute and it would echo musically around the hill tops. Even better, the surrounding area was still covered with small patches of forest that had once covered the Highlands. People come to the Highlands to marvel, but do not realise it has been raped of it's former natural beauty. During the 18th and 19th centuries, when rich English landlords cleared the people from their land by brute force, it wasn't just the communities they destroyed. Forests were cleared for the sheep they moved on to the land, which in turn slowly ate away and together this changed the face of the Highlands forever. The fertile forests and native trees, all save for a few pockets of Caledonian Pine, disappeared, along with wildlife such as wolves, bears, golden eagles and wildcats. Commercial crops of pines are all that remain.

The impatience to get to the end was winning through and I decided against any nostalgic detours, or desires to linger in the wilderness, there would be other times for that. The road to Inverness beckoned. I had sent a postcard to a friend of mine who lives there, telling him what I was doing, and my expected day and time of arrival. I had no way to verify whether he had received my postcard, or come to think of it, whether he was even in the country, (he spends a lot of time in Israel,) but if he was there, we would be sure to find each other. I knew he had a caravan up in the hills above Inverness where I could stay the night, far from the maddening crowd. After a day spent out in the big wide old cosmos, I wasn't in the mood for the clamour and chaos of the backpacker's hostel. From the top of the mountain I now had the perfect view in sight, Inverness, the town of my dreams. And now the end was also in sight. But here before me was something else I had dreamed of...this road. It was scene of my dream all those years ago, the dream that had awoken in me my love of cycling. And now I was about to do exactly as I had in my dream... freewheel this very same road, falling into the arms of Inverness.

* * *

After wandering around town for almost two hours and checking out all his usual hang-out spots, I was beginning to give up hope when I was 'found' by my friend Kym, who came tearing out of a café across the road and enveloped me in a bear like hug. Kym's praise, which came by the lorry load, bowled me over; he thought I was so marvellous to cycle all this was, and on my own, (hmm, I ignored that last bit.) He was very saddened to hear about the death of Princess Diana, as he himself is an avid fundraiser for her charity, (just one of the many things he campaigns for.) He was all for telling the whole world about what I was up to, although I didn't realise he meant literally...that was until he dragged me off to the local radio station to do an interview.

I sat rooted to the spot in Kyms' van, refusing point blank to come out. I'd cycled all this way without media fuss, so why on Earth would I want to start now? But just as I was defiantly thinking these thoughts, Kym reappeared.

'Sarah, they'd LOVE to interview you.'

God knows how, but eventually he persuaded me to go in, albeit with heels dragging. I had never been inside a radio broadcasting studio before, and actually it was quite exciting. We sat in a sound-proof box room with earphones on recording the interview, whilst I tried desperately to stifle nervous giggles and convey the facts about landmines. 'God I hope they don't ask me about Princess Di.' I suddenly thought.

'And Sarah, what are your thoughts about the death of Princess Diana?...'

Alas, I managed to miss most of the edited one-minute interview the next morning; a tractor working in the field next door to the caravan started up, right in the middle of the broadcast. (Though I later understood it was repeated every hour on the news that day.) But what I did hear of it was very spooky. I cannot begin to describe how odd it is to hear ones own voice coming from the wireless, but I was also surprised, not to mention delighted, at just how professional I sounded and as though I actually knew what I was talking about for a change!

Right: My first mountain pass by bicycle. The Lake District

Below: I made it. Kirkstone Pass from the top

187

Above: Safely over the border!

Left: The End...cold, exhausted, and poorly (but happy)

Right: On the edge of the world in the Orkney Isles

Below: New to this cycle touring lark; my mate Sarah takes a break

Above: The very end of the British Isles…The Shetland Isles where the locals lay out a place for weary cyclists to rest

Below: The winds in The Orkney Isles induce many a 'bad hair day.' Spending the night in a rat-infested Bothy

Day 36. Pounds and pedal-stools (41 miles)

It was a bright and sunny morning as I sat in 'Billy's Café'; Kym insisted on spoiling me with a cooked breakfast, and I wasn't the only one who was about to benefit from his generosity. As I sat trying to pick as many limited vegetarian options off of the typically meat-soaked Scottish menu, I watched with amusement as a local homeless man who was passing and had spotted Kym, now came in to openly ask him for a breakfast treat too. As I ate, I could hear Kym's thick loud Highland accent dealing with the situation.

'Och, I'm a bit skint at the moment, me busking's not doing too well see…aye…aye…ye had to ask…och aye…aye well o.k., this is the last time…'

Dear old Kym Avis Gordon. A heart set in gold. Living primarily off what he makes as a busker, (not very much I can tell you,) and living in an old caravan in the hills. Why is it so often those who have the least that seem to give the most? Kym spends most of his time, either going into the Highlands to pray for the needy and to pray for the salvation of Mother Earth, and when he isn't praying, he is actively campaigning for everything from Amnesty International to C.N.D. Now here is a use of religion that I cannot fault. Kym gave up a long time ago trying to convert me. I have no problem with learning about another people's beliefs, I would even go so far as to say I find them intriguing, but I do not delve; I have my own way of thinking. Kym says as Christians we should be trying to save the planet and help others; that is what God wants. Where as I say I will do these things anyway, simply because I believe it is the right thing to do. Without wanting to sound disrespectful to the religious, I personally do not believe that God dictates what happens in the world, Mother Nature does that, and I cannot help but feel it unlikely that there is a God, or salvation in another life …there is only this life.

Outside of Marks and Spencers in the high street, I tried to make myself look as noticeable as possible: charity bib on, bicycle by side with all panniers attached, and for good measure I pinned my permit to collect for Landmines Clearance International on to my chest. Kym also did his best to attract as much attention to us as possible by playing his guitar in his unique, self-taught style, and between us we had two buckets plastered with Landmines Clearance stickers. Within minutes, the money came pouring in thick and fast. Everyone seemed to have heard my broadcast on the radio that morning, and the people of Inverness came over to share their personal thoughts whilst dropping several pounds at a time into the collection, and each and everyone of them mentioned the death of Princess Di. By the end of it we had collected the grand sum of £70.72 in just two hours; more than I had collected in the last two weeks. I was thrilled and took Kym off to a café to buy a round of coffees to celebrate, (from my own pocket of course.)

All too soon it was nearing time to hit the road again and time for goodbyes. Time to say goodbye to Inverness, the town that I loved, and time to say goodbye to Kym, a man I held a deep respect for. But as I prepared to leave, I couldn't help notice how distant Kym suddenly looked, and where as I was fighting back tears at the thought that it might be years before we would see each other again, he looked quite unbothered. I know I can't expect others to share my feelings, but all the same, when I thought how close we had once been, it saddened me.

I left Inverness on the hazardously busy A9 by way of the Kessock Bridge, a huge and impressive structure that spans the gap between the Beauly and Moray Firth. As I went, I kept an eye out for those ever illusive dolphins that frequent the bay. I danced and diced with the deadly traffic until the dual carriageway ran out in a place named Tore, but disappointingly the traffic remained as heavy as ever it was. It was about this time I began to notice a lot of cars beeping their horns at me as they passed, and quite naturally, I took this as an act of aggression, reacting accordingly by shaking my fists and growling obscenities. How comical I must have looked! It wasn't until a few hours had passed, I noticed the cars passing on the other side of the road were doing the same and it finally dawned on me they must have known who I was and were tooting in greeting and encouragement. Talk about fame! I returned their greetings by waving back enthusiastically. I was even more taken aback when a women in an old Renault pulled over and produced a ten pound note for my collection tin, I listened aghast as she told me she'd heard me on the radio and had just driven almost one hundred miles to come and find me. I thanked her profusely, but when she stood back grinning at me, I thought, 'What do I say now?' Was she expecting a sermon or something? I suddenly felt very awkward and put on the spot and said nothing.

'So how's it going?' she persisted, so I jabbered on about the hills and the weather, and about how everyone in Inverness had been very generous that morning. But on the whole, I think my words came out as uninteresting, wooden and terribly unwise...BANG...I could literally hear my pedestal falling over.

'Well thanks again' I repeated, 'I'd better get going, what with the late start this morning and all'...One hundred miles to meet me? She must have been disappointed!

I hadn't strayed north of Inverness in years, but as I rounded each corner, the landscape bought back memories I had been looking forward to jogging. The Highlands flatten out into more gentle hills and an eerie isolation falls over the land, so much so that I actually began to feel comforted by the motorcars zooming past; they some how made me feel less alone. Although in a sense I was very alone in my endurance, it suddenly hit me that this last 150 mile stretch, far from being the easy last leg I had imagined, would in fact be very punishing. The shock of realisation hit me very hard. Throughout Scotland I had been keeping up a tremendous pace, keen to reach my next favourite place and the next, (for I have lots of them in Scotland,) but on leaving Inverness, all that changed. This enthusiasm which had drawn me on, no longer applied, all I had left was to push on through this unfamiliar and rather unwelcoming landscape, and I journeyed simply to reach the end. As if to confirm my anxieties, the bright sunshine that had smiled on me for the first twenty miles, disappeared behind a wall of black anger in the sky, and barely before I had time to think, 'where's my waterproof coat?' a torrent of unforgiving water began to hammer to earth around me; beating the ground, beating my head and blanking out the world around.

And suddenly I began to act quite strange. Each time a car or motorcyclist roared passed splashing me with spray, I was hit by a powerful wave of emotion, each one different from the last. One minute I was waving and grinning and beckoning them to stop, as if they were an old friend, then a few minutes later another would pass and I suddenly found myself erupting in a vile temper that made me curse and gesticulate at them, even getting off Lucy and hurling her down to the ground in the road, hoping to lure a passing motorist into an argument. I couldn't believe myself, all I knew was I no longer had control over my actions. There were no tears, no self-pity, I was just temporarily deranged. I had gone from being a celebrity one minute, and the next I was just a lonely stranger, soaked to the bone and shivering uncontrollably, who's one and only thought was...'I've got days more of this isolation ahead of me.'

I must have looked and sounded very comical. And when the energy ran out and I was no longer able to continue with these fluctuating waves of emotions, I sunk into the unpleasant position of having to just grin and bear the cold and wet and let my stream of consciousness take over my brain and mouth. As my legs, forever on auto-pilot went round and round, my eyes stared straight into the distance, and my mouth began to move and twitch until the words of a song formed and released themselves. Unfortunately it was only a childish song; 'The wheels on the bus go round and round...' I sung first in my own accent, then a Glaswegian, followed by German, South African, and Australian. And when I became tired of this, my brain began to fantasise about the impending campsite, now only six miles away, whilst the tired mouth translated the fantasy into a song.

Please, please let it be a goody campsite,
With room for me to lay my bed,
A hot shower for me to warm my toes,
A working tumbledrier to dry my clothes,
A place to lock up Loopy Loo,
Not forgetting a cheap rate too,
Cause I'm so cold and tiiieeerd...

Waffle, mumble etc. Perhaps it was fate because I some how deserved a break, or more than likely just good old fashioned luck, for when the campsite at Tarlogie finally appeared around the corner, every wish in my campsite song came true.

The campsite owner took one look at my blue lips and uncontrollable shivers and ordered me to go and sort myself out and come back and pay later. Numb hands made the usually easy task of putting up my tent nigh on impossible, and I felt a panic welling up inside that I might just die of hypothermia right here right now. I felt sick, but using the last bit of concentration I could muster, I was able to force myself to stay calm, and finally I succeeded. From there on, things got easier as routine took over; place sleeping bag and roll mat at the back of tent where they would stay dry and could be rolled out later. Put my rear panniers in the tent entrance and leave front panniers, (my larders) on bike. Stuff face with a pasty if required to keep me going, (optional) and grab wash things: towel, clean clothes, toiletries and dirty laundry bag, and make a mad dash for the shower block. On this day, however, that walk from my tent to the showers felt like the longest walk in history, and finally I was there; standing under the shower, stripping off sodden wet clothes. And the water that cascaded over my naked body was hot…so deliciously hot.

Three-quarters of an hour later, I finally felt warm enough to face getting out and return to the cold world outside. I towel dried myself thoroughly, and gave my hair a blast under the hand drier for good measure. I pulled on warm clothes, leaving the wet ones rumbling in the drier and went off to see the proprietor. As I sat in his warm office, he slowly filled out a mountain of forms and he spent a long time telling me about the left-over unexploded Second World War bombs that were regularly found in the area. (I felt glad I was sticking to the roads.) And then because I asked, he described in detail the sort of wildlife I might see up here whilst on the road. As I patiently listened to him ramble, it occurred to me that this was the way things are done up here in the isolated north, there was a real need to talk. The content wasn't important, but general chat was vital for mental wellbeing. After the afternoon I had just had, I could fully appreciate this.

I gathered my clothes from the dryer and went back to my tent to diary write and eat cheese and onion pasties. As I snuggled up in my draughty but dry sleeping bag, I worked out my distance and times for that day and was amazed. Despite not leaving Inverness until the afternoon, and despite the weather and almost freezing to death, this was by far my fastest daily average speed of the whole trip.

Day 37. Penultimate Day (53 miles)

You know when you've already decided in your mind how rubbish something is going to be, and then to your unexpected delight you find it is actually far nicer than you dared hope. All I remembered of this place was the bleak, hollow emptiness of the land as we'd driven as a family to see the famous John O'Groats all those years ago, but this time it would be different. By the speed of a car we had raced between the two landscapes. One minute in amongst the beauty of the Highlands, the next, reeling from the shock at the bleakness of the upper lands. But by bicycle, my speed was slow enough, humane enough, to witness the subtle changes clearly, nurturing eyes and senses from one landscape to the next, appreciating every tiny detail, every changing contour, every contrasting colour of the land around me.

From my position bent over the handlebars, I could see before me the long road as it snaked it's way along the coast of the far flung north. The sea to my right reflected the sun that shone across the land, making me squint in the brightness of the day, and every happy and contented thought I had was answered by the waves, as they crashed down on the pebbled beach, dragging them backwards and forwards, creating a constant rhythm in which to dream to. Above me in the skies, buzzards hovered on the lift of the breeze, surveying the land below as if they were the mighty dinosaur rulers of the skies and we were the mere mortals. The scene that filled my head, now I was nearing the end, ironically seemed to mirror the beginning. It reminded me of Cornwall in many ways, except here everything was on a much larger scale. I realised how much I had missed the sea, which had been hidden from my sight for pretty much most of the trip, and with the sea so big and blue by my side, I felt for the first time in my life that I was actually living on an island.

Something made me feel as though I had stumbled on a secret new world; a beautiful world, only I knew about. Like a child who dares to go exploring further than they would normally venture, and suddenly stumbles upon a fantastic new place in which to play. A place they keep secret from adults and the other children, save for a privileged few they trust, relishing in their secret. I felt, because I had dared to venture past the well beaten tourist trail, I had discovered this new and secret land, where the beauty of it was known only to me, and enjoyed only by me. And well I may have thought this, for I certainly saw no others out doing the same.

I had been advised by another cyclist to detour off the A9 in Helmsdale and instead cycle directly north on the A897. Studying my maps, (just two sheets left to go,) I saw this road was a single track, cutting across a mountainous region. The cyclist had argued that to follow this route would mean traffic-free cycling, but it didn't take me long to realise it would mean something far more worrying...isolation. The road in question ran through the arse-end of nowhere, (to use the technical term,) and where as I once would have welcomed this kind of remoteness, now though, more isolation was the last thing I could stand. After over a month, I was sick of talking to myself. I wanted to sit in a group and laugh like mad about a common experience. I longed for someone else to do the talking, someone else to keep me entertained other than me! Kym had also wanted me to stick to the main roads; he thought a single-track road would be too windy and dangerous, (although he was probably judging everyone by his own standards of reckless driving, but I took on board his point.) He had also pointed out that if I stuck with civilisation I may even collect a few more donations. I had virtually made my mind up when I also noticed that the further north I went on the A9, the lighter the traffic became anyway. The decision was made...the A9 it would be.

It was around two o'clock when I reached Helmsdale, and decided to use it as a lunch stop as it had all the right facilities: public loos for easy peeing, (I had been struggling all day to find convenient places to hide,) there was a garage selling cheese and onion pasties and a phone box to ring my mother. I dialled her number at work and she dutifully rang me back. The trouble was, now I had taken a minute to stop and take a step back from the task in hand, I suddenly realized just how exhausted and how terrible I felt. Up to now I don't think I'd taken the facts into consideration, but now I cast my mind back over the last week, I realised how hard I had been pushing myself since Glasgow. I had come over 300 miles in six days, come rain or shine, and regardless of whether I had been tired or not, hurting or not. And yesterday I had received the drenching of my life. If I didn't know any better, I would say I had caught a chill. I felt almost annoyed at my lethargy and my aches and shivers; why did they have to arrive now when I was so close to the end. Just one more day and I could be as ill as I liked, it wouldn't matter one iota...just not today. I wondered if maybe this was half my problem, I was so close to the end that maybe I had started to mentally relax just that bit too soon. And like what often happens, once the mind gives out, the body soon follows suit.

After Helmsdale the road left it's path of following the coastline, instead bending away from the cliff edge and meandering its way inland, up and over the mountains. So much for no more steep hills! I had to negotiate my way up and over several steep rises and drops in the mountain pass, and slowly climb the switchback road leading up to the famous Berridale Hill, a road most cars could only do in first gear. I thought how things had changed since Devon and Cornwall. Back then I had painfully panted to the top of each rise, and had lain exhausted and disheartened, barely able to move at the end of each day. One thousand miles later and at the other end of this island, I could now handle such hills with ease, and (even with a dose of the flu,) barely break into a sweat. As I thought about this, I finally began to get some sort of sense of what I had accomplished. But there was something else that did a far better job.

I began to see the odd cyclist heading in the opposite direction. We would always grin at each other, and after the fourth one passed that day, I became convinced that they too were just starting their own 'End to End' trips, (although I didn't see anyone loaded up with gear as I was.) But, you know, I didn't envy them one little bit; starting out when I was feeling only relief at having nearly finished. I thought of the intrepidity and naivety I had set out with at the beginning, it had been enough to get me to the start line at least, whilst my strong will and sense of adventure, plus a promise to myself had got me the rest of the way. I also started to notice how car drivers were beginning to grin at me the nearer the end I got. It was a good job there was something strong to draw me on in my weakened state, and I sang terrible songs to myself in an attempt to get the miles ticking by a bit quicker.

The A9 swung round and approached the sea again, which I greeted warmly like an old friend. I stopped off in the next village to use the public lavs, (conveniences were certainly abundant in the far flung north,) and it was here, a passing gentleman stopped to talk to me in one of the most incomprehensible Scottish drawls I've ever heard. My first reaction was to think that this man was drunk, and I tried every trick in the book to politely leave…I was about to be taught a severe lesson; for when I stopped trying to flee and actually listen to him, albeit as best I could, it slowly dawned on me that this guy was anything but drunk. His slur was just because he was old and had very few teeth left, and he had a strong accent to boot. And what was more, he mercifully chose to put aside my rude and ignorant attempts to ignore him, and placed a pound in my collection tin. What could I do? I smiled and thanked him before cycled away, loaded down with guilt. I had been too quick to judge on first impressions, when all he had wanted was to stop for a chat, that old comfort factor of the north again. I just wish I'd been able to understand what he had been telling me.

At last Dunbeath was within a stones throw, and I stopped off at a garage to stock up on tonight's pasty dinner. The mother and daughter who ran the show, asked me to sign their visitors book, a sure sign that not too many people pass this way. Whilst I scribbled, they bemoaned their customers. Tourists, they announced, were on the whole rude and obnoxious and did nothing but complain because their humble store didn't have as much stock or choice as a larger supermarket would. I was all too happy to sympathise with the shopkeeper's gripe, when she suddenly stopped off mid-moan to enquire where I was heading. I couldn't help feel proud as punch to announce I had just cycled here from Land's End; so was gobsmacked when the daughter sneered,

'Oh that must have been easy. I knew a man who once ran it,' in a manner that was clearly meant to belittle my feelings of achievement. After a long days cycle, I took this slap across the face and left the shop, clutching my cheese and onion pasties and wishing a coach load of 'obnoxious tourists' to descend upon her shop immediately.

The Dunbeath campsite was run by a lone but welcoming guy, who told me to pitch my tent and head straight off to the wee pub down the road for a celebratory drink. I guess on the outside I must have been looking every bit confident that I would finish the journey tomorrow with 'nea' problem, but on the inside lay a very different story, where self doubt and negative emotions had me wondering if it would be the cycling that finished me off tomorrow, rather than the other way round. I decided to give the celebratory drink a miss until I could be certain of reaching my destination tomorrow, and let my mind drift on to other comfort factors; namely food and rest.

This would be the last night, and tomorrow the last day. It was hard not to get too excited, but I stuck solid to my well-worn routine. The tent pegs went into the ground with an unusual ease, and I realised the whole of the camping field was covered in six inches of beautifully soft, springy moss. Now this surely was reward enough for any long distance cyclist, only one day out from John O'Groats? I trundled the Holy Grail to the shower blocks for the daily blast or trickle, depending on the plumbing. It made me smile when I remembered as a kid, I had always resented giving up play or reading time for self-hygiene purposes, and saw baths as boring and laborious. (Until I learnt to take my book with me into the bath.) Now though, I could find non-stop pleasure in my daily bathing ritual, as it washed away the grime of the road, and neatly divided the work from the rest.

I ate my cheese and onion pasties with little enthusiasm. My throat was sore and I felt my bones aching, a deep and chilling ache, and I cursed the weather that had brought the rain that had soaked me to the bone, which in turn had brought the aches to my body, when I was so close to finishing. I climbed wearily into my sleeping bag, but at least I could expect a good night's sleep on my soft springy natural mattress, and now I was out of the Highlands, I had the added luxury of FM stations back on my radio, and I looked forward to a good dose of radio 4 once again. But a comfortable and relaxing night it was not. As darkness closed in around my tiny tent, gale force winds lifted out of nowhere. As I lay intermittently dozing in between the great roars of wind, I fidgeted and longed for that deep sleep I needed to take my tired mind and aching body and separate them from reality. But it did not come. So much punishment before the end; that old adage…so near yet so far…reared it's ugly head.

Day 38. The End of the Road.   (45 miles)

Boiling up a saucepan of water in the shelter of the toilet blocks and engrossed in an enormous yawn, I remember my predominant thought as I listened to the wind raging outside…this was it, this was my last day, and I was suddenly overcome by an attack of what I was later to deem as 'last day nerves,' something I noticed in years to come I would always suffered on the final leg of a long distance tour.

However weird it sounds, something seemed to be blocking out the full reality of my situation and it was hard to put it all into perspective, similar in many ways to the beginning of my journey. As far as I was concerned that morning, I may as well have started my journey from twenty miles down the road. All the miles that had passed; that had been eaten up by simply working my legs round and round, all that sweat and energy now paled into complete insignificance by one domineering worry that pricked my conscience…I had a 45 mile cycle ahead of me, and physically I felt like shit. Every aching bone seemed magnified as I went to pay the guy for my pitch, but like so many before him, he waved away my offers of payment. He would be the last one to do this. I did relish his optimism when he said he didn't think it would rain on me today, and with crossed fingers I swung myself into the saddle.

Twenty-three miles of dreary A9 passed, grey and unchallenging, heightening my melancholy mood. The legs were still working; round and round and round, until the town of Wick appeared in the road before me. Here I stopped for what I hoped would be the last of the pasty lunches for a while, (I intended to shop for something a little more exotic for my tea tonight.) As I surveyed the scene around me, memories of Wick from a sixteen year olds point of view came flooding back, and what I remember most was the graffiti ridden walls in the stinking public toilets; a message from the bored youth of Wick, and maybe a measure of how dull a place is to live?

In hindsight, this was another ill judged conclusion I had come to as we had sped through on our way north. Now I sat with time to observe properly, I sensed a close-knit community, as gatherings of locals appeared for a lunchtime natter in the main square, seemingly oblivious to the autumnal wind now biting. I watched as people's eyes followed me casually around the high street, and suddenly I lost all nerve to go and ask for donations. For surely this town must have been witness to every single 'End to End' expedition that ever was, and I was just one more in a big long chain, stretching back to 1863, when an American by the name of Elihu Buritt walked from London to John O'Groats, and then from London to Land's End.

Moving on again, I looked ahead to the Spartan road, then up at the heavy grey sky, and suddenly I remembered why I had found this place so bleak. When travelling through this environment, desolation is very much a real emotion, though it is not without it's beauty; grassy hills, dark and moody reflecting the sky gently rolled away, reaching the horizon long before I would. The only thing to break the invariable scene was the odd painfully lonely house, but worse were the dozens of ruined and long ago abandoned buildings and farm houses crumbling to dust, soon to be no more a symbol of times gone by. I had a strong sense that this landscape would be far less depressing had there been no houses here at all. The ruined Crofter's farms were a sad reminder of the past. But the vision that filled my mind was not of a community driven out by the hostile environment, for these were hardy folk that had once lived here, born and bred to cope with the elements. But the picture I began to see was that of a beaten community, forced to abandon their homes and flee from poverty, a fight of modern life that is surely one of the hardest of them all…how could this community of hardened self sufficient Crofters earn a respectable living from the land, when the jaws of capitalism are slowly engulfing every traditional way of living left in this country. This was reality at it's harshest and it bought a lump to my throat.

When I passed a sign that told me I was only two miles from the end, I tried to use my old mind tricks again, reading the sign as five instead, but on this occasion it was not to work. I guess what I was really hoping for was to top a rise and unexpectedly come across John O'Groats, laying in wait at the bottom of the  hill, bathed in golden sunshine. But two miles from the end, things had never been so tough. A cold wind blew in from the north, straight off the Pentland Firth and straight into my face. It was doing it's damndest to blow me off balance, and I zigzagged across the empty road in an attempt to lessen its force upon me. Only two miles from the end and the heavens cruelly opened their flood gates as they had enjoyed doing on so many occasions before. The sting of cold rain on my hands and face made me gasp in sudden pain. With only two miles to go, and the elements couldn't spare me from this one final punishment. Only two miles...just two more damn miles.

If I had been thinking straight, I would have barred all thought of John O'Groats from my mind and let the motion take over, but after five weeks alone I had no mental energy left and my mind was devoid of anything other than what was written on that last sign post...only two miles to go. It seemed as though every last ounce of the summer that had been holding bravely on, was now being squeezed out by the snarling and salivating dark winter months that came galloping in to consume the land.

Straining my eyes for sight of the end, the sea suddenly came into view and with it a small group of buildings appeared in the distance. But feeling sadistic enough, I decided I wanted to do this properly and delayed the end by taking a right hand turn down a single track road and headed for Dunshead, ANOTHER TWO MILES away! The last two miles, which had seemed to have taken an eternity to cover, didn't have a patch on these two miles. These two miles could only be measured in light years, they were so, so long, as the steep road ran sharply up and down and around, and the weather joined in with the road to laugh at me, as rain drops turned to hail stones, smashing into my face and eyes…

…Then very suddenly it ended. For the first time in 1205 miles, there was no more road to cycle on. I dismounted, pushing Lucy across the grass towards the cliff edge in a spectacular and sudden burst of sunshine. The only two other people to be seen disappeared back off to their car, and I stood alone (except for Lucy,) alone on Dunshead, staring out to sea at the nothingness ahead. No more land, just sea. We were now the most northeasterly person and bicycle in the whole of the mainland British Isles. There were no cheering crowds, no flashing photographers; just me with some sixty million people behind me. I marked my territory as an animal would by squatting down precariously on the cliff edge, and took a desperately needed pee. Satisfied but shattered, I pushed Lucy most of the way back along the steep winding road and into John O'Groats.

John O'Groats, (or Jan de Groots, as it was originally called after the Dutch settler who had first resided here) was chilly, grey and filled with none of the magic I had promised myself for a thousand odd miles. And what was worse, there appeared to be a dozen or more cyclists hanging around the place and I was hit by a sudden wave of insignificance that my tired mind and body felt hard to take. I paid to pose in front of the official John O'Groats sign post which pointed back to were I had been five weeks ago, and the 874 miles as the crow flies. I had the photographer post up my own version of things so it read…SARAH'S CYCLE 1205 MILES. I took off my coat and posed with a fake smile and cold clenched knuckles. And that was all there was left to do.

I was not so miserable that I didn't treat myself to a pint of beer in the hotel bar, which needless to say went straight to my head. I could easily have stayed there for the afternoon, but I made myself stop at one in order to go and sort out some accommodation first. Outside in the blustery wind, I took one look over at the campsite by the sea edge. It didn't look in the least bit romantic, and I could see myself trying to hold down a wind blown tent with one arm, and trying to fight off flu with the other, and decided I would treat myself to a bed and breakfast for the night. In hindsight it was a very wise decision, and helped me to shake off the chill I had acquired. For sixteen notes, I was as pleased as punch with my room. I had a double bed all to myself, and I recreated my camping routine within the sanctuary of those four walls; panniers all tidied and sorted and wet clothes hung out to dry. I set up my camping stove and boiled up some blue cheese pasta brochettes whilst I had a shower, then sat in bed to eat dinner and watch rubbish in the television. The wind continued unabated outside, but I could hardly even hear it, frozen fingers and numb lips for now became just a distant memory. I don't think there was another soul in Scotland that night who could have appreciated that comfort and luxury as I did.

Later on I snuck out to use the phone box and reserve two beds at the backpackers hostel in Inverness for the following night. Looking forward to my friend's arrival tomorrow, I chatted eagerly to the Australian voice on the other end of the line that was making the booking. Before we had time to go into the formalities he asked,

'Is your name Sarah?'

'Yes.'

'Did you stay at the Isle of Skye Backpackers last winter?'

'Yeah'

'I thought so,' he said, 'I'd recognise your voice anywhere.'

I eventually remembered Colin too, who had worked there when last I visited. I found it curious that he remembered me so well, despite the fact we'd only met the once for about ten minutes nearly a year ago, and felt flattered by the attention. On that windy dark night, it felt good to hear a familiar voice and to feel some sense of recognition in an otherwise lonely moment. My journey suddenly felt complete.

* * *

Next morning, everything had changed. For one, the sky was predominately blue, and I wasn't used to the sun glaring directly into my face. Something else that was directly in my face was the wind, hitting me smack on and I got a measure of just how different things may have been had I chosen to cycle the country the other way around. But the main change was that I was no longer going northwards. Thurso lay distinctly to the West, and that was where I was heading. And from there I would be taking a train South. I said the word aloud. South to where there were people who knew me and would welcome me, and where there was fun to be had.

The streets of Thurso were deserted when I arrived, and surprisingly for a Saturday morning, all the shops were shut too. I couldn't help but get a feeling of post-nuclear holocaust doom, but just as I was about to start feeling depressed and isolated again, I spied some local kids playing in the street, who came bounding over like puppy dogs to see me. They agreed to guide me through the deserted streets to the railway station, and they asked me why I wasn't in London for Princes Diana's funeral. Of course, that explained why everyone was holed-up indoors watching the televised events.

As the rest of the nation thought about her, I thought about them. The people I had met, the words of encouragement, the looks of disapproval, and the money donated to Landmines Clearance International, and the very many miles between there and here. I sat on the empty railway station awaiting my train. From behind the closed shutters of the ticket office, Elton John's 'Candle in the Wind' floated across the concourse, as I reflected upon my journey.

Epilogue

Despite all the complaining, I was pleased I wasn't heading straight home to hang up my wheels, and it was with real heart felt joy that I met my friend Sarah off of the Kings Cross to Inverness train, from where we launched ourselves into a two week cycle tour of the Orkney Isles. Rich in bird life and ancient monuments that scatter the land, this really was a magical place to come to. I have never seen the end of so many rainbows, nor experienced such a rapid change in weather conditions, usually from one minute to the next. In fact one day it got so indecisive, we had everything all at once, and I clearly remember cycling along getting drenched in the rain, and at the same time feeling my skin burning in the sunshine.

A year later and I was determined to complete the dream; I found myself in the Shetland Isles, cycling to the true most northerly point of the British Isles (that the road would allow). I should have taken heed of one comment I found in a visitors book which read, '...to cycle in the Shetland Isles, one needs thighs like Fatima Whitbread and a head shaped like an axe...' But I didn't let it put me off, and despite rain flooded roads, and tree toppling gales; I finally reached the most northerly point of the British Isles. As I stood there panting, with the rain pouring off my nose and chin, something caught my attention opposite. Blinking the rain from my eyes I saw a bus shelter that someone had decked out like a comfy living room. There was a settee, television set, cups of tea and cream buns, (all plastic of course) and I laughed very hard. It was as if someone had known I was coming, and I took shelter there accordingly; comic relief is never too far away when you need it the most.

So at the end of one thousand two hundred and five miles, I had spent around three hundred pounds of my own money on the trip, and had raised around eight hundred for the charity. My body had never been in such a physically fit state, but what about the psychological effects? At twenty-one I, perhaps was a little young to appreciate all

I had done, seen and learned, but the fact I had actually completed the challenge I had set myself certainly gave me a new inner strength.

In fact I knew something inside had already changed, because after the weeks of solitude, when I started mixing with people again I did so with a renewed ease and confidence, and before I knew it, I would find myself in the thick of conversations which before I probably would have avoided. I was suddenly happy to be there, raising constructive points in discussions, and what took me by surprise was when I suddenly noticed that people were actually listening intently to what I was saying.

I have to say the end of a journey is a funny business, it is like the end of an era and can take longer than you realise to adjust. At first I felt indifferent; I'd done what I set out to do and now it was over. Sarah and I had to wait three days for a ferry to Orkney, as the strong winds had cancelled all ferry sailings. We pitched our tent at the campsite, but after an invitation, we quickly moved into a large caravan with some Australian surfer types. For three days I relished in the novelty of not having to move, and Sarah and I barely got out of bed. We kicked back in the caravan, listening to music, smoking and eating, and watched out of the window as my little tent flapped wildly in the storms outside; I felt only relief that I know longer had to be out there.

Strange then that only a week later I found myself feeling rather deflated, whilst my body, at the peak of fitness, now had little more than ten miles a day to do, and felt useless and without purpose. I can only compare it to losing a job, I had not adjusted back to 'normal' life and I worried that what I had fought so hard to achieve, now seemed almost insignificant.

But eventually it did begin to register what I had personally achieved, and I began to feel very proud of myself. I first noticed it when I went on long train journeys. I'd sit and stare out of the window for hours on end and suddenly think, 'I've cycled further than this.' And once this had dawned on me, for months afterwards I would settle down to sleep each night; turn off the lights and enjoy running through each and every day of the trip, remembering the roads I had cycled and the places I had camped. And this is where I found self respect.

There are, I am sure, some who will think I hadn't exactly achieved much, after all I hadn't broken any world records, and being that it was Land's End to John O'Groats, I am sure plenty would scoff and say 'Oh everybody does that,' (usually people who could never be motivated enough to do it themselves.) But I never set out to prove myself to anyone else, I did it for me, and as far as I am concerned, I achieved everything I wanted. Quite frankly, I can't imagine anyone would go to so much trouble just to prove themselves to someone else, and if they did, believe me they would be unlikely to succeed. If you have ever dreamed of doing your own journey, be it cycling, running etc, you will probably encounter people who will try to belittle you and scoff, 'what is so tough about going cycling, or walking?' And they'd be right, there is nothing tough about it, but try doing it day in and day out, walking with five blisters or cycling with a sore arse, and you will soon get the measure of what testing yourself is really all about. And it won't just be your physical strength that gets you through, but what stamina and will power you have. As something I have learnt is; the body is only as strong as the mind is.

I am sure that almost any healthy adult can train up their bodies to perform a surprising number of tasks, but what appears to stop them is these modern beliefs that, if you can get a machine to do the work for you, then why bother. But what happens when we use the legs we were given less and less or the muscles in the arms we once needed? Do our spirits evaporate with it? It just seems to me, that for most labour saving devices man invents, it kills off a bit more of the life and spirit around.

Take the modern motorcar as an example. You could say, great, now we don't have to walk or cycle anywhere again if one doesn't wish too, and now every man has access to an entire combustion engine to take him to the shops up the road if he so wishes. But is this really necessary when you take into account that when he fires up his labour saving machine, the poisonous fumes, the laying of the roads, the digging up of the oil, and the unsociable isolation the car puts you in, not to mention the aggression behind the wheel, all comes into play. And can any of this be regarded as positive attributes to humanity? When a child uses the labour saving device of a calculator, does he not lose the ability to think arithmetically in his head? And take farming. Where many men once gathered to harvest the fields, they had a vitally important job within the community that gave them self respect. They worked hard together, they laughed together, and gathered in their local for a drink at the end of a hard day's graft, and they reaped enough crops to feed their families. Now one man does all the work with his labour saving machine, growing industrial size crops in a way that damages the land, producing too much food so a lot of it is simply thrown away. And what of the other men that once worked the land? They had to find menial, soul destroying work in the factories instead, making bits of things, insignificant to their lives, which go to be sold on another continent.

When I choose to fight the natural human desire to be lazy and take the easier option, (something modern marketing takes full advantage of,) and instead make the choice to use my own energies, walking or cycling, rather than jumping into a car; there is never a time when I don't feel a sense of strength, a sense of really being in control of my life, not whisked away by someone else's ideals about the way I should live my life, or ideas about what they think will make me happy. I wish I could teach kids to understand these things; to be in control of their lives by using the free physical and spiritual energies we are blessed with at birth. Life was never meant to be easy, and if we try to cheat and make it easy, we miss out on the fantastic opportunity to grow and really feel free. By nature we are animals and let us look at the rest of the animal kingdom. If life was meant to be easy, why do they all go to so much trouble? The salmon, risking life and limb to return to their place of birth? But most glaringly obvious, the lion. If the ultimate goal is a life of ease, why is he still far happier out hunting his own prey and struggling to survive; and is miserable being spoon fed in the zoo? Because ultimately life is a struggle; but rewarding with it. And these are the natural laws of nature we should not try to defy.

5% of the author's profits from this book will go to MAG

MAG (Mines Advisory Group) is a humanitarian organization clearing the remnants of conflict for the benefit of communities worldwide. MAG is co-laureate of the 1997 Nobel Peace Prize for its work with the International Campaign to Ban Landmines (ICBL), which culminated in the 1997 Mine Ban Treaty.

MAG moves into current and former conflict zones to clear the remnants of those conflicts, enabling recovery and assisting the development of affected populations. MAG consults with the local communities and works to lessen the threat of death and injury, while releasing reclaimed and safe land and other vital resources back to the local population, helping countries to rebuild and develop their social and economic potential.

MAG has worked in over 35 countries since 1989 and currently has operations in Angola, Burundi, Cambodia, Chad, Cyprus, Democratic Republic of Congo, Gaza, Iraq, Jordan, Lao P.D.R, Lebanon, Republic of Congo, Rwanda, Somalia, Sri Lanka, Sudan and Vietnam.

For more information, or to support MAG's work, please visit www.maginternational.org

Registered charity number 1083008

About the Author

Sarah was born in 1976 in South London, but at the age of just one the family moved to a house in the Sussex countryside, where she grew up; falling in love with natural history, horses, and adventure.

Since cycling 'End to End' she has completed many more tours in the U.K, especially in Scotland, and it is her ambition to, bit by bit, cycle right around the world. Beginning in Brighton, Sussex, she has over the last few years traversed: England, Wales, Ireland and the United States, and looks forward to writing more about further cycling adventures.

If you would like to contact Sarah on a cycling matter, please email her. scareyfairy1@tiscali.co.uk

Lightning Source UK Ltd.
Milton Keynes UK
19 December 2010

164553UK00007B/26/P